Quilts and Other Bed Coverings in the Canadian Tradition

Quilts

and Other Bed Coverings in the Canadian Tradition

Ruth McKendry

Photographs by Blake McKendry
Foreword by Dr. William E. Taylor, Jr.

KEY PORTER·BOOKS

Canadian Cataloguing in Publication Data

McKendry, Ruth, 1920-
    Quilts and other bedcoverings in the Canadian tradition

Reprint. Originally published: Toronto: Van Nostrand
Reinhold, 1979.
American ed. published under title: Traditional quilts and
bedcoverings.
Bibliography: p.
ISBN 0-919493-66-1

1. Quilts — Ontario. 2. Bedding. 3. Quilting — Ontario —
History. I. McKendry, Blake, 1919- II. Title.

NK9113.M24 1985   746.9'7 C85-098411-4

Acknowledgments

The author and publisher wish to express their gratitude to those who have provided photographic and other material for use in this book. For a complete list of acknowledgments, please see page 231 which for legal purposes is considered to form part of the copyright page.

Editorial Consultant: James T. Wills
Design: Howard Pain
Typesetting: Fleet Typographers Ltd.
Film: Colourgraph Reproductions Inc.
Printed and bound in Italy
85 86 87 7 6 5 4 3 2

Contents

foreword

In her book on Canadian quilts and other bed coverings, Ruth McKendry gives us the newest of a rare kind of book, one that presents Canadian history in a loving, personal way. Here we meet ordinary yet fascinating Canadians – our predecessors – rather than politicians and constitutional issues. From a reference perspective, this book is even more rare, for it is a study in that still young discipline, material history. It joins, as well, that remarkably rare genre of studies in immigrant Anglo-Celtic craft and folk art. Those of us with an Anglo-Celtic, or even a simply Anglo-Saxon background need no longer wonder if our ancestors made anything other than money, laws and war – and the churches to validate them all. Clearly, the following story reflects a time when thriftiness and hard work were, in fact, next to Godliness.

Perhaps the book's most relevant and persistent historical theme is the brutal, isolated struggle that English, Scots and Irish immigrants endured pioneering in Upper Canada. The habitant in Lower Canada had already experienced a like life. Subsequent waves of westward-moving immigrants from many European backgrounds came to share the same struggle, following those who were previously driven out by starvation, industrialization and the profiteering of landowners who invested in sheep rather than people. This hard, lonely pioneer life is a principal theme in Canadian history. The remarkably large British share of it is often forgotten, as if the Scots, Irish, English and Welsh were all alike, all urban, educated and mercantile.

We are fortunate to be able to benefit from Ruth McKendry's years of dedicated collecting and studying of the quilts and bed coverings shown here. Through them, she introduces us to the common people at work in their own homes. These are non-verbal documents, expressive and evocative media for social, economic and craft history. Until recently, written records were the historian's main resource, but the pieces pictured here clearly point out that material history often contains insights that are far different and far more personal than those of more formalized documents.

For such reasons, Ruth McKendry's work will stand not only as a monument to Canadian history, but also as a history of the individual woman labouring to provide comfort for her family.

The National Museum of Man deeply appreciates that the McKendry Collection, part of which appears in this book, has been added to Canada's national collections. The McKendry Collection will maintain its identity and integrity in perpetuity as a distinguished resource for future scholars and students of Canadian crafts, art, society and history, and for those of us who appreciate its quiet beauty.

William E. Taylor, Jr., PH.D., F.R.G.S., F.R.S.C., D.U.C.
Director,
National Museum of Man, Ottawa

Preface

Years ago, when I went to auction sales in the country, I used to be intrigued but also saddened by what I saw. The pattern was often the same. There would be a small farmhouse set among peaceful green fields. Mouldering nearby in the empty barnyard was the original log hut built more than a century ago by the first young couple from the old country. In the little fenced yard stood the house to be sold, the second log cabin, now neatly covered with wooden clapboards. Piled around the house were the remnants of the household furnishings of all the generations that had lived and raised their families there.

What touched me most was the bedding made through the years by the women who had helped wear down the threshold at the sagging kitchen doorstep. High-backed wooden bedsteads of the nineteenth century, piled high with feather ticks and homemade pillows, stood in solemn squalor among the day-lilies and peonies along the straggling fence. Scattered everywhere were boxes and trunks filled with crumpled pillowshams and handmade, lace-trimmed pillowcases, which at one time were the starched and gleaming pride of the owners of these same beds. The ironing board leaning against the kitchen wall was padded with the remains of a fine handwoven coverlet. On the dining room table, there were always quilts thrown in tangled, graceless heaps, glorious quilts, shining with colour.

Out at the back, from woodsheds and lofts, came the moth-eaten homespun blankets and woollen quilts, "so heavy that, two of them on you, you couldn't turn over to save your life" as the old women say. From the granaries and machine sheds were dragged the broken spinning wheels and scattered pieces of a homemade loom.

The homespuns had come from the untidy backs of family sheep that used to crop the bright green grass growing among the boulders. The feather beds were plucked from the breasts of geese that used to run shrieking through the back yards and lanes. Almost everything had come from the fields, transformed into comforting household articles by the hands of the hard-working women of the house. All, in the end, would be offered along with the farm at three o'clock in the afternoon on the day of the sale.

After the auction was over, the spinning wheel would be piled into the back of one car, the wool-winder into another, and the loom would be left lying in the barnyard until the grass grew high enough to cover it. The beautiful quilts were carried away to be scattered from here to everywhere, with nobody remembering and nobody caring about the women who had sat sewing them by the sunny kitchen window through the long winter afternoons.

I began to think then that someone should record the love and labour that went into the making of these Ontario bedcovers before their history was lost

10

forever. So I began to collect nineteenth century bedding together with all the stories and histories about its making that I could obtain. I became more and more fascinated as I discovered the extra hours of work that the women had put into even the most utilitarian items to make them attractive to the eye as well as functional. Their days were short and filled with labour, but they took the time to weave coloured bands into their blankets, to trim the pillowcases made from humble grain bags with handmade lace, and to arrange their patchwork quilts into pleasing designs. It seems to us today to have been an impossible accomplishment.

The life of the pioneer was hard. Apart from the bearing and raising of many children, there were the endless chores. A woman had to help care for the poultry and sheep; to hackle and sort the flax; and to wash, pick, grease and card the wool. Then she had to spin the wool into thread, dye it and weave it into cloth from which she made ticking, sheets, blankets and quilts. Linen had to be prepared for the marriages of daughters, and mothers and daughters worked from dawn to dusk and, later, by candlelight. They would spin until their fingertips were raw and bloody, rinse them off and then keep on spinning.

Many of these tasks were unpleasant. The grease that had to be worked into the fleece was usually rancid, and the fleece itself was dirty and full of parasites. Recipes for making dyes called for constant stirring over an open fire, and the mordant most commonly used to set the dye was urine, or "chamber lye" as it was called. Little girls of four wept over their pricked fingers as they struggled with their first quilt patches, but they learned at an early age that they must do what was expected of them, just as their mothers did. Despite all these things, the quilts and bed coverings in this book show that these women took pride and joy in the results of their work. It satisfied their love of beauty in a world that afforded little time for luxuries.

The women made more quilts than anything else and probably took the greatest pleasure in their making. Quilts were made primarily because warm covers were needed for the beds. There were two kinds: the "good" quilt made for special occasions, and the everyday one for common use. Utility quilts were used daily, washed every spring, and replaced, when worn, from a supply kept ready and waiting in the blanket box. The few "good" quilts that a woman might make were cherished and taken out only on important occasions, such as when the minister slept over. These special quilts were seldom washed and were carefully passed down to the next generation. A fancy quilt was prepared by a girl in anticipation of her marriage, and although she might make hundreds of everyday quilts in her lifetime, often only her treasured marriage quilt survives. Thus, more of these quilts have come down to us, though fewer were actually made.

As I continued my research and collecting, however, I found that some of the most interesting quilts were made for everyday, "just quilts" as many old people say. I have included as many of these as possible in this book. The majority of the bed coverings shown were made in the last quarter of the nineteenth century. This is because more were made then, and certainly some of the finest seem to have come from this period. All are a silent and glowing testimony to the patient and hardworking women who sat quietly by those sunny kitchen windows.

There have been many people who have helped me with this project. Those who have helped most are the women who have "remembered" for me, in particular, the few who are gifted with memories for what seem to be inconsequential details, like the smell of a bed tick newly filled with corn husks. I am grateful to the women of the community of Latimer who have helped me in many ways, and I should especially like to thank Jessie Ritchie, who is blessed with one of those memories. Others who have supplied me with information include: Dorothy Burnham of the Royal Ontario Museum, Toronto, who kindly shared her great knowledge of handwoven fabrics with me; Marjorie Dissette of Upper Canada Village, Morrisburg; Jeanne Minhinnick, Picton; Nancy-Lou Patterson, University of Waterloo, and Russell and Elizabeth Harper, Alexandria.

Of great assistance was my daughter, Jennifer McKendry, whose many hours of patient research among early newspapers and books brought forth much valuable information. For local histories I am also indebted to John Russell, Gananoque; Mrs. James James, Brockville; Paul Byington, Portland; Marjorie Larmon, Burgessville; Margaret McGuire, Cornwall; Blanche Connell, Kemptville; and Edith and Helen Dewar, Endicott, U.S.A.

Tim and Gerda Potter of Odessa were of great assistance in obtaining accurate information about various items, as were Richard and Christine Bird, Corbyville; Grant Eskerod, Newboro; Michael Bird, Kitchener; Robert Lambert, Orono; and Margaret Rhodes, Helen Holliday, Margaret McLean, Elsie Davidson and Ila Wood, all of Kingston. Our friends Ralph and Patricia Price of Port Perry were of great help, contributing valuable information and their infectious enthusiasm to this book.

I should like to acknowledge the cooperation of various museums and their staffs: the Archibald Campbell Museum, Perth; the Prince Edward County Museum, Picton; the Scugog Shores Museum, Port Perry; the Royal Ontario Museum, Toronto; the St. Lawrence Parks Commission and Upper Canada Village, Morrisburg. Grateful thanks are also due to Dr. William E. Taylor, Jr., Director, National Museum of Man, Ottawa, and Wesley C. Mattie, Curator of the Canadian Centre for Folk Culture Studies, National Museum of Man; their continuing interest has been a source of inspiration and confidence to me.

I should like to thank the many people who have lent us their treasured bedcovers, often family heirlooms, to be photographed for this book. Their names are listed on p. 231. I would also like to express my gratitude to editor James T. Wills for his patient and sympathetic help in smoothing out the rough spots. Designer and collector Howard Pain has been of great assistance throughout the entire project.

My very special thanks are reserved for my husband, Blake McKendry, who did the photography, helped with the writing, and cooperated every step of the way, along with our four-legged editor-in-residence, B.C., who sat on a chair beside me sharing my travails through the long hours that went into the preparation of this book. All the photographs used were done by Blake McKendry, except for the following: Plate 260 was furnished by the National Museum of Man, History Division; Plates 79, 87, 88, 102 and 259 were supplied by the Royal Ontario Museum; Plate 239 was taken by Arnold Matthews, Toronto; and Plates 235 and 236 were shot by Ron Liss, Fine Arts Archives, University of Waterloo. Plates 39 and 201 were provided by Jennifer McKendry.

Last of all, my gratitude should be expressed to the many women, too often nameless, who created the bedcovers shown here. They have left us with a legacy of beauty and joy.

R.M.
Tunis Snook Farm
Latimer, Ontario
April 1979

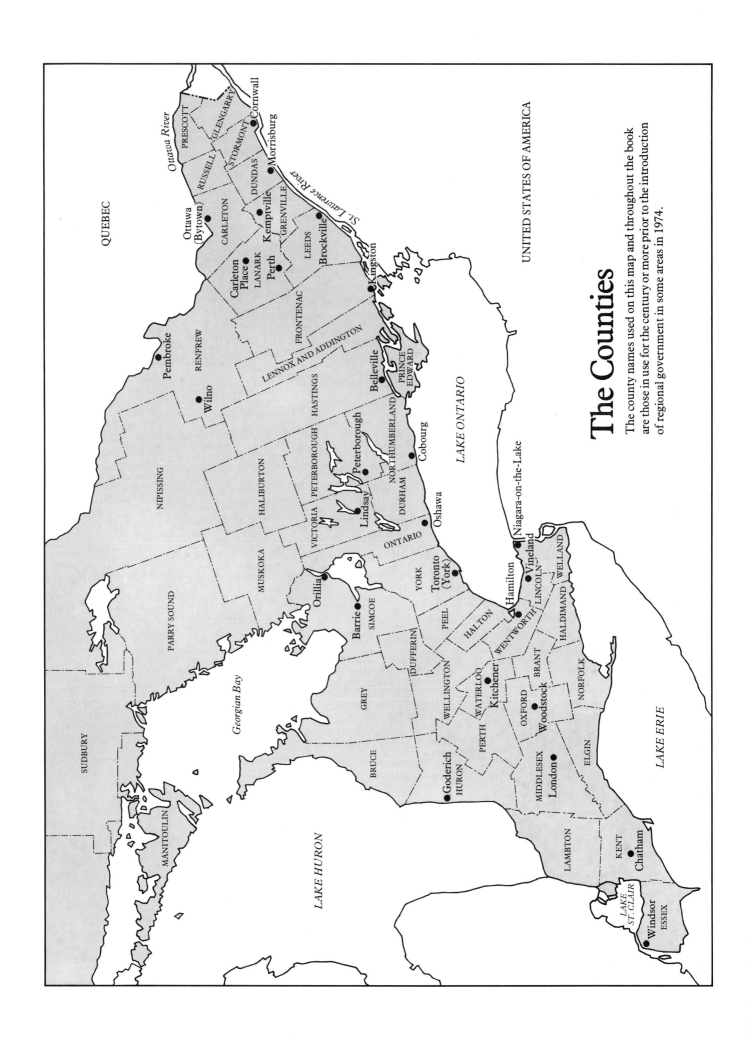

The Counties

The county names used on this map and throughout the book are those in use for the century or more prior to the introduction of regional government in some areas in 1974.

1 Immigrants & Imports: The Loyalists and After

Find me the men on earth who care
Enough for faith or creed to-day
To seek a barren wilderness
For simple liberty . . .

"The Pilgrim Forefathers"
Helen Hunt Jackson (1831-1885)

Before 1780, the area that was to become Upper Canada was a vast wilderness of dense forest, interwoven with threads of bright streams and rivers joining brilliant patches of blue lakes. A few isolated forts had been established for the protection of the fur trade, some of which were already quite old by this time. Fur traders and voyageurs, many of whom were from French Canada, paddled the main waterways where they met with the Indians to trade manufactured goods for the furs of wild animals. For the most part, the Indians were nomadic, moving their villages and campsites as the seasons changed and hunting and fishing conditions varied.

As might be expected in such an isolated environment, bedding was extremely important, and it consisted of the bed-rolls of the traders and the imported woollen blankets that the Indians received for their furs. In 1780, the "Haldimand Papers" listed "sundry goods in possession of Robert Macaueley [sic] Carleton Island, 20th April 1780, 2 bales of blankets . . . 1 Trunk Irish linen, 1 ball coarse cloth . . . FOR THE INDIAN TRADE."[1]

Although they came to prefer the white man's colourful blankets, the Indians traditionally worked the pelts of wild animals to make them soft and pliable for bedding and sometimes decorated them with paint, porcupine quills, beads or other trinkets. Trade blankets were useful for making coats and leggings as well as for bedding. Up to 1780, the population, based largely on the fur trade, was sparse, depending on the relations of the traders and the Indians.

During and after the American Revolution in the colonies, there were many people who, because of their loyalty to the Crown or because of their unwillingness to take part in revolution by violence, were unable to remain in the new republic. Many had already lost their lands and possessions to the patriots and were forced to flee to Canada and other British possessions. First called Loyalists (later United Empire Loyalists), these people settled along the shores of the St. Lawrence River and the lower Great Lakes.

This group of people was remarkable for its cultural diversity. There were Germans from the continental Palatine who had sought refuge in the American Colonies many years before, religiously based Pennsylvania-Germans, Highland Scots who had settled in the colonies so recently that they did not speak English, and people of Dutch, Irish, English, and French Huguenot backgrounds. Those of

Indians dressed in trade blankets; from a lithograph, *Indian Wigwam in Lower Canada,* by Cornelius Krieghoff.

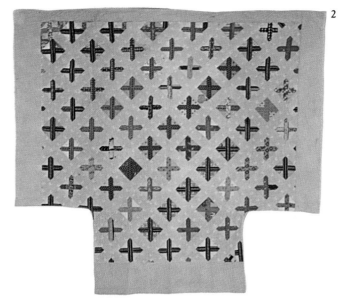

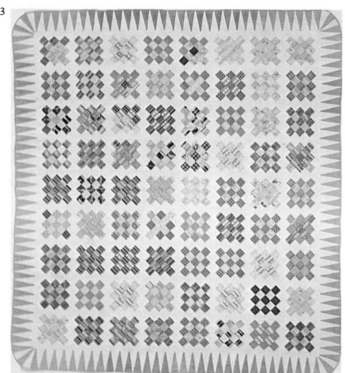

1 Pieced Pineapple: quilt, pieced and appliquéd; cotton; hammock border; greens and yellow; ca. 1820. W. 196 cm, L. 210 cm (77, 83 in.). This quilt was brought from Pennsylvania to Kent County with the original settlers. The back is fine home-spun linen or cotton. Lotus flowers form clusters between the crossed pineapples. [M.L.]

2 Cross: quilt, pieced; cotton; found in Pembroke, Renfrew County, 1st quarter 19th century. W. 250 cm, L. 270 cm (98, 106 in.). This very large quilt has notches for a four-post bed and a wide border that acts as a flounce. Although possibly American in origin, this quilt has been in the Pembroke area for some time. [C.C.F.C.S.]

3 Chimney Sweep: quilt, pieced; printed cottons and white linen; made by nuns in a New York convent, 2nd quarter 19th century. W. 236 cm, L. 262 cm (93, 103 in.). This large quilt was given to Lydia Ann Holliday, Wolfe Island, Frontenac County in the 19th century. She also made fine quilts. Quilts like this one undoubtedly influenced those made in this country. [H.H.]

4 Prince of Wales Plumes, Prince's Feathers, or Princess Feathers: quilt, appliquéd; cotton; made by Frances Rowland Stewart, Pittsburgh, Pennsylvania, ca. 1830. W. 217 cm, L. 220 cm (85, 87 in.). This quilt was brought up to Canada many years ago. Until recently it was in the possession of the former owner, Virginia Urlson Baird, a great-granddaughter of the maker. The feathers are blunt indeed. [P.E.C.M.]

5 *Encampment of the Loyalists at Johnstown, a New Settlement on the Banks of the St. Lawrence River, June 6, 1784,* by James Peachey.

6 Interior of a Settler's Home in 1812, from a sketch by Thomas Conant.

7 A certain amount of bedding was required on the emigrant ships, and one would expect to find tucked in the great bundles they carried some items brought over for sentimental reasons, for example a treasured family counterpane. *Canadian Illustrated News,* 1874.

common ethnic origin tended to settle together, usually by choice but occasionally by recommendation. When Sir John Johnston led a large group of Highlanders and Palatinates to Upper Canada from the area of Johnstown, for example, he is reported to have said that he must separate the two groups, lest the Palatinates pick the eyes out of the Highlanders.[2] The Scots chose to settle in what are now the counties of Glengarry and Stormont, and the Palatinates settled in western Stormont and Dundas.

Another large group of Loyalists of English, Dutch and German descent settled in the Kingston area as far west as the Bay of Quinte, and another group settled in the Niagara Peninsula. After the initial Loyalist immigration, American settlers continued to come to Upper Canada for many years. Especially in the case of the dispossessed Loyalist groups, there was relatively little baggage brought along. Doubtless, household goods of some emotional significance were carried, but of prime importance would be bedding to defend the family from the harsh North American climate.

Shortly after 1800, the Highland clearances in Scotland resulted in the dispossession of many families who eventually emigrated to Canada. Other small groups began to drift over in search of land. Like most national groups, the Scots tended to settle where their own people were already established. After the Napoleonic Wars came to an end in 1815, the armies began to disband some regiments and more or less organized groups of soldiers and their families came to Canada. During the depression that followed the wars, the poor began to pour into Upper Canada from Ireland, Scotland and England.

These later immigrants were able to bring little with them, since, unlike many of the Loyalists, they were extremely poor. A certain amount of bedding, however, would be required on the ships, and one would expect to find tucked in the great bundles they carried some items brought over for sentimental reasons, for example, a treasured family counterpane. The early Loyalist settlers had taken up lands in the front townships along the shores of the St. Lawrence River and lakes Ontario and Erie, and those who arrived later had to find land in the still unsettled back townships. Each wave of settlers, as they moved into a newly opened township, endured the same hardships as the first settlers.

Each distinct ethnic group had its own traditions, resulting in distinctive bedding patterns in the different districts. These traditions were modified to suit the conditions of a new land, and in the course of time there was a gradual infusion of new ideas from other groups when they began to mingle and exchange ideas.

Loyalist settlers were supplied by the British government with rations and clothes for three years, or until they were able to provide these articles for themselves. Each person above the age of ten received one blanket; those under ten were given one blanket between two children. Men and boys above ten years each got a coat, a waistcoat, breeches, a hat, a shirt, shoe soles, one pair of leggings and one pair of stockings. Each woman and girl above ten was allowed two yards of woollen cloth, four yards of linen, one pair of stockings and one pair of shoe soles.[3] This was virtually all they had in the way of textiles. Out of these they had to clothe themselves and provide their bed covers.

Over the years, the clothing became too worn to use in any other form, and pieces of it found their way into the earliest quilts made in Upper Canada. Those settlers who came later often brought their own bedding, including quilts, with them. Today, one occasionally finds a quilt that is said to have been brought up with the settlers from the United States.

The history of such a quilt is generally known by the family, and it is a treasured family keepsake. These quilts, such as the Pieced Pineapple in Plate 1, were brought up at a later date when the settlers were not under so much pressure to get away as they were at the time of the revolution, unlike the Loyalists who were described in a 1784 letter as having "not So much as a blanket to Cover them . . . Strange is the Collection of people here."[4]

Among the supplies given to the Loyalists were "Indian blankets" which, one can assume, were made in Scotland or England for export by the Hudson's Bay Company. These were woollen blankets of varying weights and colours, such as the example in Plate 8. Some were very colourful; Elizabeth Simcoe wrote in her diary that the Indians she and her husband, Colonel John Graves Simcoe, met in Upper Canada near York (Toronto) wore scarlet leggings or pantaloons and black, blue or scarlet broadcloth blankets.[5]

At that time it was virtually impossible to buy cloth in Upper Canada, but goods could be bought in Lower Canada if one had sufficient money. Mrs. Simcoe purchased an eiderdown quilt in Quebec City in 1792 for £4.16s,[6] which was an enormous amount for that time.

Early accounts suggest that the skins of animals were used by the Loyalists to supplement the insufficient bedding and clothing supplied by the government. William Canniff wrote that a settler's ordinary costume was made from coarse cloth and Indian blankets, but the most common and serviceable garments were made from deerskin and worn by both sexes — breeches for the men, petticoats for the women.[7] The historian Walter Herrington quotes from a document, "The Testament of Roger Bates," in which an old man, telling of the making of dresses from deerskin in the early days, added that, "At night they were extremely comfortable for bedcovers."[8] In 1792, Mrs. Simcoe wrote that the Indians gave Colonel Simcoe, first Lieutenant Governor of Upper Canada, "a beaver blanket to make his bed,"[9] an article that they considered fitting for the governor of the country. When travelling, she too sometimes slept fully clothed on a folding bed under a fur blanket.[10]

Great hardships were endured by the less fortunate early settlers, since the skins of wild animals were difficult to obtain in order to supplement their inadequate bedding and clothing. William Canniff describes the extent of the situation in 1790 in the tale of a Kingston man, an important official, who became acquainted with the fact that his own brother was living in a house near the head of the Bay of

Quinte in a state of nakedness. The brother had to remain in that condition until the Kingston man was able to rescue him. He was only a boy at the time, but there were plans for him to be apprenticed to a carpenter, so he must have been nearly fully grown.[11]

A great deal of ingenuity was displayed in making clothing and bedding during these early, difficult years. Blankets were said to have been made out of hair picked from the tanners' vats combined with a hemp-like weed that grew wild. The blanket in Plate 9 was made from horsehair and wool.

The lot of settlers had improved somewhat by 1823. In that year, Peter Robinson brought a contingent of Irish immigrants to the Pakenham District, Lanark County, and each family received two bolts of cotton, serge and flannel from the government.[12] This caused some resentment among earlier settlers, who were not allowed such bounty.

Some settlers wrote home that bedding was extremely important in Upper Canada, because of the

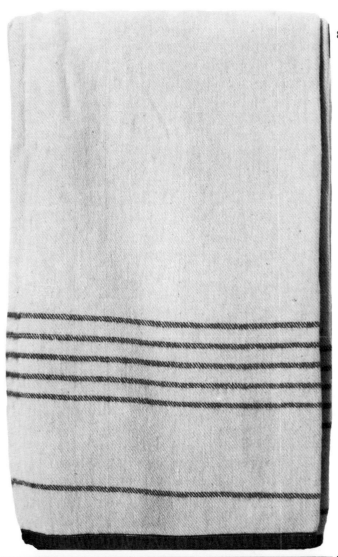

8 Blanket: cream coloured wool with blue stripes; found in Leeds County. W. 163 cm, L. 224 cm (64, 88 in.). This was the type of blanket used by the first settlers who came to Upper Canada. [P.C.]

9 Blanket: horsehair and handspun wool, handwoven; brown; Renfrew County, 3rd quarter 19th century. W. 143 cm, L. 211 cm (56, 83 in.). In times of economic necessity, blankets were made from hair taken from the tanner's vats. [P.C.]

cold that had to be felt to be believed. Anne Langton wrote in 1839 that,

> within two or three inches of the chimney which feels quite warm to the touch, our water becomes ice, and notwithstanding an excellent fire night and day the thermometer will remain sometimes ten, twelve or fifteen degrees below the freezing point. But this is on our colder days, and even then we have rarely been otherwise than warm in bed, though in covering we have never exceeded two blankets and the down quilt.[13]

Later, she mentioned that one of the men, upon counting, had found he was using eight blankets.[14] Another day she wrote: "The thermometer was twenty below zero, with a strong wind. It blew very hard during the night, the mercury stood only three degrees above zero in our room while we were dressing."[15]

Deaths from cold were also described:

> Her mother died in her confinement last year, leaving this poor girl of ten years of age with several younger brothers and sisters to take care of. Another woman died under the same circumstances, literally of cold, and the baby was, while in the charge of another woman, found one morning outside the family group in bed, and frozen to death. This was one of the coldest nights this winter.[16]

It is difficult for us in the twentieth century, with our central heating and electric blankets, to imagine what pioneer life was like and the crucial importance of good, warm bedding. In her *Backwoods of Canada,* Catherine Parr Traill gives us a graphic picture:

> The 1st of March was the coldest day and night I ever experienced in my life; the mercury was down to twenty five degrees in the house; abroad it was much lower. The sensation of cold early in the morning was very painful, producing an involuntary shuddering, and an almost convulsive feeling in the chest and stomach. Our breaths were congealed in hoar-frost on the sheets and blankets.[17]

She warned settlers to bring out to Upper Canada, "a good stock of wearing-apparel, and shoes, good bedding, especially warm blankets; as you pay high for them here, and they are not so good as you would supply yourself with at a much lower rate at home."[18]

The warning to bring blankets is repeated in all the early guide and travel books, with the advice that the precaution should not be omitted on account of the difficulty in carrying them. John Howison wrote, "Those who have money to spare should lay in a quantity of wearing apparel before leaving this country as alternatives of this kind cost very high in Upper Canada. A stock of broadcloth, cotton, bedding, etc. can be carried out at a trifling expense and will prove advantageous to the settler."[19]

A descendant of the McNicol family from Lanark County related in a family history that the Scottish women brought out with them great hanks of woollen yarn; they passed their time on board ship knitting socks, mittens and stockings. They also carried bolts of cloth to make pants, coats and waistcoats for the men, preparing for the cold Upper Canadian winter ahead.[20]

In *A Pioneer History of the County of Lanark,* Jean McGill relates that the societies organizing Scottish emigration to the Lanark area had been advised that little girls should be taught to knit coarse woollen stockings and to spin wool and linen yarn for family use.[21]

Considering the importance and scarcity of cloth during the pioneer era, it is little wonder that all scraps of worn clothing and remnants of tattered blankets were used to make patchwork quilts. True, by about 1820 clothing, fabric and bedding could be bought in local stores, but it was difficult for settlers to do so because they lacked both money and goods to trade. Also, the stock at a backwoods store would vary considerably; it might carry tea, dyes and blankets, but it was unlikely that all three would be available at any one time. There was a great deal of waiting for the next shipment to come from across the ocean and through the miles of bush.

At a very early period, settlers responded to these problems by beginning to cultivate flax and to establish flocks of sheep. Most of the women who came to Upper Canada from the American Colonies, the early American republic or from European countries were accustomed to providing both bedding and clothing for the family. They knew how to prepare yarn from the fleece of sheep, how to make linen thread from flax; many had had looms and had done their own weaving. Highland women, for example, had been making woollen cloth for generations, jealously guarding their localized patterns and designs. Loyalist women had been making quilts for some years out of worn garments, since cloth had been scarce in the colonies from the beginning; they were accustomed to "making do."

Out of scarcity, deprivation, dispossession and sheer need among immigrants from many ethnic backgrounds grew the unique Upper Canadian tradition of quilts, bedding and cloth that is the subject of this book. Although they were in part responses to the necessities of Canadian life, they are also the beautiful expressions of traditional craft, made with both joy and pride.

2 Making Cloth at Home

She seeketh wool, and flax, and worketh willingly with her hands.

Proverbs 31:13

Throughout the nineteenth century, most Upper Canadian bedding was made from homespun materials. Large numbers of flannel sheets, homespun blankets and coverlets have survived and are to be found in almost every home where succeeding generations of the same family have lived since pioneer days. A large proportion of early quilts contain homespun cloth and are still to be found in the countryside, despite the fact that these heavy quilts have received little care during the last fifty years.

Due to the scarcity of cloth, the early establishment of a home industry of cloth making was of prime importance. This meant acquiring a flock of sheep and clearing land to grow flax. Because cotton could not be grown in the Canadian climate and flax was one of the first crops that could be brought in after the land was cleared, linen was used to make the earliest clothing and bedding. Mrs. Sarah Slaght, an early Norfolk County settler, described in detail the making of her linens during the first winter of her marriage in 1825:

> In the barn there was a quantity of flax . . . Job broke it for me, and then I took off the shives, hetcheled it, takin' out the tow, which was carded and spun on the big wheel like wool, and which furnished the fillin' in weavin' the coarser cloth used for towelling, tickin', baggin', etc. The flax was spun on the little wheel. We were married in October and during the winter I made up forty-three yards of cloth out of that flax, and this gave us a supply of tablecloths, towels, sheets, tickin', bags, etc.[1]

The use of linen had been established quite a bit earlier, however, and a 1795 account book kept by Samuel Sherwood in Belleville, Hastings County, lists charges for "spining 14 rum linen yarn /8 . . . . 0-9-4, Do [ditto] 10 tow Do /9 0-7-6 for Nicholes Lake."[2] There is no mention of cotton yarn being sold at such an early date, but by 1829 a Mr. A. Jones of Prescott recorded in his account book the sale of "2 yards" of "loom cotton" to a Mrs. Jessup.[3]

Because of the extremes of heat and cold, linen did not turn out to be the most comfortable fabric for wear in Canada. About the end of the first quarter of the nineteenth century, cotton yarn became generally available in the general stores, and people began to use it to replace linen thread in weaving. In 1827, Roderick Matheson, a storekeeper in Lanark County, wrote to his supplier in Scotland that, "the little bitts of stripes will not do, wool and flax does not answer this climate, it must be all wool or wool and cotton (not flax)."[4]

Flax was still in widespread use by 1832, and there

A woman spinning at the door of her cottage; from an early engraving.

was some thought given to making it into a cash crop. In that year, Tiger Dunlop, an employee of the Canada Company, wrote,

> Flax would be a profitable article, but as yet there is not a single flax-mill in the province. All that is raised is used for domestic purposes, and is dressed by a hand-brake, by the farmer who grows it, and spun, and in many instances woven, by the women of the family.[5]

It is difficult to imagine today just how widespread the home weaving industry really was in pioneer Upper Canada. In 1812, when he was staying with a family of Dutch origin near Cornwall in Stormont County, an area settled by the Loyalists in the late eighteenth century, Dunlop reported that,

> I had the shew [show] room of the establishment for my sitting parlour ... and the walls [were] decorated with a tapestry of innumerable homespun petticoats, evidently never applied to any other (I won't say meaner) purpose, declaring at once the wealth and housewifery of the gude vrow.[6]

People in Ontario continued to grow, spin and weave some linen until the third quarter of the century. Many quilts and a few coverlets made of homespun, handwoven materials do contain linen thread, but it is difficult to distinguish cotton thread from linen in cloth composed of linen and wool or cotton and wool. In general, cloth with linen in it feels colder to the touch than cotton cloth. It is important to remember that linen could be grown and prepared at home, while cotton had to be bought at the store. Upper Canadian farmers liked to be self-sufficient, and did not pay out cash if they could avoid it. However, because cotton yarn was cheap and much easier to handle, it was used by the majority of people after 1830.

10

Nevertheless, flax growing and weaving was an important occupation for entire families. The McDiarmids, who had a son called "Hughie the Weaver," bought four hundred acres from Sir John Johnston in 1811 which were located in an area near Martintown, Glengarry County, called "The Island." Another Hugh McDiarmid on the Island was also a weaver, and his brother, Donald, was a hackler who retted and hackled the flax to prepare it for weaving.[7] The coverlet in Plate 16, which is made of heavy handspun linen and trimmed with indigo blue wool along the side borders in the Scottish fashion, was made by the McDiarmids for the Ross family near Williamstown.

In the first twenty years after the settlers arrived, implements for preparing, spinning and weaving cloth were probably homemade and crude. Some implements, such as spinning wheels, may have come over with the immigrants, but most of them had to start over with new tools. Distaffs were improvised from the branches of trees, and crude skeiners were carved by the men of the household. There was one man skilful with his hands in many districts who began to make wheels and equipment to sell to the surrounding settlers.[8] Of course, some implements were sent over from the old countries, witnessed, for instance, by an 1823 letter from Alexander Cameron of Aberfeldy, Scotland, who was replying to a request from his brother-in-law, Robert Dewar, who settled in 1817 near the border of Glengarry County:

> And if you wish to get one of the Heckles, you may have it, should a proper and sure conveyance for it occur, which, although we have it not at present, may in the course of time present itself.[9]

The "proper and sure conveyance" presented itself about twenty years later. In any case, Dewar's request for the family hackles gives some idea of the importance attached to these implements, which seem today to be of little significance.

The widespread use of home-woven wool materials did not begin as early as flax weaving, since it

---

10 "The walls [were] decorated with a tapestry of innumerable homespun petticoats ... declaring at once the wealth and housewifery of the gude vrow." Tiger Dunlop, 1812. [P.C.]

11 The spinning room in the attic of Fairfield House, Bath, Lennox and Addington County. The great wheels stand silent in the dust. The room once hummed with activity while the yarn was prepared to make cloth for a large family and numerous servants. [S.L.P.C.]

12 The weaving room at Fairfield House, Bath, Lennox and Addington County. Here the cloth was woven for clothing and bedding. A plentiful supply of bedding would have been needed, because the house was once an inn. [S.L.P.C.]

took longer to establish a flock than it did to grow a crop. By 1803, a carding mill was built at Martintown, Glengarry County, and it was not long before the people of the area were almost independent in cloth making. The Glengarry settlers carried on commerce with Montreal rather than with Ontario towns, and it is probable that they profited by proximity to Quebec where flocks of sheep already existed. Dependence on Quebec had lessened by 1820, when John Howison wrote,

> That I may make you acquainted with the blunt and uncultivated inhabitants of Glengarry, which is the first regular settlement in the Upper Province, and contains a large proportion of Scotch, as you can conceive from its national appellation. I entered the settlement in the evening, and the first person I met was a common labourer, whistling and walking gaily along, with his axe over his shoulder. I accosted him, and had some conversation with him, in the course of which he informed me, that he had commenced farming two years before, not being then possessed of subsistence for two months; but things had prospered with him, and he now owned a house, three cows, several sheep, and seven acres of very fine wheat.[10]

Since settlement was considerably earlier in Quebec, weaving was well established when Mrs. Traill came up the St. Lawrence River in 1836. She observed,

> Many a tidy smart-looking lass was spinning at the cottage door, with bright eyes and braided locks, while the younger girls were seated on the green turf or on the threshold, knitting and singing as blithe as birds.
>
> There is something very picturesque in the great spinning wheels that are used in this country for spinning the wool, and if attitudes were to be studied among our Canadian lasses, there cannot be one more becoming, or calculated to show off the natural advantages of a fine figure, than spinning at the big wheel. The spinster does not sit, but walks to and fro, guiding the yarn with one hand while with the other she turns the wheel.
>
> I often noticed, as we passed by the cottage farms, hanks of yarn of different colours hanging on the garden or orchard fence to dry; there were all manner of colours, green, blue, purple, brown, red, and white. A civil landlady, at whose tavern we stopped to change horses, told me these hanks of yarn were first spun and then dyed by the good wives, preparatory to being sent to the loom. She showed me some of this homespun cloth, which really looked very well. It was a dullish dark brown, the wool being the produce of a breed of black sheep. This cloth is made up in different ways for family use. "Every little dwelling you see," said she, "has its lot of land, and, consequently, its flock of sheep; and,

as the children are early taught to spin, and knit, and help dye the yarn, their parents can afford to see them well and comfortably clothed."[11]

Despite some difficulties, flocks of sheep were being gathered together in the Kingston area. In an 1825 diary, a farmer complained of the wolves on several different occasions,[12] but the list for an 1829 auction sale held near Adolphustown in Lennox and Addington County shows clearly that farmers were prospering. The list describes a flourishing household containing a bountiful supply of homespun bedding. Several sheep were sold, and, among the household effects, were listed fourteen good white flannel blankets, eight checked blankets, three striped blankets, one plaid blanket, several quilts and other textile items.[13] Other household inventories, such as that of John Meyers from Hastings County (1821), include a good supply of flannel (homespun) sheets.[14] The ability to manufacture such quantities of homespun cloth in the home was probably due in part to the carding machine which was in operation in the Kingston area as early as 1817; it carded wool for nine pence per pound. In the neighbouring districts, there were several additional carding machines and fulling mills; Isaac Fraser, for example, advertised his operation in the *Kingston Gazette* for June 29, 1814:

> The subscriber informs his friends and the public that he has removed his carding machines to the second concession east of Ernest Town, where those who may please to favour him with their custom will have their work done in the best manner — Prices for breaking and carding into rolls, seven pence half penny per pound.

By 1840, woollen mills had begun to make what was often called "country cloth." The Britannia Woollen Mills, Gananoque, Leeds County, advertised that they "made goods of similar quality to American manufactures," on shares or by the yard. At Cobourg, the Ontario Mills made: "Heavy Winter Woolen Goods, Etoffe-du-Pays; Broad and narrow Pilot Cloths, Cassimeres, Doeskins, Satinetts, Blankets, & C." According to W. A. Thompson, author of *A Tradesman's Travels in United States and Canada in 1840, 1841, and 1842*,

> In Upper Canada there are seventeen or eighteen of these woollen mills, equally scattered about the province, some of them employing eight or ten men. The hands are mostly paid by the month. From eighteen to twenty dollars with board is about the ordinary wages, but frequently one third to one half is paid in cloth or yarn. There is not other but water power, and this they have in abundance . . . I have learned

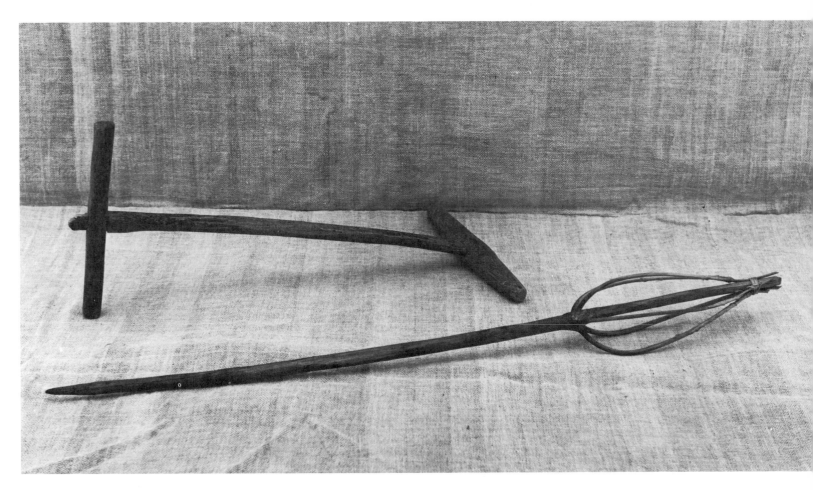

13 The Rock and the Reel, old names for the distaff and niddy-noddy or skeiner, implements used in preparing yarn at home. Simple tools such as these were probably homemade and crude. [P.C.]

14 An old photograph of a woman using a big walking wheel to spin yarn in a Leeds County dooryard. [P.C.]

what I did not expect – they get their machinery from the States... These establishments are of great value to the farmers, many of whom have looms in their houses, from which they have a supply of home-made stuffs: and here too as in the States, there is a numerous class of country weavers who make a good living from the farmers and cultivating a piece of land for themselves.[15]

These mills continued to rely heavily on the custom work done for local residents: carding, fulling, weaving and dying the wool brought to them and taking wool in payment for cloth or services.

Lanark County, an inland section of the District of Bathurst, was not settled until 1816, and even by 1827 the farmers were still struggling. In that year, a Montreal newspaper published the account of a traveller to the Lanark backwoods who related that his host "had no sheep. There were few of these in the township, but it is the intention of the settlers to set speedily about the rearing of these useful animals after which they expect to make the greater part of their own clothes."[16] The inhabitants of some Lanark townships, however, had sheep and were already weaving in 1823. The Reverend Bell wrote in his diary, "I came next to the house of Mr. McNab, the Baptist preacher, where the good man was busy at his loom."[17] Duncan McNab was a weaver in Beckwith Township until 1833 when he moved to Port Elmsley. The blankets in Plate 15 belonged to the Farmer family in Lanark County and were made by Duncan McNab. The quilt in Plate 17 was made from pieces of homespun cloth by the same family; they prepared the yarn and McNab did the weaving.

It was not easy to maintain a flock of sheep in a little clearing in the bush, because of the depredations of wild animals. Sheep were scarce and flocks suffered as a result of inbreeding. Besides this, the sheep coming from England and Scotland were not

15

16

15 Blankets: handspun and handwoven by weaver McNab; originally owned by the Farmer family, Lanark County, 2nd quarter 19th century. Left: W. 168 cm, L. 194 cm (66, 76 in.). Centre: W. 150 cm, L. 172 cm (59 ,68 in.). Right: W. 150 cm, L. 192 cm (59, 75 in.). Duncan McNab was a weaver in Beckwith Township until 1833 when he moved to Port Elmsley. He was a Baptist preacher and wove as a sideline. In an 1823 diary entry, the Reverend Bell mentioned visiting McNab's house where he found "the good man at his loom." [P.C.]

16 Coverlet: homespun, handwoven cream coloured linen with a blue wool border; by weaver McDiarmid, Martintown, Glengarry County, 1st quarter 19th century. W. 160 cm, L. 200 cm (63, 79 in.). Acquired from the Tom Ross family, Williamstown, Glengarry County. [P.C.]

17

17 Central Square: quilt with borders and block corners, pieced; handspun, handwoven wool with cotton warp; Farmer family, Lanark County, 2nd quarter 19th century. W. 162 cm, L. 192 cm (64, 75 in.). The weaving for this family was done by weaver McNab, Lanark County, from yarn prepared at home from the family flock of sheep. This quilt is made of material from worn clothing. [C.C.F.C.S.]

accustomed to the severity of Upper Canadian weather, and the lambs were born into a cold and snowy world. The little flocks had to be tended solicitously, a job that often fell to the women, while the men were engaged in the hazardous and never-ending task of clearing new land. During the first quarter of the nineteenth century, a few settlers had managed to maintain enough sheep to produce wool, which together with the flax they grew themselves, provided some cloth for clothing and bedding.

Many of the settlers coming from England, Ireland and Scotland had been employed as weavers in the old country. As landowners, they had to devote their time in Upper Canada to clearing and cultivating the land. The women took over the weaving in many cases, although traditionally they had been in charge of preparing the yarns. In most districts, one man or woman would set up as a custom weaver in his or her own home. Settlers who had no loom or did not have time to do all the weaving brought them their prepared yarns, and the custom weaver would make the cloth for a fee or sometimes for part of the yarn. As well, there were itinerant weavers who would take orders or who would work on people's own looms. As the century progressed, it would appear that one member of the family took charge of the spinning and weaving, probably because she had a special talent for it, or possibly because she was unmarried and did not have to bear a child every year or so. Edith McEwen, who was born in 1893, remembers that, "Aunt Bella[born 1866] used to make the yarn and card wool for comforters. My mother was always too busy to do these things."

The home making of cloth was being encouraged during these years. The Bathurst District Association of Lanark County was offering prizes in 1832 for the best twenty yards of linen, the best twenty yards of flannel and other domestic manufactures.[18] At its first fair, the Niagara District Agricultural Society offered prizes of £1, 10s. for the best piece of woollen cloth, not less than fifteen yards long.

By the middle of the century, the home industry of making cloth was flourishing. The agricultural census of 1851 listed the amount of fulled cloth, linen and flannel made on the farms. According to the census, there were thirty-one yards of flannel made on the Tunis Snook farm in Frontenac County. This represents a tremendous amount of labour. Home production was sufficient by 1848 for fulled cloth to be bought from local farmers in Leeds County and sold in the village stores.[19] While visiting the mid-century Provincial Agricultural Show in Toronto, Susanna Moodie was led to remark that, "The vast improvement in home manufactured cloth, blan-kets, flannels, shawls, carpeting, and counterpanes was very apparent over these same articles in former years."[20]

Spinning, this "important part of our domestic economy," in the words of Major Samuel Strickland, produced so many home comforts that, "the single ladies are literally spinsters."[21] The carding and weaving were usually done by the local weavers with yarn prepared by the housewife. Strickland mentions, too, that, "the common Canadian grey cloth, generally worn by the settlers of the Western province, is a strong, warm, servicable [sic] fabric, costing about four or five shillings per yard, Halifax currency."[22]

In *The Canadian Settlers' Guide*, first published in 1855, Mrs. Traill described a well-established home industry for producing cloth, or yarn for cloth to be woven by the weaver. She also wrote that very few people carded at home during that period, although it was commonly done when she first came to Upper Canada in 1832.[23] Despite this statement, the number of people living today who remember wool being carded and woven at home would seem to refute the idea that this was an uncommon occurrence.

Through extraordinary, sometimes backbreaking effort in the production of raw materials and actual manufacture, the home industry of cloth making was flourishing and of considerable economic importance by the middle of the century. The amount of cloth produced was not overwhelming by any means, but it was sufficient to supply an ample amount of cloth for the quilts and blankets covering the bedsteads of Upper Canada.

3 The Bedstead

Let his bed be hard, and rather quilts than feathers. Hard lodgings strengthen the parts, whereas being buried every night in feathers melts and dissolves the body. . . . Besides he that is used to hard lodgings at home will not miss his sleep (where he has most need of it) in his travels abroad for want of his soft bed, and his pillows laid in order.

Thoughts Concerning Education
John Locke (1632-1704)

The bedstead was one of the most important possessions of a family in the early days of Upper Canada. In their one-roomed shanty in the bush, the whole family would huddle together in a crude homemade bed. Enclosed in the snug, curtained haven, with the firelight dancing on the log walls, a body was safe, warm and comfortable beneath the pile of heavy blankets and quilts. Here, the family found rest and a renewal of strength to face yet another day of scanty food, merciless cold and back-breaking labour.

Traditionally, the bedstead had always been a significant possession, but here in this cold, hard new country it was of even greater and more immediate importance. A good bed might mean the difference between life and death; people were known to have frozen to death without its protection. As time passed, life became a little easier and the cabins were gradually replaced by more substantial houses, but the traditional centrality of the bedstead continued unabated. Large sums of money were spent by otherwise frugal people to acquire a prestigious bedstead and the fabrics to cover it.

Bedstead was the term used to describe the wooden or metal parts of what we now simply call a bed. Then, the bed was the tick or mattress; the bedding consisted of the pillows, bolsters, sheets and blankets; the top cover was the coverlet, counterpane, quilt or bedspread. The bed furniture included the curtains (until 1840, bedsteads were usually curtained), the tester cloth, valance, head cloth and dust ruffle. Curtains were necessary to insure a degree of privacy in accommodations shared by several members of the family and to keep out drafts.

Generally speaking, the first beds in Upper Canada were platforms or boxes, and the tick or mattress rested on planking. In rural areas between 1780 and 1820, use was occasionally made of woven hemlock or elm bark or canvas webbing to support the bedding, especially in small beds. Trundle beds, for example, often had cloth tacked to the side rails. During the same period and as late as 1860, the most commonly used mattress support or "spring" was made of rope, which went in and out of holes drilled in the rails or, in some cases, passed around knobs. Bed ropes were sold pre-cut in general stores as early as 1820 and as late as 1860. "Manilla bed cord" was advertised in an 1847 Kingston newspaper. On the other hand, some beds had cleats nailed along the inner surfaces of the rails to support the wooden slats on which the mattress rested. In the latter half of the century, wire springs came into use, the first ones

A kitchen bed with homespun curtains in nineteenth century Upper Canada.

being wire mesh tacked to a heavy wooden frame, while later ones were made entirely of metal, and from this many different types evolved, ranging from metal strips to coils.

Early Upper Canadian shanties have been described in many early books. Indeed, there are a number of shanties still standing today that have changed little over the years, and one can easily visualize the conditions faced by the first settlers. J. F. Pringle, author of *Lunenburgh* (1890), described the typical log shanty built by the Loyalists in Glengarry County:

> These houses were small, the largest not more than 20 feet by 15, built of round logs notched at the corners and laid one upon another to a height of seven or eight feet. The roof was made of elm bark, an opening for a door and one for a window was cut, the floor was made of split logs, the hearth of flat stones, the chimney of field stone laid up with clay for mortar as high as the walls, above which it was made of small round sticks plastered with clay; the spaces between the logs were "chinked" with small pieces of wood and daubed with clay, a blanket did duty as a door until a few boards could be cut with a whip saw, the window was fitted in course of time with a rough sash, and four lights of glass seven and a half inches by eight and a half, and the log house would be complete. Bed and bedding the settlers in most cases brought with them . . . and a few poles could be put together to form a bedstead.[1]

This is the type of shanty that would be found in any district (see Plate 26).

The first bedsteads were more or less built-in affairs occupying one or, occasionally, two corners of the room. Usually, they were "roughly hewn out with a felling axe, the side, the posts, and ends held together in screeching trepidation by strips of basswood bark; . . . [covered with] a bed [mattress] of fine feathers"[2] (Plate 19). Earlier and even cruder examples found in a sugar-house were described as "made with poles covered with bark and raised about fifteen inches from the ground; these had evidently served as seats as well as beds."[3] Their crude appearance is explained by Mrs. Traill: "The shanty, or small log-house of the poorer immigrant is often furnished by his own hands. A rude bedstead, formed by cedar poles, a coarse linen bag filled with hay or dried moss, and bolster of the same, is the bed he lies on."[4]

It was customary for a young couple who were setting up housekeeping to be equipped with a good bed and a sufficient supply of bedding. From the time she was about six years old, a girl and her mother would spend part of each day preparing for her marriage. This was doubly important in Upper Canada, and the custom persisted even into the depression of the 1930s when the village priest would provide a penniless couple with a bed and stove if they wished to marry; these were the only two items considered essential to setting up housekeeping.

When Job and Sarah Slaght were married in 1825, one of Job's first tasks for their Norfolk County home was building a primitive bed for his cheerful young wife. It sounds to be both comfortable and bouncy in the following description:

> A bedstead was made by fitting small poles into auger-holes bored into the logs. These poles were about six feet long, and were small enough to have a good spring. The lower ends of these spring poles lay on a cross piece, one end of which was inserted in an auger-hole in the wall and the other supported in an upright. Job got a feather bed and some bedding from a man who owed him for work done.[5]

In the early days of the nineteenth century, people did not travel extensively. They did not go to hospital during illness, and they gave birth at home. It was quite common for a man and his wife to sleep together every night of their married lives in the same bed in the same house. A bridegroom brought his bride home to their own bed, newly made up with bedding of her own manufacture and adorned with her marriage quilt. There the children were conceived and born. In the course of time, the man and woman grew old and died one after the other in the same bed in the same room. The bedstead was passed down to a favourite child, usually the son who was inheriting the homestead, and the bedding was divided among the daughters.

Early letters tell us of bedding sent across the seas to a daughter in the new land whose mother had died. Alexander Cameron, for example, wrote from Scotland to inform his brother-in-law in Upper Canada that, "their [sic] are some articles such as muches [caps or house bonnets] to be sent my sister of her mother's linen which will be welcome on arrival."[6] By passing the bedstead and linen down, the chain of marriage, birth and death was renewed with each generation.

In some areas, it was customary to burn the bedstead in which someone had died together with

---

18 A slip bedroom opening off the parlour, large enough to hold a bed and a chair, circa 1820. [U.C.V.]

19 An early homemade bed laced with woven elm bark, Lanark County, 1st quarter 19th century. W. 70 cm, L. 160 cm (28, 63 in.). Similar beds were described by Edward Talbot (*Five Years Residence in the Canadas*, 1823) as, "roughly hewn out with a felling axe, the sides, the posts, and ends held together in screeching trepidation by strips of basswood bark." [C.D.]

18

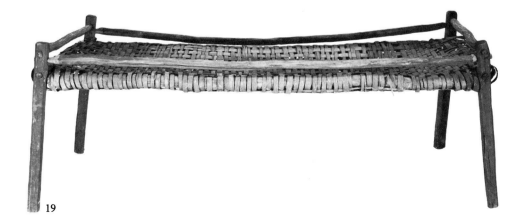

19

20

20 By day the cradle was placed in the midst of family activity so that someone could keep an eye on the baby. There was usually a grandmother, a brother or a sister ready to start the cradle rocking and hum a lullaby if the baby cried. [P.C.]

21 A *banc lit* in a kitchen with a man sleeping in it. *Canadian Illustrated News*, December 6, 1873.

22 A *banc lit* or bunk-bed from Lanark County made up for sleeping. When not in use, the hinged box can be folded up to serve as a bench. Lily Jane McLeod, born 1888 in Glengarry County, remembers visiting cousins when she was young; the children gave up their beds to the visitors and slept in the *banc lit* in the hall. [P.C.]

23 In the early days, small children slept in trundle beds, which were pushed under their parents' bed during the day and stood near it at night. [P.C.]

24 Hired man's bed, Lanark County, 2nd quarter 19th century. Old quilts were kept long after they were considered too shabby even for the children's beds. They were still good enough for the hired man, who usually had to sleep on a short narrow bedstead in the kitchen or the hall. [P.C.]

25 A low-post bed made to fit under the eaves, Lanark County, 2nd quarter 19th century, covered with a handwoven checked blanket. [P.C.]

21

23

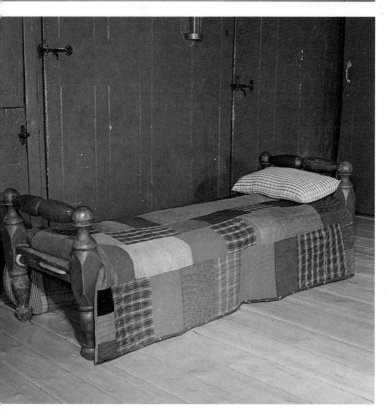

all the bedding which had been on the bed. Until the third quarter of the nineteenth century, Glengarry County Highland Scots continued this homeland tradition,[7] but fortunately all the best family bedding was not on a death bed, and some of it has survived.

There are reports in the early days of women dying from the cold during childbirth. It is probable that they were lying on the floor to give birth, while the rest of the family lay huddled in the only bed. Describing an episode in the Talbot Settlement, John Howison wrote in 1821 of the "inmates" of a farmhouse who "consisted of a family who recently emigrated from Scotland, and the Mother was dying in childbed. Supported by pillows, she reclined on a mattress in the middle of the floor."[8]

A "shake-down" on the floor was a common enough bed for the men and older children, and travellers were accommodated in this fashion. For the traveller, this would be more comfortable than a bed in the average inn, since there one must expect what early writers called "nuisances," or what Sir Richard Bonnycastle described as "fleas and bugs and such small deer." In his *Reminiscences of a Canadian Pioneer,* Samuel Thompson described a tavern, so called, at which he spent the night:

> It was a log building of a single apartment where presided "the wife" — a smart, plump, good-looking little Irish woman, in a stuff gown and without shoes or stockings . . . the floor was of loose split logs, hewn into some approach of eveness with an adze. The hearth . . . of bare soil . . . revealed to our eyes an extraordinary piece of furniture — a log bedstead in the darkest corner.[9]

The reports of the beds and bedding to be found in the early inn vary somewhat, but most are disparaging. Usually, the inn was no more than the dwelling place of a farmer or other settler, and members of the family gave up their beds to sleep on the kitchen floor when business was brisk. Sir James Alexander reported on the accommodations in Upper Canada in 1833:

> The ladies usually on the journey occupied the best bed-room in the house, whilst the gentlemen stretched themselves on a "shakedown" in the sitting room, preferring this method for the sake of sociability and to take advantage of the fire. Most of the bedrooms in country inns in Canada are mere closets with curtainless stretchers containing feather-bed nuisances, and very small pillows.[10]

This is rather mild criticism when compared to Mrs. Moodie's report of a friend's experiences while travelling in 1832:

> I thought to get a private room to wash and dress in, but there is no such thing as privacy in this country. In the bush, all things are common; you cannot even get a bed without having to share it with a companion. A bed on the floor in a public sleeping room: — men, women and children, only divided by a paltry curtain.[11]

After various experiences, such as a "miserable, dirty, wretched room at a Highlander's," Mrs. Simcoe learned in 1794 to take her own folding bed with her.[12] Mrs. Traill was dismayed with the cool reception she got at an inn in Cornwall, where she was offered the choice between a room which was a "mere closet, in which was a bed divested of curtains," or "a four-bedded room, which has three tenants in it — and those gentlemen."[13] Similarly, John J. Bigsby describes one of his Upper Canadian journeys in these words: "We at length arrived at Andrew's Inn, near Mallory's Town on the highroad to Kingston . . . . This family . . . took to us cooly. . . . My blankets here were again thin and few and the crannies in the wall wide and many."[14]

Comfort was not to be found in bed while travelling Upper Canadian roads, but some descriptions of the inns are almost pleasant: "the bed chamber commonly contains four or five beds, clean and plain, with cotton sheets and linsey-woolsey coverlets, but having neither posts nor curtains."[15] No doubt some of the criticism was due to very real conditions, such as the "small deer" mentioned earlier, but it was probably also due to the fact that many immigrants were used to old country inns

26

26 The settler's first shanty in the bush. (Detail of a naïve painting from Eganville, Renfrew County.) [P.C.]

where the accommodations were considerably better.

Once travelling and living conditions in Upper Canada were accepted, however, the immigrant's attitude probably altered. Even the fastidious Mrs. Moodie set up her bedstead in the corner of the single room of her first cabin in Upper Canada, "I left off arranging the furniture of a bed that had been just put up in a corner."[16]

One of the first improvements made by the early settler was to set up more comfortable sleeping quarters. In 1817, a few days after settling in his primitive one-roomed shanty, the Reverend Bell, the first minister of Perth in Lanark County, began to partition off small bedrooms. These partitions were only one board thick and afforded a scant amount of privacy. Mrs. Moodie had a bed-closet built around the bed of a male friend who was living with her and her husband. This was a windowless cupboard just about the size of a single bed.[17] A similar "room" was found in a Frontenac County kitchen added to a farmhouse about 1830. It was probably here that the hired girl slept on a crude, narrow bedstead, or on the floor.

Within a few years, a second room might be added, or a larger log cabin built. The second cabin usually contained two rooms and a loft, one room being a kitchen-living room and the other a parlour or a parlour-bedroom. In some cases, small bedrooms were partitioned off each room. These were called slip-rooms and were hardly larger than a bed (Plate 18). The same floor plan was retained in the more substantial early houses, the downstairs bedrooms becoming a little larger as the century wore on. It was still customary during the first half of the century to sleep downstairs near the sources of heat. When stoves began to be used to supplement fireplace heat, stove pipes were run through the upstairs rooms, which were finished as bedrooms for the older children. Only the houses of the wealthiest people had stoves in the upstairs bedrooms.

The built-in homemade beds of the first shanties were soon replaced with high-post beds often built to order by the local carpenter or furniture maker. The earliest beds were heavy structures with squared posts and sometimes with wooden cornices at the ceiling. They had curtains that pulled closed to provide both warmth and privacy, and they were usually very large, accommodating mother, father and some of the children.

Based largely on research among the older people in the Niagara Peninsula in 1905, Michael Scherck included in *Pen Pictures of Early Pioneer Life In Upper Canada* (1905) an interesting, complete and valuable description of sleeping arrangements in the area:

> In the sleeping apartments of the family was to be seen the old family bedstead with high wooden framework on top enclosed by damask curtains, and with a white linen curtain or valance around the bottom of the bedstead, as well as the low trundle bed on wooden castors or rollers, in which the children of the family slept in the same room with their parents, often until they were twelve or fourteen years of age, and which in daytime was shoved underneath the large bed. When the farmer was short of bedroom space there was to be seen in the dining-room or kitchen, the old-fashioned bunk, which served as a seat or bench in the daytime and a bed at night, the lower part being in the shape of a box, which when opened up, disclosed a quantity of bedclothing and made a comfortable place for sleeping.[18]

Plate 21 shows a bunk-bed opened to make a bed, while Plate 22 shows a man sleeping in a bunk-bed in the kitchen of a farmhouse as late as 1873. These beds were known as bunk-beds, bench-beds, settlebeds or *banc lits,* the latter term being used in Quebec and Glengarry, and they are common in areas settled by Scottish people who had used them in the old country. In the same areas, we find small homespun quilts that are just the right size to fit a *banc lit* and were probably made for this purpose (Plate 27).

The settle-bed started out life in the kitchen, but, as bedrooms were added, it was relegated to the upper hall where it was used for the children when there were visitors. A few old people can still remember sleeping in the settle-bed and that they were not very comfortable as benches.

Quilts made for the early, large four-post beds were themselves very large, and, since these beds rarely had footboards, the quilts had cut-outs at the bottom corners to fit around the bottom posts, leaving the tail of the quilt to hang down (Plate 28). A bed without a footboard shows a quilt off to advantage. The early four-poster was almost immovable, and it began to be replaced by a lighter, smaller four-post bed in the 1830 to 1840 period. These beds, which usually had footboards, were still curtained, but the curtains became shorter, and the foot curtains had begun to disappear by 1840.

Built-in wall beds are scarce in Canada, although they were common in Scotland. It is possible, of course, that some Upper Canadian wall beds have been removed over the years to make more room in the kitchens and parlours. Some support for this idea comes from the fact that blankets with coloured

27   Fence Row, or Shoo Fly: quilt, pieced; handspun, hand-woven wool; Norman Kent family, Consecon, Prince Edward County, 2nd quarter 19th century. W. 155 cm, L. 167 cm (61, 66 in.). Suitable in size for a *banc lit*. [C.C.F.C.S.]

27a   Detail showing handspun, handwoven and home-dyed cloth, probably dress goods.

28   Eight Point Star: quilt, pieced; cotton; Lancaster, Glengarry County, 2nd quarter 19th century. W. 205 cm, L. 217 cm (81, 85 in.). This is a large quilt with the corners adapted to fit a four-post bed. [C.M.]

28a   Detail showing the simple, old-fashioned pattern and colour scheme.

29 Blanket: detail; handspun, handwoven wool; Glengarry County, 2nd quarter 19th century. W. 163 cm, L. 186 cm (64, 73 in.). This example is characteristic of blankets found in Scottish areas with its borders of broken herringbone weave along the sides and the lack of bands across the ends. [P.C.]

30 Wild Goose Chase: quilt top; black and red to set off a shining brass bed; pieced by Mrs. Saphronia Pearson, Kingston, Frontenac County, ca. 1905. W. 192 cm, L. 240 cm (76, 95 in.). [P.C.]

31 Drunkard's Path: quilt, pieced; red and white cotton; made by Elizabeth Brooks Stedman, Perth, Lanark County, the great-grandmother of the present owner. W. 167 cm, L. 195 cm (66, 77 in.). This quilt won first prize for quilting at the Lanark County Fair in 1881. [M.J.L.]

32 Crazy Quilt: pieced; velvets; Glenburnie, Frontenac County, 1st quarter 20th century, W. 155 cm, L. 190 cm (61, 75 in.). An interesting arrangement and a galaxy of colour. [L.A.S.]

borders along the sides only are said to have been made for wall beds (Plate 29) and are found in districts settled by Scottish immigrants. However, such blankets may also have been made for beds merely placed against a wall.

High-post beds were being sold as early as 1798 in a general store in the Bay of Quinte district of Lennox and Addington County. In this year one Archibald Chisholm bought a high-post bedstead from Samuel Sherwood,[19] although it was more usual to order a bed to be made by a cabinetmaker. Even as late as 1860, it was possible to buy a bedstead at the village store. It is probable that these large bedsteads were becoming old-fashioned by the first quarter of the nineteenth century; this is perhaps why John Duncan of Kingston auctioned off his excess stock in 1822, including "five large bedsteads, roped and reeded."[20]

When bedrooms began to be used in the upper story of a story-and-a-half house, low-post beds were made to fit under the eaves. These were attractive beds usually with turned posts topped by a finial and often with a blanket rail instead of a footboard. The purpose of the rail was for rolling the blanket around it so that it could be pulled up at night if one became chilly and preventing the discomfort of having it across one's feet when not in use. These beds were often painted red or blue, and, when covered with gaily coloured quilts, they were bright and charming in the dark, low-ceilinged bedrooms (Plate 25).

Houses built after 1840 tended to have higher ceilings and many could accommodate a high-post bed upstairs. The sad state of four-post beds whose tops have been lopped off testifies that many beds did not make the move unscathed.

By the middle of the nineteenth century, beds were being made in furniture factories, and it was possible to buy suites of bedroom furniture. Iron beds began to be sold around this time, and brass beds soon followed, while spool beds were popular between 1850 and 1860. Quilts were made to suit the styles of the new beds, but still keeping, nevertheless, to the traditional patterns. The quilt top in Plate 30, Wild Goose Chase, was made in 1905 for a brass bed. It is a traditional pattern, yet it is made in colours that would complement the shining metal — red flannel print on a black background.

Bedsteads that came with suites were very elaborate. The headboards, which often reached almost to the ceiling, were machine carved and florid. They contrasted strangely with the clean, uncluttered lines of the quilts being made at the same period, since some of the finest and most graphic pieced quilts were made in the last quarter of the century. For

example, the quilt in Plate 31, Drunkard's Path, won the prize for quilting at the Lanark County Fair in 1881.

Many fine red and white quilts were made between 1880 and 1910, a period when taste in furniture was not nearly so good. Publications such as *Godey's Magazine and Lady's Book* tried to persuade women that pieced quilts were hopelessly outdated, but their taste remained constant and they continued to make quilts in the traditional patterns. New patterns were introduced which were in keeping with late Victorian tastes, but they were in the minority. Instead, fancy Crazy quilts became popular. Originally, they had been made as the most economical method of using scraps of scarce material that were too small to cut into a pattern. Now they were being made as ornamental throws in velvets and silks. Some are very beautiful, obviously made by women who had an eye for texture and colour (Plate 32). Even the most haphazard of them are glorious conglomerations of shapes and colours.

Some people began to make quilts that were as much feats of endurance as anything else. Many were made of tiny pieces of silk in beautiful, shining colours, such as the Pineapple Log Cabin in Plate 33; it won first prize at the Canadian National Exhibition in Toronto during the early 1900s. Although it is beautifully executed and coloured, like most silk quilts it is quite useless since the silk cuts and rots even without being used.

Several new patterns that appeared about this time, such as Colonial Lady and Sunbonnet Sue, clearly show that the art of quilt making did not entirely escape from the deterioration of taste that characterized the late Victorian and early Edwardian periods.

By the 1920s and 30s, iron beds painted with a white enamel that usually peeled were in common use. They were not very handsome in themselves, but, enlivened by red and white Irish Chain quilts, they achieved a cheerful, homey look that gives them a certain charm in retrospect.

The high-post bed style, which became popular once the early large and heavy four-poster was outdated, was lighter and smaller in both width and length, since the addition of extra bedrooms at this time meant that children did not sleep with their parents any longer. This size is considered today as somewhat small for two people, but it was used as a double bed for more than a hundred years, and it may have something to do with the fact that people were accustomed to sharing beds from their childhood. During the nineteenth century, it was thought unkind to make a small child sleep alone, lest he be

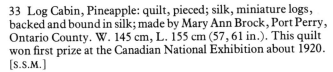

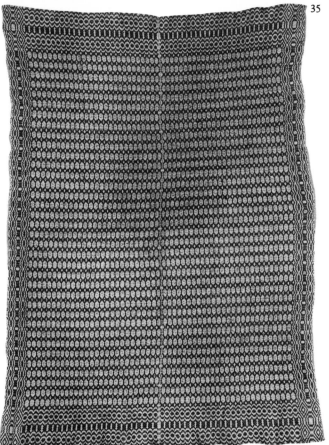

33 Log Cabin, Pineapple: quilt, pieced; silk, miniature logs, backed and bound in silk; made by Mary Ann Brock, Port Perry, Ontario County. W. 145 cm, L. 155 cm (57, 61 in.). This quilt won first prize at the Canadian National Exhibition about 1920. [S.S.M.]

33a Detail. Incredible patience and skill were required to make this intricate pattern using tiny pieces of silk.

34 Cradle Blanket: homespun wool, cream with blue bands;

eastern counties, 19th century. W. 72 cm, L. 82 cm (28, 32 in.). Small blankets were made to welcome a new arrival in the family. [P.C.]

35 Dog's Tracks: coverlet; handspun, handwoven, medium indigo blue wool on white cotton; Carleton Place area, Lanark County, ca. 1870. W. 100 cm, L. 145 cm (40, 58 in.). This coverlet was made for a child's cot, and the pattern, with its centre seam, has been scaled down appropriately. [C.D.]

afraid, or cold or lonely at night. Children slept together, and spinster aunts or widowed grandparents shared a bed with a child.

The cradle or cot was kept beside the parents' bed, and by day the cradle was placed in the midst of family activity where someone could keep an eye on the baby. There was usually a grandmother, a brother or a sister ready to start the cradle rocking and to hum a lullaby if the baby cried. Several years ago, I went to a French-Canadian farmhouse in Ontario to see the new baby. The parents were in the barn doing the milking. I went into the big, warm kitchen where the baby was sleeping in the family cradle by the wood stove. It was dusk, and the only sound was the soft singing of the kettle on the back of the stove. A dark-eyed boy of three sat on a little stool close by the cradle ready to set the rockers going at the slightest whimper.

Cradle quilts and little homespun blankets (Plates 34, 35) were always made to welcome a new arrival in the family. In the early days, small children slept in trundle beds, which were pushed under the parents' bed during the day and stood near it at night (Plate 23). Young unmarried girls slept in small rooms which could be reached only through the parents' room. This was considered a wise precaution in the days when hired men slept in the house and casual visitors were common.

Because very few people slept alone, single beds were scarce. Almost the only ones to be found were very narrow and intended for the hired help who slept in the kitchen, in the back hall or over the back kitchen. Any sleeping quarters were considered good enough for the unfortunate hired hand. One theory often held was that he or she would not linger too long in the mornings if the bed was sufficiently uncomfortable. This attitude continued into the late 1930s when, not surprisingly, hired men became hard to get. Old quilts were kept long after they were considered too shabby even for the children's beds and passed on to the hired man. We can thank him for the survival of many tattered old quilts that are historically interesting despite their condition.

Besides the fact that it was lonely and cold sleeping alone, sleeping together saved on labour in the days when washing had to be done under difficult conditions. In very large families, it was not uncommon to put the children to sleep like knives and forks in a box, head to toe, using both ends of the bed.

4 Bed Furniture

A curtain lecture is worth all the sermons in the world for teaching the virtues of patience and long-suffering.

Rip Van Winkle
Washington Irving (1783-1859)

Bed furniture was the term used to describe all those appurtenances of the bedstead that were separate from the actual bed (tick or mattress), bedding (pillows, bolsters, sheets and blankets) and top cover (quilt, counterpane, etc.) The bed furniture consisted of a top, back, two head curtains, two foot curtains, one top outer and one top inner valance, one bottom valance and sometimes extra drapery laid on the back of the bed.

Early four-post beds had curtains which were meant to be drawn, although as time passed they became merely decorative. From about 1830 on, the custom of drawing the curtains began to die out, yet between 1840 and 1860 there were still people who regularly slept with their curtains drawn. As stoves came into common use, however, and bedrooms were separated from communal living quarters, bed curtains were no longer so necessary for warmth or privacy.

There were three main types of curtained beds in use around 1820: the four-post bed with straight hangings, the tent or field bed with an arched canopy, and the Empire or French bed as it was called in Upper Canada.

The top or tester cloth, sometimes lined with cream coloured cotton, was tacked to the tester frame. The frame used with most early bedsteads was made up of four narrow strips of wood with holes in the ends which fitted over pegs in the tops of the posts. Existing examples of Canadian tester frames usually have one or two cross pieces to help support the cloth. The tester cloth, itself, did not necessarily match the rest of the bed furniture.

The upper valance, or short curtain, was tacked to the tester frame and was usually lined. In early beds before 1820, the valance was not gathered, although it was often scalloped or shaped. Inside the tester frame was an iron or brass rod from which the long bed curtains were suspended by rings or tapes running along the rod when the curtain was pulled. Later, the head curtains were diminished until eventually just a cascade remained, the foot curtains having been omitted first.

The head cloth was attached to the tester frame at the head of the bedstead and came down to just below the headboard. When a dust ruffle or lower valance was used, it was tacked below the rails or gathered on a tape and tied. Sometimes it was made in three pieces to avoid covering the legs of the bedstead at the foot. Occasionally, this lower valance would be attached to the bed cover as a flounce rather than to the bedstead.

A tent bed with an arched canopy; from an early engraving.

36 A curtained high-post bedstead hung with rose and blue on white printed Indian cotton. The bolster and pillow are in original homespun linen cases. [U.C.V.]

The tent bed was an early fashion, coming in about 1790, and it was said to be very popular in Upper Canada. In his *Journal of a Tour of North America* (1832), Thomas Fowler stated that tent beds were commonly used in Canada and could be bought for three to six dollars.[1] The posts of the tent bed were lower than other types, and an arched canopy was used to support the tester cloth. On some, the canopy could be folded; for example, on officers' beds that had to be moved frequently. Tent bed curtains were looped back with ties that went around the posts or buttoned onto the cloth itself.

French beds had foot and head boards of equal height. This kind of bed was placed against the wall and the curtains were suspended from an arrangement, such as a pole or hook, attached to the wall above the bed. Early homemade beds, really boxes built in a corner, had curtains suspended from a wooden canopy attached to the ceiling. It is probable that a homespun blanket tacked to a beam often served this purpose.

The Workwoman's Guide (1840) suggested suitable materials for bed hangings:

> Beds for common use were hung with linen or cotton check, or stripe, print, or stuff, but for better purposes, with dimity, fine stuff, moreen, damask chintz, Turkey twill, and lined with glazed calico or muslin of various colours, and for state rooms, fine silk, satin, and velvet is employed.[2]

All the parts of the bed furniture did not necessarily match, except in very fashionable beds. The tester cloth and dust ruffle were sometimes of plain material, while the rest of the material was patterned. In 1829, for example, three families in Prescott, Grenville County, each bought "1 psc. furniture calico 28 yds., 10s . . . £ 1-3-4"[3] (ten shillings . . . one pound, three shillings, four pence). Twenty-eight yards of bed furniture calico would be sufficient to make curtains and valances for a high-post bed, but would not be enough to make a bedspread as well. In these cases, quilts, coverlets or bedspreads of different materials must have been used.

Moreen, a heavy woollen, or woollen and cotton material, is one of the most commonly mentioned fabrics for bed hangings in Upper Canada. According to an 1818 auction sale bill,[4] General Widdpington of Kingston had crimson moreen hangings, as did the Turnbull house in Belleville[5] in 1827. A Mrs. McCauley of Kingston bought green moreen curtains in 1838.[6]

Of course, other materials were used, but, no matter what the fabric, a great deal of care was exercised in making hangings. A bedroom in the Niagara area, for example, had damask curtains with a white linen dust ruffle,[7] while in 1838 Mrs. Moodie used "snow white fringed curtains with bed furniture to correspond."[8] Anne Langton bought her bed hanging fabrics in Manchester (U.S.A.) and spent a considerable number of months making them.[9]

From the turn of the nineteenth century, bed hangings were advertised in Upper Canada, and among the materials offered were moreens, serges, chintzes, India calicoes, prints and checked calicoes. Dimity and muslin were used, and among surviving bed hangings, which are very rare, are those made of copperplate English cotton and a fine set of crewel-worked cotton thought to have come from the Maritime Provinces.

The bedstead shown in Plate 36 is now in Upper Canada Village and is hung with a printed India cotton, daintily sprigged in rose and blue on white, made in the same way it was over a hundred years ago. Another bed (Plate 37), also in Upper Canada Village, has a netted, fringed canopy. The spread on this second bed has a netted fringe added to match the canopy. There is some evidence that lighter hangings were used in the summer, supported by the fact that both light and dark hangings are listed in one 1829 home inventory from Lennox and Addington County.[10]

Large amounts of money were spent on bed furniture. A stylish bedstead was considered to be very important in the early nineteenth century. Those who could afford to buy material at the store for this purpose probably did so even if they had to do without other important items in order to find the money. Those who simply could not afford to buy imported materials, or who would not do so as a matter of principle, undoubtedly made their own hangings from homespun linen and wool.

Early bed hangings are very difficult to find today, although there is no doubt that they were used extensively in both rural and urban areas. As fashions changed and as the early, complete sets of bed hangings passed out of style, the valuable materials were likely put to other uses and the remnants worked into quilts. Inventory lists of household effects and auction sale bills indicate that almost every house in the first forty years of the nineteenth century had at least one high-post bed complete with hangings. The 1811 William Firth sale at Holyrood House in York (Toronto) lists among articles for sale, "superb four-post bedsteads on castors, with large bordered, prime goose feather beds and pillows, best Whitney [sic] blankets, hair mattresses of very first quality."[11] Prosperous farmers, such as John Meyers in Hastings

County[12] and Daniel Haight in Adolphustown[13] listed bed curtains in their inventories as well.

Even after the days when curtains were no longer necessary, vestiges of curtains were retained by old-fashioned people who believed that their heads had to be protected from drafts. This was a widespread opinion, and most people wore night caps for the same reason. As late as 1920, people with brass beds padded the headboard to keep their heads warm.

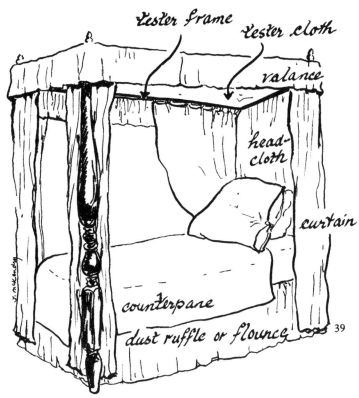

37 A cherry four-post bed with netted canopy and white Bolton counterpane trimmed with matching handmade netted fringe. Lighter canopies were used in the summer. [U.C.V.]

38 A high-post bedstead in the parlour bedroom, Fairfield House, Bath, Lennox and Addington County. The heavy wooden canopy reaches to the ceiling. The bed has been left as it was, with the headboard at the foot of the bed. It was used by the family well into the twentieth century. The Delectable Mountains quilt was made around 1860 by a member of the Fairfield family. [S.L.P.C.]

39 A high-post bedstead complete with bedding and bed furniture. Sketch by Jennifer McKendry.

5 The Feather Bed

Go tell Aunt Nabby,
Go tell Aunt Nabby,
Go tell Aunt Nabby,
The old gray goose is dead.

'Tis the one that she was saving,
'Tis the one that she was saving,
'Tis the one that she was saving,
To make a feather bed.

This lullaby has been used to sing babies to sleep for countless generations. It came over to Upper Canada with the settlers, who continued to croon the sad little song to their babies in the strange new place, just as they continued to make the traditional feather bed of their homelands.

The feather bed is a bag made of cotton ticking or, in the early days, of homespun linen stuffed with goose, duck or chicken feathers. The aristocrat of feather beds was the goose feather bed. There has always been prestige connected with the possession of one of these beds, and folk songs are filled with references to them as symbols of luxury and comfort:

> Last night I slept on a goose feather bed
> With the sheets turned down so bravely O,
> Tonight I shall sleep on the cold, cold ground
> Along with the raggle-taggle gypsies O,

and,

> Feather beds are soft, and painted rooms are bonny,
> But I shall leave them all to live with my love
> Johnny.

Since feather beds were difficult to handle aboard ship, most settlers emigrating to Upper Canada had to leave them behind in the old country. Both during the crossing and in their new homes they had to use more durable hair mattresses, straw ticks or even pallets made of blankets. Books by early travellers and published guides for emigrants advised settlers to bring mattresses with them, for, as Anne Langton wrote, "The aching of the bones when obliged to toss upon a hard surface for some days, is no trifling inconvenience."[1] Doubtless knowing this, Catherine Parr Traill brought with her a straw mattress, the price of which was one shilling.[2]

During the cholera epidemic in the early 1830s, all bedding had to be washed at Grosse Isle, while the emigrant ships were halted there for a quarantine period. Susanna Moodie described the scene:

> The women, with their scanty garments tucked about their knees, were tramping their bedding in the tubs or in holes in the rocks which the retiring tide had left half full of water. Those who did not possess washing tubs, pails, or iron pots, or could not obtain access to a hole in the rocks, were running to and fro, screaming and scolding in no measured terms. The confusion of Babel was among them.[3]

Because her luggage had been removed to customs, Mrs. Moodie, herself, spent one of her first nights in Canada aboard a ship lying off Montreal sleeping on a pile of Union Jacks,[4] a most appropriate bed indeed for the very British Mrs. Moodie.

Running goose; from an engraving in an early children's book.

Whether it was brought from the old country or made by early settlers, the feather bed would be placed on a mattress of hair, moss, straw or some material acting as a substitute. This mattress was supported by a rope or woven elm bark lacing which was the forerunner of modern springs. If one did not have a feather bed, a straw or corn husk tick replaced it. Early settlers arriving without a mattress had to make do with what they could find in the woods and fields. In 1839, for example, Samuel Strickland reported that, "My bed was composed of hemlock picked fine and covered with a buffalo robe."[5] A description of a shanty built by settlers in the Peterborough area reads, "On top of this [planking] they placed grasses and cedar boughs for a mattress, and made pillows from down of bullrushes."[6] Mrs. Traill noted that a coarse linen bag filled with straw or dried moss, and a similar bolster, was often the bed of the poor immigrant. It had the singular advantage that it could be made by his own hands — "Little enough and rude enough...better things are in store."[7] Such information was picked up and passed on in books published in the old countries. The Scottish *Information for the People,* for instance, suggests that, "the mattress needs consist of nothing more expensive than the boughs of the spruce fir, or dry beech leaves."[8]

It was not, however, all a big camping trip in the bush. As early as 1811, town houses had "hair mattresses of the very first quality,"[9] but there was a great discrepancy in living conditions in different regions depending on the length of time the area had been settled and, of course, the amount of money the individual settler had. As a result, there were fine hair mattresses and goose feather beds in the towns where wealthy army personnel lived and home-made mattresses in the country whose materials had been gleaned from field and bush. During his first month in Upper Canada, for instance, Edward Talbot's bed was "composed of a few withered leaves, while 'a log contriv'd a double debt to pay/By night a pillow, and a seat by day'."[10]

As soon as a settler was able to do so, he gathered a few geese together and these supplied him with feathers for his bed. As might be expected, the problems encountered in the more remote areas were quite similar to early attempts at raising sheep in the small bush clearings. Wild animals made it difficult to keep enough geese to supply great amounts of feathers, and hence wild fowl feathers supplemented the meagre domestic output.

Nevertheless, household inventories reveal that feather beds were being used in prosperous rural homes at an early date. By 1821, John Meyers of Hastings County had in his household six feather beds, four bolsters, ten pillows and thirteen straw ticks.[11] The Hurd family of Augusta, Grenville County, had in 1839 eight feather beds (valued at £3 each) with twenty-six pillows. There were fifteen bedsteads listed for this household; presumably they also had ticks of some kind not considered worth mentioning.[12] In 1850, the Cronkhite family of Prince Edward County had four bedsteads and a lounge, five feather ticks, four feather bolsters and four husk ticks. The five feather ticks were listed at forty dollars for the lot.[13]

Early travellers were not so fortunate as the prosperous Meyers, Hurds and Cronkhites, and they complained of the scarcity of feathers in their beds. Describing his voyage on the first steamship on Lake Ontario, a gentleman wrote, "The beds and pillows have a scarcity of feathers. If one passenger tells a correct story, he took the trouble to count and found the pillow under his head to contain only nineteen feathers and a half."[14]

Mattresses were available in Upper Canadian stores. The ones used even in the early days looked much the same as felt mattresses do today, since they were made with boxed sides. In 1857, the Penitentiary Cabinet Warehouse in Kingston, Canada West, advertised:

Hair mattresses,
Moss Do.,
Straw Do.,
Spring Do.[15]

Horse, cattle and hog hair, treated and curled, was also used in mattresses; one example was ordered from a Kingston merchant specifying the use of twenty-three pounds of hair.[16]

Throughout the years, it was known that only goose feathers were suitable to make a good feather bed. Chicken, duck and wild fowl feathers were used, but these tended to lump and get hard. The practice of plucking geese live for the down on their breasts, so that they might live to give more down another day, continued from ancient times into the first quarter of the twentieth century when it became less common in Upper Canada. Some people had a knack for plucking live and drew no blood. The unfortunate bird was placed on its back with its head bent down and held beneath the knee of the woman who was doing the plucking. With one hand, she held the bird's legs and, with the other, plucked the down feathers. A woman who remembers her mother regularly plucking live geese said that she herself had tried it only a few times and did not consider the small amount of down one got to be worth the distress it caused the creature. The small amounts of down obtained had to be carefully saved up until there was enough to make a down quilt or pillow. Because collecting it was such a time-consuming process, down was worth a considerable amount of money, as it still is today.

Happily for the old gray goose, it was usually dead before it was plucked. The dead bird was scalded with boiling water and then plucked. The feathers were picked over, all soiled or "thatch" feathers being discarded. Thatch feathers were those found on the back and parts of the wings. The usable feathers were placed in bags, usually old grain bags, and hung from the rafters to dry for about a year. If they were used before the drying process was complete, they would smell. The dry feathers were then stuffed in a bag of ticking to make a bed.

As in modern down clothing, the feathers had a tendency to work out of the tick. To combat this problem, some women rubbed the inside of the ticking with homemade brown soap, while others used an inner bag of thin, unbleached muslin as an undercover. Early mattress ticks were made of coarse linen tow or tightly woven cotton; Plate 41, for example, shows part of a homemade tick which is made of linen and has dark stripes of wool.

On the other hand, ticks for straw and corn husk mattresses often had an opening in the top where one could reach in with a smoothing stick to settle the stuffing when it lumped. This opening could be buttoned shut or pulled together with ties. Some women had a way of tucking in the corners of the bag or tick to make a neat squared corner. Others made boxed ticks by setting pieces in the sides. A good feather bed, however, was plump, shapeless and completely soft wherever it was squeezed, and sufficiently thick and resilient that the surface beneath could not be felt.

Some people piled two or more feather beds on a bedstead; some slept with one over and one under. The upper one was called a feather comforter, or comfort. In some areas, these were called feather quilts, although they were usually not quilted. Thin muslin was used for the "tick" of the comforter, covered by a calico print. This was done so that the cover could be washed without the fuss and bother of washing the feathers. However, without changing the feathers, feather beds could be washed. They were scrubbed or even put into a tub and hung on the line; their position had to be changed frequently and the tick rubbed between the hands to fluff up the feathers while they were drying. From time to time the tick would be opened, if it seemed to be getting thin, and the feathers were replenished. Bolsters,

long pillows shaped like sausages that were laid across the bed to support the head, and ordinary pillows were made and cared for in much the same way as the feather bed and comforter.

During the 1920s, salesmen came to farmers' doors soliciting the business of remaking feather beds into mattresses. The result was a feather bed sewn by a heavy machine into tubes. These had a neat appearance, but were nothing like a proper feather bed. The luxurious softness, the overabundance of comfort and the voluptuousness which one associates with a feather bed were gone, leaving only a mattress pad.

People who were not fortunate enough to own a flock of geese had to substitute corn husks or straw to fill their ticks. The husks were gathered in the fall, the inner leaves were dried and these were used to fill the newly washed tick. A light cotton, such as a factory cotton, was sufficient covering for a corn husk mattress. Despite the fact that country people considered a tick filled with corn husks to be inferior to those filled with feathers, a husk tick is firm, even and surprisingly comfortable. It does not rustle like a straw mattress and is not dusty. A woman who slept on one regularly in her youth told me that she remembers the good aroma of a corn husk bed newly filled in the fall, like sheets dried in the sunshine.

In place of feather beds or stuffed ticks, quilted pallets were sometimes used. There is some evidence that quilts or quilted pads were used to sleep upon rather than under in very early times. I have seen a homemade mattress of quilted, unbleached cotton stuffed with cotton wadding which was being used on a sofa belonging to the Robert Blakey family of Prescott, Grenville County, while quilts sewn in a plain diamond pattern are occasionally found that have no decoration. It is probable that these quilts were used on top of mattresses or feather ticks much as we use machine-quilted mattress pads today.

Feather bolsters and pillows were made with narrow striped ticking in the early years; wider striping came later. Very early examples were covered with tightly woven homespun cotton cloth, often made by the local weaver, and sometimes of beautifully woven linen, firm and tight, which would be light brown or gray in colour. Usually, the bolster went right across the bed and took the place of a second pillow. Thus, on a double bed two pillows and one bolster were used, one pillow for each person, the bolster being shared.

The earliest pillows, especially in settlements of Germanic people, were large and square. A woman born in 1894, whose mother's people were Quakers, remembers one of these large pillows being around

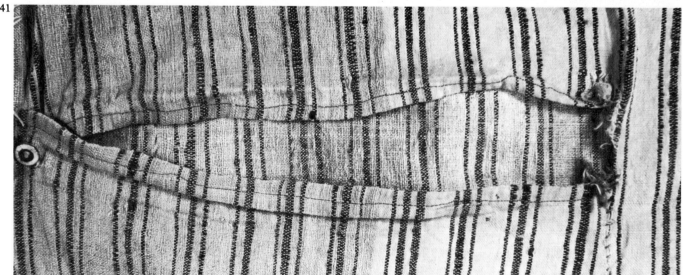

40 Bunk bed at Cook's Tavern, Dundas County, ca. 1835; opened up to reveal a straw filled mattress tick. The straw can be seen poking through the opening in the top, which was used to stuff the tick and then drawn shut with tapes. [U.C.V.]

41 Tick: detail; handspun, handwoven linen with cotton warp and wool stripes; Renfrew County, 3rd quarter 19th century. The buttoned opening allowed easy access for stuffing the tick with straw or corn husks or for smoothing out bumps with a stick while the tick was on the bed. [P.C.]

42 Feather Pillow: homemade, covered with handwoven linen ticking; eastern counties, 19th century. W. 38 cm, L. 71 cm (15, 28 in.). The pillowcase, which has been pulled back to show the pillow, is made from a sugar bag trimmed with handmade knitted lace edging. There is also a pillow protector made from a sugar bag. The pillow itself appears to have been made to a size which would allow the use of an uncut sugar bag as a case. [P.C.]

43 Feather Pillow: homemade, covered with ticking, which is probably cotton and imported; Wellington Thorpe estate, Spencerville, Grenville County, ca. 1870. W. 37 cm, L. 60 cm (15, 24 in.). At the auction of the Thorpe estate, there were two dozen feather beds and numerous pillows. The author remembers her mother and the hired girl making pillows from wild duck feathers each autumn; it was a messy job and done out in the woodshed. [P.C.]

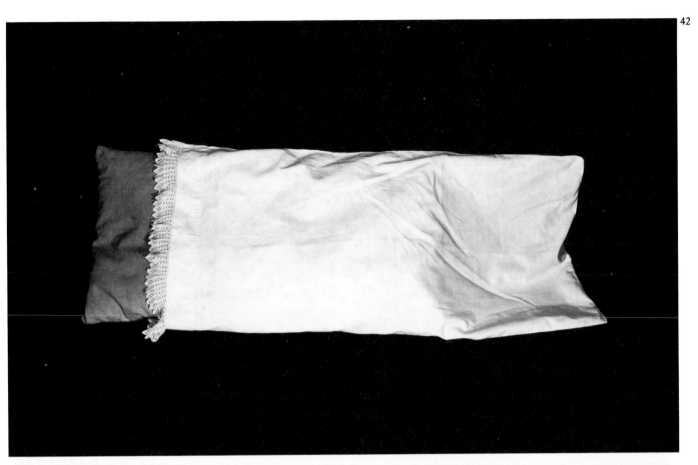

42

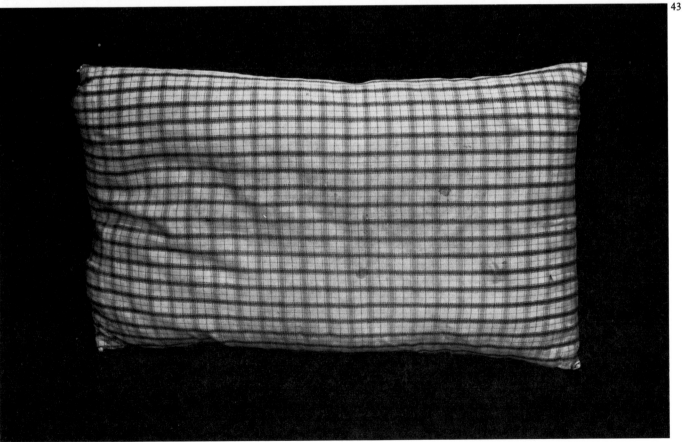

43

the house. It was covered in the old style with narrow striped cloth ticking. This pillow was not in use even during her mother's time but by the generation before her. Very few of these large, early pillows seem to have survived, and few people can remember them being used.

People who had sheep but no geese made mattresses stuffed with wool. Anne Langton described the process in 1846:

> There is bedding to be overhauled, pillows to fill, mattresses to take to pieces and remake, and a new one to manufacture. I ... well remember the last time we had this work to do. We were in the midst of hair and wool when our only servant fell ill, and besides the business on hand and no assistance except that of a little girl who was helping to pull the wool.... It was a right busy time.[17]

The reference to hair in this quote may have something to do with the fact that the Langtons had brought their beds with them from the old country.[18] The remaking described no doubt has to do with the yearly turning out of the beds which was part of the incessant struggle to keep the bedding insect free. In May of the previous year, the Langtons had washed the walls with scalding lye to keep them clear of bugs, "a most desirable thing occasionally in sun-baked log houses."[19]

Wool filled comforters were made in the same way that feather comforters were made. They were considered more durable, especially if made of virgin wool.

Because of their luxurious comfort, however, feather beds were the most desirable type in Upper Canada, but a certain amount of affluence and hard work was necessary to obtain one. Unless such a bed is actually slept upon, it is difficult to relate just how voluptuous it feels, or how pleasing to the eye it looks placed in a handsome bedstead and covered with beautiful sheets, blankets and quilts.

6 Blankets, Sheets and Pillowcases

The cool kindliness of sheets, that soon
Smooth away trouble; and the rough male kiss
Of blankets...

"The Great Lover"
Rupert Brooke (1887-1915)

Sheep shearing; from an early photograph.

Blankets were probably the most important articles of bedding used in Upper Canada. One could do without a counterpane, white sheets or bed curtains, but blankets were essential for survival in a cold country. As we have seen, among the first to be used in Canada were those traded with the Indians and issued to the Loyalists by the government. General stores and trading posts of the Hudson's Bay Company carried these Indian blankets which came in weights of 1, 1½, 2, 3 and 4 points and which were coloured blue, red, green, white and cream with coloured bands.

Between 1784 and 1791, Samuel Sherwood sold point blankets in the Bay of Quinte area, and upon one occasion he recorded the exchange of one otter skin for a pair of 2½ point blankets.[1] In 1784, two pair of 4 point blankets sold for £3 10s.[2] These were extortionate prices for the time, especially for goods that were probably not of the highest quality.

Due to the complaints of early travellers and settlers and because of the profits to be made, better blankets were also imported directly from Scotland and England. In 1829, for example, Roderick Mathewson of Perth ordered ten or twelve pair of "ten-ounce Scotch blankets" and linen tow sheeting, both bleached and unbleached directly from Glasgow.[3] Shops advertised Mackinaw, Witney, point, and rose blankets at early dates (rose blankets were of fine quality and had a rose worked into the corner).

Inventories, such as that of Thomas Hurd, Grenville County, listed "carsey" blankets at 18 shillings each. Carsey (English, Kersey) or kearsy blankets as they were usually called in Upper Canada obtained their name from a type of weaving. This term or a corruption of it was apparently applied to a type of blanket actually made in Upper Canada. William Canniff wrote that he had seen the first kearsy blanket made in Upper Canada and that it was still in use,[4] although it may well have been either an early import or a type of homespun blanket. Whether kearsy or not, homespun blankets were made to supplement imports, and such inventories as that of John Meyers, Hastings County (1821), could list ten Indian, five 3 point, one 2½ point, one rose and twenty-four woollen blankets which were probably homespun.[5] This is an unusually good supply, and Captain Meyers doubtless had it because he was a successful trader of flour, grain, lumber and furs.

Most of the woollen blankets used in Upper Canada after the turn of the nineteenth century were made from homespun yarns. As noted in Chapter 2, many farmers had looms and the women made their own blankets. After the cloth had been taken off

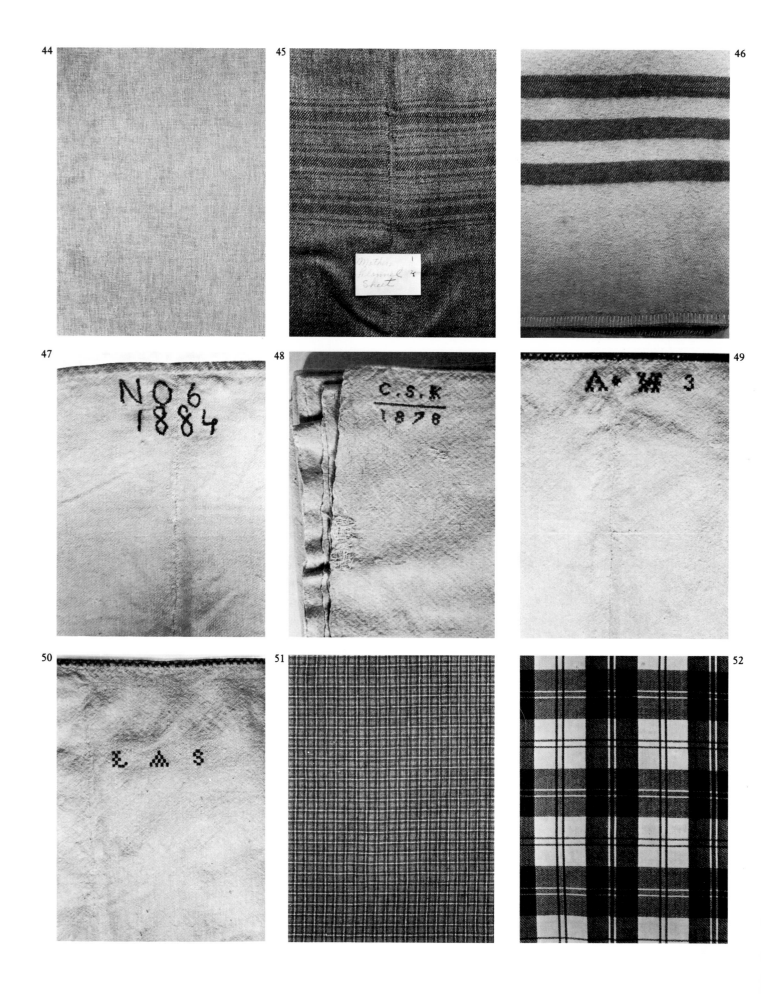

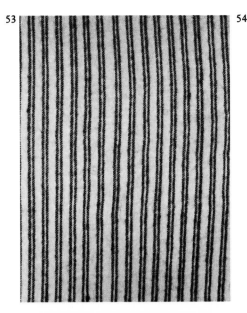

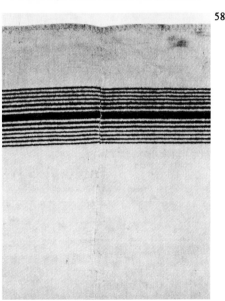

44 Sheet: homespun, handwoven gray linen, tabby weave, centre seam; McMaster family, near Gananoque, Leeds County, 2nd quarter 19th century. [P.C.]

45 Flannel Sheet: handspun, handwoven wool with cotton warp, natural brown wool; made by Amelia Parks Crozier, Mountain Grove, north Frontenac County, 4th quarter 19th century. The little note pinned to this sheet indicates that the term "flannel sheet" was used as well as the more common "winter sheet." [P.C.]

46 Blanket: wool, no centre seam; made at the Stackhouse Mill, Peveril, Soulanges County, Quebec, late 19th century. [P.C.]

47, 48, 49, 50 Flannel Sheets: handspun, handwoven wool with cotton weft; eastern and western counties. Bedding to be put aside for a daughter of the house had to be made from the wool and linen that could be spared from the everyday requirements

of the family. As a result, it took some years to make the required number of blankets or sheets. In a family where there were several girls it was advisable to number, date and initial the bedding. [P.C.]

51 Blanket, or Winter Sheet: handspun, handwoven wool on cotton; western counties, mid-19th century. A colourful, light weight blanket resembling dress goods. Weavers in the western counties used colour lavishly. [R.P.P.]

52 Blanket: handspun, handwoven wool, twill weave, centre seam; indigo blue and cream plaid; Leeds County, ca. 1860. [P.C.]

53 Blanket: handspun, handwoven, indigo blue striped wool, centre seam; Hastings County, 3rd quarter 19th century. Blankets woven at home can sometimes be identified by the uneven selvages (outer edges). [P.C.]

54 Blanket: handspun, handwoven, indigo blue and cream wool, centre seam; Glengarry County, ca. 1850. The large, bold check is typical of Glengarry County blankets. Heavier and thicker than most Ontario blankets, they are very similar in style to those woven in Quebec. [P.C.]

55 Blanket: wool, twill weave; Young family, Hastings County, ca. 1840. [R.B.]

56 Blanket: handspun, handwoven wool; York County, ca. 1850. [P.C.]

57 Blanket: handspun, handwoven wool, goose-eye twill weave; yellow and blue; Picton area, Prince Edward County, ca. 1860. [P.C.]

58 Blanket: wool on cotton; natural colour with indigo bands at top and bottom; made by Jane Hamilton, Dundela, Dundas County, ca. 1880. The girls in this family each made one red and one blue coverlet, blankets with matching red or blue bands and parlour carpets. [P.C.]

the loom, it could be taken to the mill to be finished or "fulled." Fulling was a cleaning or shrinking process. Sometimes, though, fulling was done at home, and it was customary to have a fulling bee where a group of people worked together on the cloth singing old traditional songs as they worked in order to maintain a rhythmic motion. As late as 1896, fulling bees were being held in Glengarry County: "A fulling bee took place at Mrs. Christy Morrison's, McCrimmon, last Thursday evening where willing workers soon manipulated the blankets to the required thickness."[6] The traditional songs sung in McCrimmon were undoubtedly in the Gaelic.

Usually, the cloth was woven into long strips about a yard wide. A blanket or sheet was made by sewing two lengths together, selvage to selvage, thus making a seam in the centre. Blankets were woven double width occasionally and therefore would have no centre seam, although these were ordinarily the products of a professional weaver or a local woollen mill. The blanket in Plate 46 was made at the Stackhouse Mill, which was situated on the banks of the Delisle River near the boundary between Glengarry County and Quebec. More than one generation of Stackhouses made blankets and arrow-back chairs in that location up until about 1925.

Blankets were sometimes made in double length and used folded, but these were awkward to wash and handle. Many expedients were employed in making the all-important blankets, though, and when times were hard and wool scarce, cow hair or horse hair obtained from the tanners' vats was mixed with the wool.

Once the blankets were made and the cold kept out, sheets were next on the list of priorities. According to Mrs. Traill (1853):

> the thrifty industrious farmers' wives usually spin yarn for making flannel sheets which are fine and soft for winter wear, and last a very long time; homespun blankets are made, sometimes on shares with the weaver. These are often checked with a red or blue cross bar, but sometimes are made plain, with only a broad red or blue border. Those families who know nothing of spinning can hire a spinning girl by the week, and this is frequently done.[7]

Inventories indicate that very few linen or cotton sheets were used, even in households where there were sometimes nearly two dozen flannel sheets. Linen or cotton sheets were luxuries, woollen sheets were not. In a house heated only by fireplaces during the long Canadian winter, no one was apt to complain that the sheets were too woolly. Anyone who has ever slept in an uninsulated house heated in this manner knows that no sheet is too woolly, no quilt too heavy. Flannelette sheets today are the equivalent of the flannel sheets used in Upper Canada.

Linen sheets were of secondary practical importance during the first quarter of the nineteenth century, but they were also considered luxuries and people did take great pride in their bedding. As soon as it was possible, women began to make linen sheets for their households. Period inventories indicate that a household would have only a few linen or cotton sheets at a time, since both linen and cotton were scarce and precious. From 1790 on there are records of imported linen sheeting being sold in general stores, and wealthy families undoubtedly brought a good supply with them when they came into the country.

Still, very few early linen sheets, especially those made of handspun, handwoven linen, have survived. As early as 1815, newspaper offices were advertising in persuasive terms for linen rags which they would buy or exchange for children's books or stationery. "Rags enough may be saved in every family to furnish the family with Books and Stationary. And it is to be hoped that no person will be ashamed to engage in Saving an article so much needed," wrote the *Kingston Gazette*. Many worn sheets, quilts and other bedding may have made their way into early newsprint.

When one considers the myriad uses to which old linens could be put, it is not surprising that so few early linen sheets have survived intact. Plate 44 shows a linen sheet from the McMaster household, Leeds County.

For both sheets and blankets, the wool was dyed in different colours in the yarn stage, before it was woven, hence the term dyed in the wool. Gray was made by mixing the fleece of white sheep and black sheep in certain proportions. There is a soft shade of brown that one sees in winter sheets which came from the natural colour of a certain breed of sheep (Plate 45). A darker brown was achieved by using a dye made from butternut bark, and other vegetable dyes were used to produce various colours. Indigo or dark blue dye, which was bought at the local store or from a pedlar, was traditionally used with natural coloured wool in bedding. Since linen is very resistant to most dyes, blue was one of the few colours that could be used. In addition, it was thought to have mystical powers that ensured the safety of the sleeper.

During the nineteenth century, a young woman preparing her trousseau made a dozen flannel sheets; some women carefully initialed, numbered and dated their sheets in cross-stitch pattern (Plates 47 to 50), while others embroidered them with coloured wool along the hem. The sheets were made long

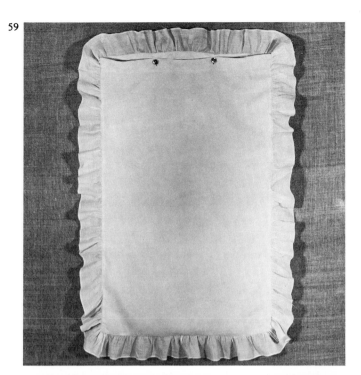

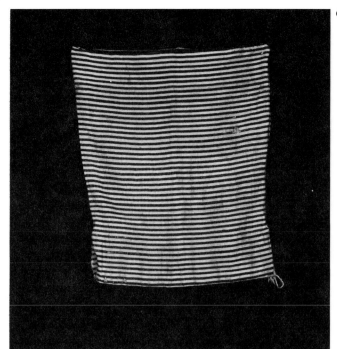

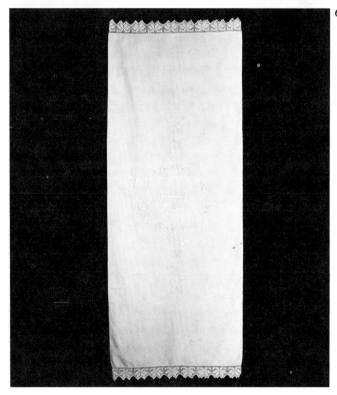

59 Pillowcase: back view; linen; Van Stranbenzea family, Kingston, Frontenac County, mid-19th century. W. 39 cm, L. 80 cm (15, 31 in.). Marked in ink "Stranbenzea 6." Early pillowcases were sometimes buttoned up the back or closed with a drawstring. [P.C.]

60 Pillowcase: handwoven, natural coloured linen with indigo banding; McLeod family, Lancaster, Glengarry County, ca 1840. W. 42 cm, L. 53 cm (17, 21 in.). This pillowcase was being used as a ragbag, and when I mentioned handwoven bedding to the family, it was hunted up and produced along with the information that grandma always said it used to be a handwoven pillowcase. Early pillowcases sometimes did have a drawstring. [P.C.]

61 Pillowcase: handsewn, made from a grain bag, trimmed with homemade knitted lace; Carleton County, 19th century. W. 48 cm, L. 92 cm (19, 36 in.). Pillowcases were made from flour, sugar and even grain bags. Bleached white, they were trimmed with crocheted or knitted edgings and were starched and ironed like fine linen and cotton cases. Women went to a lot of work to embellish everyday bedding, in many cases using materials that cost them nothing. [P.C.]

62 Bolster Case, or Double Pillow Slip: one of a pair; linen, trimmed with knitted edgings and white embroidery; Carleton County, ca. 1880. W. 55 cm, L. 142 cm (22, 56 in.). Open at both ends, this case would lie across a double bed. [P.C.]

enough to allow a generous tuck-in, but over the years some were shortened by hemming the worn edges. Linen sheets were made and used as well, although in smaller quantities. Beyond this custom, there was a considerable amount of sheeting sold in Upper Canada: the most popular was Russia sheeting made of sturdy twilled linen, but Scotch sheeting of somewhat finer linen was also sold. In the late 1800s, Samuel Sherwood sold both Russia and Scotch sheeting, which was not always used for sheets. One time he sold: "1 pare overhalls of Russia sheeting."[8] (There appears to have been a tailor working in connection with Sherwood's store, a not uncommon arrangement.) John Meyers in Hastings County listed both Russia and cotton sheeting among his trading goods, even though his personal household inventory lists only a few cotton and linen sheets.[9]

Like early linen sheets, very few pillowcases and bolster cases seem to have survived. Although bolsters were still being used in rural areas during the early years of the twentieth century, they were not commonly seen after 1900. The earliest pillowcases were made of checked blue and white homespun linen and of natural coloured linen. The bed in Plate 36 has been made up with a feather bolster in a fine linen bolster case upon which rests a feather pillow in a homespun linen pillowcase. All are made of bleached homespun linen and all are original pieces. Some of these pieces have survived accidentally, like the striped linen homespun pillowcase I found which had a drawstring and was being used as a scrap bag (Plate 60). Good quality linen pillowcases often had frills and were buttoned up the back (Plate 59). For many years, pillowcases were made at home by hand, and they were often trimmed with handmade lace. Since they were the right size, flour, sugar and even grain bags were also used for the same purpose. Sugar bag pillowcases were common during the Great Depression of the 1930s, but despite their humble origins they were trimmed with lace just like the linen or fine cotton ones, and they underwent the same careful washing, starching, drying, dampening and ironing process.

Pillowcases for guest beds were often heavily embroidered, but by about 1865 people began to use fancy pillow shams to cover the pillowcases during the daytime, since the quilts were not drawn up over the pillows until the second quarter of the twentieth century and pillowcases did have a tendency to become mussy. There was sufficient concern for this type of thing that in 1890 one could buy a hinged wire contraption to hold the pillow shams above the pillows by day and against the wall at night.

Early pillow shams were frilled and embroidered in white floral designs. Later shams had red patterns; ones with little messages were very popular:

> Sweet Lilies Close Their Leaves at Night,
> And Open With the Morning Light.

and,

> I Slept and Dreamed that Life was Beauty,
> I Woke and Found that Life was Duty.

One line of the verse was embroidered on each pillow sham. Another popular theme was "Good Night, Good Morning" well embellished with flowers, lilies, birds, deer, herons and swans. One set featured Queen Victoria as a young woman in 1837 and as an old woman in 1897. Some families used embroidered bedspreads to match the shams in the summer, and in some houses these cotton spreads were placed under the best quilt to provide a fancy bed cover when the quilt was removed at night. Quilts were usually left on the bed to sleep under, but a few people had a good quilt which they brought out only for visitors who were expected to remove it at night as one does a bedspread today. A well brought up guest was expected to realize that the best quilt in the house was not to sleep under. In cases of doubt, it was considered quite polite for the hostess to escort the guest to the bedroom on the pretext of checking that there were enough blankets and, at the same time, to remove the quilt while turning down the bed. It is still a good idea today.

---

63 Pillow sham: one of a pair; white linen with white embroidery; Leeds County, ca. 1890. W. 74 cm, L. 74 cm (29, 29 in.). Square shams such as this one had open hems, which enabled one to insert the wires for the sham holders attached to the headboard of the bed. At night they were flipped up against the headboard to avoid touching or crushing them. [P.C.]

64 Pillowsham: one of a pair; McLeod family, Lancaster, Glengarry County, 1890-1910. W. 78 cm, L. 80 cm (31, 32 in.). The design consists of Scotch thistles and *fleurs-de-lis*, typical of Glengarry County. Some young women from Glengarry, such as the original owner of this sham, worked as hired girls in Montreal before their marriages and probably did most of their shopping there. Square shams were sold as pillowshams or table covers and were used as both. [P.C.]

65 Pillowsham: one of a pair; white linen; made by Mary Shangraw, Frontenac County, ca. 1884. W. 56 cm, L. 68 cm (22, 27 in.). Mary Jane Wallace (Shangraw) married in 1884 and this was among her marriage linens. Both shams in the pair are initialed with her married name. [P.C.]

66 Pillowcase: one of a pair; white cotton; Carleton County, ca. 1860. W. 77 cm, L. 94 cm (30, 37 in.). This case was made to fit the very large pillows used, for the most part, before 1860. [P.C.]

67, 68, 69, 70, 71 Pillowshams: red embroidery on white linen; found in Frontenac County, ca. 1890. These or similar designs were available in cotton or linen from mail order catalogues. [P.C.]

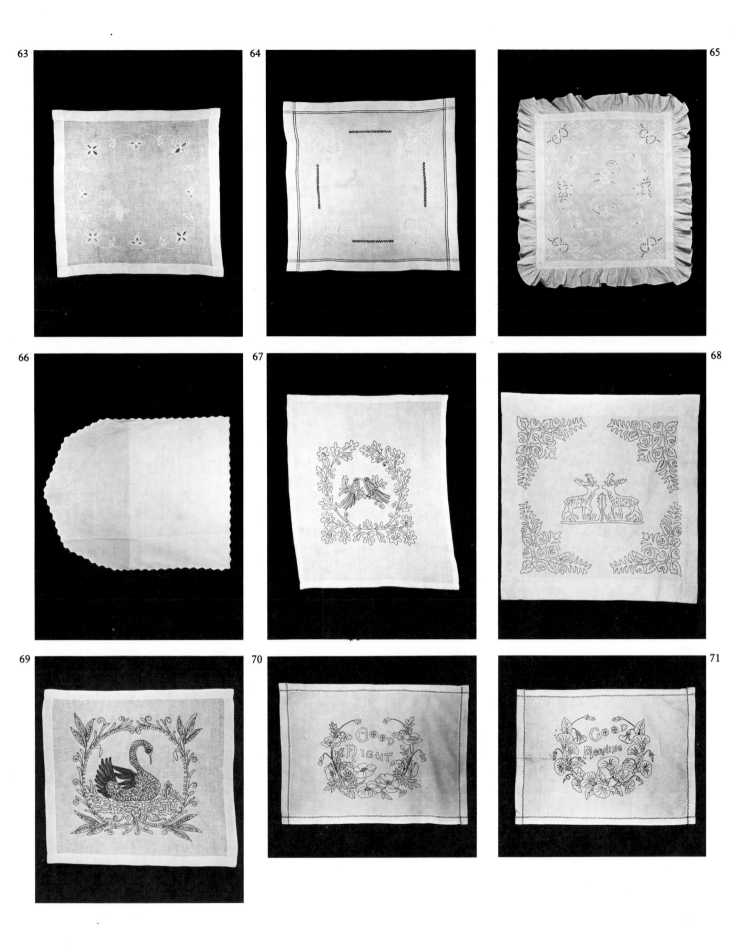

7 Quilts, Counterpanes and Coverlets

A king of shreds and patches.

Hamlet
William Shakespeare (1564-1616)

An old woman working at a loom; from an early engraving.

Today there is always some confusion among the terms used to describe bedcovers: quilts, counterpanes, coverlids, coverlets and bedspreads. All these terms were used in the nineteenth century, but often interchangeably as times and vogues altered. A woman born in 1893, for example, remembers her mother using the word counterpane, but when bedspread became the fashionable term for the same item, her mother, who liked to keep abreast of the times, began to use it.[1] In light of this, our present day confusion is understandable, but nevertheless some general distinctions may be made which clear the air somewhat.

The counterpane was the top cover, what we now call the bedspread, a term not frequently used in the nineteenth century. The counterpane was placed on top of the quilt or woollen bedcover that acted as the blanket. In the second half of the eighteenth century, cotton counterpanes or bedspreads imported from India became popular in England, and copies of these expensive imports were soon being made there. Their popularity carried over to nineteenth century Upper Canada, and as in the old country they were used for decoration. In wealthy families, the counterpanes often matched the rest of the bed furniture and might vary in weight from light cotton and silk to heavy woollens and damasks. Counterpanes were also homemade of linen or cotton embroidered in lavish and beautiful designs, often with wool threads. Some of these early counterpanes were backed and quilted in order to preserve them.

In the first quarter of the nineteenth century, a prosperous Upper Canadian family might have one or two counterpanes or bedspreads reserved for the best beds, witnessed by a household inventory (1821) of John Meyers, Hastings County, where one of each is listed.[2] In fact, all the terms used for bedcovers in this chapter appear in this inventory, but the distinction between counterpane and bedspread remains uncertain. There is considerable evidence, to be discussed later in this chapter, that the quilt was used as a bedspread in humbler homes or in secondary bedrooms. Counterpanes were considerably easier to obtain and cheaper to buy than other types of bedcovers, and by the end of the century they were used to protect quilts and coverlets which were heavy and hard to wash.

Coverlet and coverlid were sometimes used in the same way as counterpane and bedspread. A coverlet is generally considered to indicate a handwoven, patterned bedcover, usually made of wool, cotton or linen, that was either made at home or by a professional weaver. The term coverlid seems to have been used regionally to denote the same item.

It is important to realize that most quilts and woollen coverlets made in the nineteenth and early twentieth centuries were intended for use as blankets to keep the sleeper warm. A great deal of labour went into the production of even the most utilitarian ones, and women were cautious about washing them. It was advantageous, therefore, to use a light cotton bedspread to help keep them clean.

On the other hand, there were also fine and beautiful quilts made for best use, some with little or no padding, as well as expensive handsome coverlets that were either home-made or purchased, both undoubtedly intended for decorative purposes. If these were slept under at all, it was only on rare occasions when there was an important guest. It is unlikely that these decorative bedcovers would be hidden by a counterpane, although the woman born in 1893 mentioned earlier does remember that her mother used a bedspread over her handwoven wool coverlet that she had made in preparation for her wedding. Another woman of the same age recalls that in her family they used a cotton counterpane under the best quilt. The quilt was taken off at night, but the guest would still have a pretty bedcover to look at.

A quilt consists of two layers of cloth with a layer of some soft substance between them. In order to keep the filling from shifting, the three layers are tacked together in some manner. They might be tied together with little pieces of yarn, or sewn (quilted) together, usually in a pattern, by running seams through the layers.

When the top and bottom of the quilt are made from single pieces of cloth, the result is called a wholecloth quilt. The other main category is the patchwork quilt, which is divided into the two main classes, pieced and appliquéd. The top of a pieced quilt consists of many small pieces of cloth seamed together in a manner which may or may not form a pattern, while in the appliquéd version small pieces of cloth are sewn onto a large single piece of cloth to form a pattern. Both types may be made as over-all patterns or they may be assembled in units which are then seamed together to form the whole. These units are called blocks, and they are used in both types of quilts but not in wholecloth versions.

Wholecloth quilts were favoured in the immigrant homelands even though patchwork quilts had been in use there for many years. In the United States and Canada, however, the patchwork quilt was the most popular, and it was in these countries that the art achieved its zenith. At least in Upper Canada, it is likely that one reason behind the preference for patchwork was the important part that quilt making played in the social life of the nineteenth century,

and the second was probably the high-spirited competition engendered by the fairs and exhibitions where prizes were given for the best quilts.

The art of quilt making became closely tied to the feat of catching a man. The unmarried state was not a happy one for a woman in the nineteenth century, since there was almost no way for her to make a living, and until she was settled she had to remain in the home of a relation as an unpaid servant. In the second quarter of the nineteenth century, Samuel Strickland described this particular aspect of quilting:

> Among the many home productions of Canada, the counterpane, or quilt holds a conspicuous place, not so much in regard to its actual usefulness, as the species of frolic 'clept [called] a Quilting-bee, in which the young gentlemen take their places with the Queen-bees, whose labours they aid by threading the needles, while cheering their spirits by talking nonsense.
>
> The quilts are generally made of patchwork, and the quilting, with down or wool, is done in a frame. Some of the gentlemen are not mere drones on these occasions but make very good assistants under the supervision of the Queen-bees.
>
> The quilting bee usually concludes with a regular evening party. The young people have a dance. The old ones look on. After supper, the youthful visitors sing or guess charades. Mirth, good humour, and pleasant company, generally abound at these quilting-bees, which are not liable to the serious objections which may be made against other bees in Canada.
>
> If several gentlemen receive an invitation to a tea, they may be assured that their services are required at a quilting-bee, which often is followed by courtship and matrimony! Indeed it is one of the methods taken by the Canadian cupid to ensnare hearts and provide work for Hymen.[3]

An invitation to participate in the making of a girl's marriage quilt was equivalent to putting an announcement in the local newspaper. A girl did not quilt her marriage top until she was engaged. In some instances even the everyday quilts were not finished until a marriage appeared imminent, since completing them involved the greatest expenses for buying stuffings and backing material. This custom was not always followed, however, and most Ontario women made backings from cotton bags in which flour, sugar and grain arrived from the store or mill. These bags, of good unbleached cotton, were stamped with the name of a mill and were often bleached and then dyed by the women. Other women used them unbleached, knowing that a few washings would soon render them white and soft.

Around 1850, Eli Merkley, a farmer in the

Williamsburg area, Dundas County, married the daughter of a neighbouring farmer. They had twelve children of whom nine were girls. Following the family tradition, the mother and daughters made quilts, and it would appear that many of the tops were folded away to be finished at a later date. Only one girl married and the boys died early in life. When the youngest daughter, Ella May, died in 1974 at the age of ninety-eight, a niece found one hundred and fifteen quilts neatly folded in blanket boxes in the attic. Examples of these quilts are shown in Plates 290, 329, 337, 356.

Since most of these quilts were never used due to the fact that eight of the daughters remained unmarried, they are in remarkably good condition, appearing to have been quilted during one great bee around the turn of the century. Ella May was born in 1876, and by the turn of the century it was probably becoming apparent that only one of the daughters, Estelle, would ever marry, so the girls probably decided to finish the quilts. One pair of exceptionally fine quilts in the Baby Blocks pattern bears two dates, one above the other in the centre of the quilts – 1876 and 1900 (Plate 290). It is likely that these are the dates that the tops were made and the quilting finally finished. This theory is supported by the fact that all the quilts appear to be quilted in a uniform manner in straight lines. All have similar or identical material used for the bindings, and they are universally backed with mill bags; some are dyed but others still show the mill stamps which have not washed out (Plate 78).

Because the ancestors of both parents were United Empire Loyalists of Lutheran-German stock and because ties were maintained with either Lutheran or Mennonite communities in Pennsylvania (George, a son, attended a small private school in Bethlehem, Pennsylvania, and one of the daughters, Drusilla, taught there for several years), one would expect to see some similarities to Pennsylvania quilts in the products of the Merkley sisters. In fact, the patterns used are the same as those employed in that state; these were commonly used in many areas during the late Victorian era. Still, there is a love of bright colours and lively form which is a feature of Pennsylvania quilts. The Merkley quilts, however, do not show the perfection and intricacy of early

72

73

72 Double Hearts and Tulips: quilt, detail of Plate 294. In this quilt, the design has been sewn down on the foundation cloth with a neat herringbone stitch. Sometimes a button-hole stitch was used.

73 Garden Wreath: quilt, detail of Plate 135. This shows how a design was appliquéd to the foundation cloth. Here, an almost invisible catch stitch was used.

Pennsylvania examples; they are everyday quilts made in a rather plain and utilitarian manner, although the use of contrasting colours in designs that have a definite movement to them enhances their beauty. Beyond these possible connections, it is difficult to say whether any other outside influences were involved in the making of the Merkley quilts.

Despite the large number of quilts that have been found in this household, it would be a mistake to assume that the Merkley sisters did nothing but stay home and make quilts; they lived busy lives teaching, painting, dressmaking and mingling with the community. The story of these quilts, though, is a remarkable instance of how quilts were made in anticipation of marriage, and the fact that only one daughter married has left us with an invaluable collection.

The survival of the Merkley quilts is very unusual, and it is important to note that quilts are generally very perishable. Most of the early Canadian examples have been worn out and discarded. Of the quilts photographed for this book, one was found lying in an abandoned cutter to make a bed for the dog, another was found in a heap on the floor of a loft where squirrels were starting to nest in it, and several were on top of springs protecting mattresses. Everyday quilts were not used kindly when they became outdated or worn. Heavy woollen ones were used to put under the baby on the floor and for children's picnics in the orchard. Fortunately, homespun quilts are durable; they have survived many indignities, but cannot tolerate washing machines and detergents.

Every woman had her "good" quilt, though, usually her marriage quilt, which she protected by using it only on special occasions and by washing it as seldom as possible, if at all. One finds a surprising number of such quilts that have never been washed.

These best quilts were always made in traditional patterns, unlike everyday ones which tended to be truer expressions of the creativity of the women of the nineteenth century. Hence, everyday quilts include some of the finest and most interesting examples of the art. It is unfortunate that this latter type was discarded when worn, although, like the Merkley quilts, some made by women who never married have survived in very good condition.

In theory at least, a good quilter was more apt to make a suitable marriage than a poor quilter, because she would be invited to all the quilting bees where the girls met the young men. Life is unfair, however, and the good quilter might well be plying her needle in the parlour, while a girl with curls and dimples, who could not sew a straight seam, was flirting with

the boys in the kitchen. Whatever the reason, many fine quilters did not marry and their products, prepared since childhood, remained folded in the blanket box. These women often continued to make quilts for friends and relations, but rarely parted with those prepared for marriage.

Given the quilting bee tradition, it would not be strange for a mother to insist that her daughter learn to sew and quilt. What she made as a young girl would be necessary to keep her future family warm, and her popularity as a young woman might well depend on her skill. A good quilter still commands respect in the rural areas of Ontario.

Despite the fact that quilts were the most commonly used bedcovers in Upper Canada, there is relatively little mention of them in early diaries and travel books. They were commonplace objects and of little interest to the average writer in the early days. One can learn more about quilts talking with the old women who remember the days when quilting was an important part of life.

An early mention of quilts in Canada was made by a German officer travelling in Batis Township, Quebec, in 1776. He wrote an interesting and detailed description of beds, furnishings and quilts:

> In every room one will find at least one bed capable of holding two persons. As a rule, these beds have a large square canopy, fastened to the ceiling, with curtains which are generally drawn up. All bedsteads are square, but without posts. The best of them have a bed well filled with straw nearly a foot in thickness, and over which is thrown a nicely stuffed feather bed. For the head, is a bolster nearly a foot in thickness (rouleau is the name given them in the inns in France). The bed, also, has two linen sheets; and for covering there are four thick woollen blankets. Furthermore, every person receives a pillow a yard long by three quarters wide. . . . As soon as you are out of bed, it is made up and covered with a quilt of silesia, calico, or wool, with the ends hanging down over the sides. The poorest inhabitant has such a covering for his bed; nor indeed have I seen cleaner beds in any country. In the houses of the poor people all the beds are placed in one room.[4]

Although this description is of early Quebec, the details are typical of bedsteads and quilts in Upper Canada, a fact that is borne out by the inventories of many nineteenth century Upper Canadian residents.

It is interesting to note that quilts in Quebec were being used in the eighteenth century much as we use them today. That is, the quilt was taken off the bed at night and used only as a coverup during the day. Naturally, this keeps the quilt in better condition than if it were used as a covering at night. By the nineteenth century and into the early years of the

74 Quilting Frame. Although some quilts were made at quilting bees by several women, most were done over a period of time at home by the women of the family. Quilting frames such as this one were used at home. Because the frame took up a great deal of space, a room of the house would be used for little else while quilting was in progress. The author can remember being present at a bee when the women bounced the family cat on the finished quilt; the person in whose direction the cat landed was next in line to be married. [P.C.]

75 Elizabeth Aikey (1840-1923), maker of the Harvest Sun and Dutch Tulip quilt in Plate 256. She married David York around 1860, and this was her marriage quilt, which was saved for posterity. The illustration is from a charcoal drawing in the possession of her great-granddaughter, Ann Davison. [J.D.]

76 *Crazy Patchwork*, canvas, by W. Brymner, 1886 [N.G.C.]

77 Eli and Almita Merkley of Williamsburg, Dundas County, and their nine daughters: Edith, Anne, Sarah, Josephine, Estelle, Drusilla, Maud, Louise and Ella May. These nine sisters' lives spanned the years 1850 to 1974. The mother and daughters made quilts, twelve for each girl. Only one daughter married, and one hundred and fifteen unused quilts were found in the family attic after the death of the last sister. [P.C.]

twentieth, this custom had changed, and it was usual to sleep under a quilt. If it is used at night, a quilt does not need to be as long or as wide as one used for covering the bed during the day. Indeed, it is a nuisance to sleep with an overlong quilt in a roll beneath one's chin. Neither version was intended to be pulled up over the pillows, since they were placed on top of the bed by day.

Such well-to-do immigrants as Mrs. Moodie did not have to make bed coverings, since they were in a position to bring theirs along from the old country. Mrs. Moodie was not inclined to associate with the class of people who held quilting bees and took a rather dour view of bees in general, but she did mention that her servant was away overnight at a quilting bee.[5] She also described a visit with an old woman who lived in a log cabin so small that the bed filled half the room. The old woman's bed was "covered with an unexceptionably clean patched quilt."[6] On another occasion, she referred again to quilts when she found the impoverished wife of a fellow officer of her husband's regiment in a log dwelling that had "a rude bedstead of home manufacture, in a corner of the room, covered with a coarse woollen quilt, which contained two little boys, who had crept into it to conceal their wants from the eyes of the stranger."[7]

Quilts are sometimes mentioned in rather odd circumstances and not always with the disdain of Mrs. Moodie. In 1836, Catherine Parr Traill described the interior of a log house in which were, "two beds raised a little above the ground on a frame of split cedars. On these lowly couches lay extended two poor men, suffering under the wasting effects of lake-fever. Their bilious faces strangely contrasted with the gay patchwork quilts that covered them."[8] Less strange, perhaps, but more unusual is Samuel Thompson's account of travelling in 1833 in the vicinity of Barrie, where he found deep in the forest the one-roomed tavern of Yankee David Root and his wife:

> Bedtime drew near. A heap of odd-looking rugs and clean blankets was laid for our accommodation and pronounced to be ready. But how to get into it? We had heard of some rather primitive practices among the steerage passengers on board ship, it is true, but, had not accustomed ourselves to 'uncase' before company, and hesitated to lie down in our clothes. After waiting some little time in blank dismay, Mr. Root kindly set us an example by quietly slipping out of his nether integuments and turning into bed. There was no help for it: by one means or another we contrived to sneak under the blankets; and, after hanging up a large coloured quilt between our lair and the couch occupied by her now snoring spouse, the good wife also disappeared.[9]

While Mrs. Traill did not share Mrs. Moodie's disdain for quilts in general, she was not so sure about homespun cloth. She recommended that the settler's wife weave her own flannel for her house dresses, because it "is very durable lasting two or three seasons. When worn out as a decent working dress, it makes good sleigh-quilts for travelling."[10] Mrs. Traill may have considered pieced homespun quilts as suitable only for travelling, but the majority of Upper Canadian women used them for years on their beds. They were still being used as extra quilts in the first quarter of the twentieth century.

This scorn for homespun cloth, though perhaps unconsciously expressed, was not uncommon among country people, and many in the second half of the nineteenth century were ashamed to use it. A strong indication of this kind of feeling is evident in a woollen patchwork quilt that was found recently. Several of its patches were covered with an obviously store-bought, sleazy gray flannel that seemed so out of keeping with the rest of the quilt that they were removed. Underneath was found homespun cloth in fine condition and brightly coloured. Someone had taken the trouble to cover every little scrap of homespun cloth with cheap store-bought material, perhaps in a bid to appear more affluent and less "countrified."

All bed covers in Upper Canada were not homemade. Some were imported from England, Scotland and the United States. In 1827, Roderick Mathewson ordered directly from Scotland, "one dozen $9/4$ coloured cotton counterpanes," and "one dozen $9/4$ white cotton counterpanes"[11] for his store in Perth, Lanark County. (The term $9/4$ refers to the size of the counterpane; $1/4$ meant a quarter of a yard, hence they measured eighty-one inches.) Other stores occasionally mentioned that they had bed coverings for sale: in 1816 Peter Wetsel offered three dozen coverlets in the *Daily News*, Kingston, and B. Whitney was already selling scarlet comforters and bed ticking in 1814 (*Kingston Gazette*). By 1842, a Kingston warehouse was advertising imported quilts and counterpanes:

> The Subscriber has received per Mohawk from Glasgow, Blond from Liverpool and Great Britain from London, [Mowhawk, Blond and Great Britain were the names of ships] a consignment of Dry Goods which will be found worthy of the Notice of the Trade. The goods were selected by a person long acquainted with this market and will be found in price and style every way suitable.[12]

A merchant from Oswego City, which is on the southern shore of Lake Ontario in New York State, was advertising quilts and other textiles in the 1849

Kingston newspapers.[13] Steamships went daily from Kingston to Oswego and thence to Toronto, and quite a few Upper Canadians did their shopping there.

It is probable that these imported quilts were of the wholecloth type, filled with cotton and machine quilted, similar to what we now call comforters. Old machine-made wholecloth quilts were sometimes used as fillings for handmade versions, but these imported items have largely disappeared.

At the same time, there were some fine woven English counterpanes on the market, and examples may still be found in Upper Canada. One of these was the Marseilles spread, which was woven on a loom in imitation of hand quilting. Made double width on a wide loom without a centre seam, these spreads became fashionable. Plate 80 shows an early Marseilles counterpane which was found in a trunk in Kemptville, Grenville County. It is soft and fluffy, and at first glance difficult to distinguish from an all white handmade quilt. The Marseilles spread was woven to take the place of the fine, white handmade variety, and it was so successful that women then began to make their own in imitation of it.

An American fashion magazine found in a Canadian household contains an article describing New York fashions in 1873; the article gives the following description of Marseilles and other quilts that were commercially available:

> Eleven and twelve-quarter Marseilles quilts are of spotless white and so exceedingly pretty that it seems scarcely right to use them for any other than ornamental purposes; they are worked in elaborately flowered patterns, with simple borders composed of indented squares and diamonds; they range in price from $12.75 to $13.00, but there are also some less skillfully wrought, which are sold at from $5.00 to $6.00. In this line of goods designs in foliage and flowers are every day becoming more popular.
>
> Eider-down silk quilts in numerous patterns and sizes are at present ranging in price from $30.00 to $65.00, and the same in chintz are to be had at from $12.00 to $14.00 each; these luxurious articles are eminently suggestive of a delicious repose, and seem calculated to entice the fickle Morpheus even in his most arbitrary moods.[14]

Marseilles spreads of this type were extremely popular and continued to be sold and used until the twentieth century, by which time the quality had deteriorated to that of a sturdy everyday bedspread.

Another type of white cotton counterpane also had its roots in the homemade tradition of the nineteenth century. It was a variety of woven spread that began as a cottage industry around Bolton, England, and

became known as the Bolton coverlet (Plate 81). These coverlets are made with raised loops in a pattern that has a consistent and well-defined range of motifs. Often, there is a star in the centre and a series of borders. Bolton coverlets were usually woven double width, although some of the eighteenth century ones have a centre seam. The majority have initials in the bottom corner, presumably those of the weaver.

This type of coverlet was copied in the United States, and the *boutonné* coverlets made in some areas of Quebec and the Maritimes appear to show the same influence, but it is not certain whether these later examples were developed from similar coverlets made in France or from actual Bolton influences.

The Bolton coverlet in Plate 81 came from the same Kemptville household as the Marseilles spread in Plate 80. They appeared in the same house perhaps because early members of the family ran a general store in the area before 1850. At any rate, I arrived at the estate auction sale just after a farmer had bought a blanket box full of bed covers, because his wife had wanted some extra bedding for the children. He was persuaded to sell the three top ones, and they are the Marseilles spread, the Bolton coverlet and a white overshot woven coverlet. I have often wondered what became of the rest of the quilts and coverlets in that blanket box.

Handwoven white, cotton overshot coverlets were made in Upper Canada, yet today they are rare. Three or four known examples, which were made in the area between Kemptville and Belleville, were recently acquired from the descendants of the original owners. White, woven, rag counterpanes were also made in eastern Upper Canada, especially in the region around Belleville, and these were found on the farms where they were made. Plate 84 shows an early rag coverlet with blue stripes as an example of the type just described; these were for everyday use, but they were either not commonly made or very few have survived. One very attractive and crudely made coverlet of this type that has survived comes from Glengarry County. It has a Hit and Miss pattern in which lengths of yarn are combined with rags. The person who made it simply collected bits and pieces of yarn from around the house.

Lengths of woven rag and cotton yarn were used as bed covers earlier than on the floor, since cloth of any kind was far too scarce and expensive for such an application. Harold and Dorothy Burnham write that these woven rag coverlets were called "clouties" and are to be found in areas settled by Scottish people.[15]

Probably around 1860, white candlewick bedspeads were made by embroidering white cotton

78

79

80

81

82

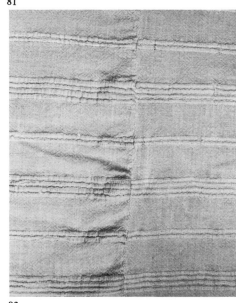

83

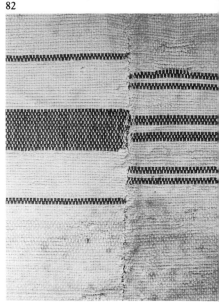

84

78 Baby Blocks: quilt back, detail of Plate 290; Morrisburg Roller Mills stamp. All the Merkley quilts were backed with material from feed, sugar or grain bags. [P.C.]

79 Quilt: white cotton; Port Elgin, Huron County, 1850-55. W. 198 cm, L. 208 cm (78, 82 in.). The field is quilted with fine lozenge lattice with decorative motifs in padded quilting. [R.O.M.]

80 Marseilles Spread: detail; loom woven, England, ca. 1830; found in the possession of the Archibald family, Kemptville, Grenville County. [P.C.]

81 Bolton Coverlet: detail; woven, Bolton, England, 2nd quarter 19th century; from the Archibald family, Kemptville, Grenville County. [P.C.]

82 Counterpane: detail; white, candlewick embroidered, cotton; Donovan family, Portland, Leeds County, 3rd quarter 19th century. W. 170 cm, L. 230 cm (67, 91 in.). [P.C.]

83 Coverlet: detail; white, handwoven cotton yarn and cotton strips in regular repeating bands; Northumberland County, 2nd quarter 19th century. W. 145 cm, L. 170 cm (57, 67 in.). Lengths of woven rag and cotton yarn were used as bedcovers earlier than they were used as rugs. These coverlets were not commonly made in Upper Canada. [P.C.]

84 Bedcover: detail; handwoven cotton with blue bands across the ends; Lennox and Addington County, 3rd quarter 19th century. W. 130 cm, L. 175 cm (51, 69 in.). [P.C.]

with a coarse cotton yarn called roving, which was similar to candlewick. These bedspreads were worked with a large needle in a design that started in the centre. The areas between the central design and the border were filled in with motifs that were sometimes drawn freehand. If the candlewicking was not sheared, the designs appeared in low relief, but in other spreads (Plate 82) the roving was cut between the stitches, and, when washed, the cloth tightened causing the candlewick or roving to fluff. These spreads were very popular between 1860 and 1890, and many traditional motifs were employed, such as hearts, stars or the open hand of friendship. There was a late revival of this style in the 1930s, but these bedspreads, usually made with a stamped transfer pattern, lacked the strong exuberance of the earlier ones, since they did not have a powerful central motif and the designs were generally rather skimpy.

Woven and embroidered candlewick counterpanes may look fairly similar, but they may be distinguished by looking at the backs; the woven variety is smooth, but the stitches can be seen on the back of an embroidered one.

A type of bedcover which rivaled the quilt in popularity was the woven bedcover or coverlet. It was always used as a "good" covering, being more expensive and difficult to make than a quilt, and it would be a source of pride and satisfaction to its owner. It was unusual for a family to own more than one of these, and, although a girl might have several quilts in her trousseau, she would be considered very fortunate to have one woven coverlet. As a result, they are much scarcer today than quilts. Most coverlets were made by traditional weavers, and some kinds cost more than others. They wore well and were carefully looked after until about 1900, when they were thought to be old-fashioned and began to fall into the hands of younger women who did not care for them.

Around 1920, a needlwork magazine suggested ways to use up such old-fashioned coverlets, such as making curtains for a doorway, couch throws and cushion or chair covers:

> All old coverlets are ... not good in design or colour, and they should not be used merely for sentimental reasons, but some of them, woven in strips without borders ... may be taken apart and used as table runners, or the best parts of those very much worn will make handsome couch cushions or chair coverings.[16]

Unfortunately, some very fine coverlets were shown in this article as examples to be cut up, and such recommendations have undoubtedly contributed to their scarcity today. When it was acquired, the fine

coverlet in Plate 95 was being used as a rug in the living room of a busy farm household. Luckily, it was rescued. Coverlets are durable, but no textile a hundred or more years old will tolerate such rough usage.

Handweaving reflects the traditions of the various ethnic groups who settled in Upper Canada. The earliest coverlets were of three types, the twill diaper, the summer and winter coverlet and the doublecloth. The term twill diaper refers to an all-over repeating design in large geometric motifs, and those made by the Loyalists around 1800 are now extremely rare. Dating from 1800 to 1830, summer and winter coverlets are firmly woven and reversible, being light coloured on one side and dark on the other (Plate 87). Doublecloth versions have two layers of cloth, one of wool and one of cotton, which are woven simultaneously (Plate 88). These are also reversible, but one can actually separate the layers in the areas where they are not tied together. Doublecloth coverlets were woven during the period from 1800 to 1850, and like the other two types, they were made by people of Loyalist origin.

Out of the Scottish tradition came the technique of overshot weaving. This is one of the few methods that seems to have been shared by housewives and professional or custom weavers, since they could be made on the four-harness loom which many people had in their homes. Such coverlets have a plain ground, usually cotton, over which shoots an extra pattern of wool. Patterns formed in this way were always geometric. Overshot coverlets are most commonly found in areas where Scottish influence prevailed and are by far the most common type of coverlet to be found in the eastern part of the province, the dividing line being just east of Toronto. Successful, colourful and adaptable, they continued to be made until 1900. Most of the ones that were made at home have a centre seam. The two lengths to be sewn together had to be woven with the same tension so that the pattern would line up. Plate 89 shows an attractive overshot coverlet in a dark indigo and white pattern called Freemason's Felicity; it was made in Lanark County and as the illustration shows the pattern does not line up very well. This problem also arose in homemade blankets which sometimes have little seams taken in one side to make the coloured bands meet. Plate 90 shows a coverlet made around 1880 by Jane Hamilton (1865-1956) of Dundela, Dundas County. Very talented, although not a professional weaver, she made both an indigo blue and a red coverlet as well as blankets with bands across the tops and bottoms to match. These were made at her parents' home before her marriage. Her two sisters also had two coverlets. The example in Plate 91 was made by Peggy McGovern at the late date of 1890 in Irishtown, a hamlet in Grenville County; it has an attractive colour scheme, the colours showing variations of rosy reds, greens, blues and blue greens.

The overshot coverlets made at home have a tendency to show more imperfections than those made by professional weavers, especially because of the difficulty of lining up the centre seam. Professional weavers overcame this problem by using a flying shuttle, a mechanism which enabled them to make cloth wider than thirty-six inches, thus eliminating the seam altogether. Few home weavers had this attachment, although most professional weavers did in the second half of the century. Those shown in Plates 92 and 101 were made by commercial weavers in Glengarry County. The first was woven by John Dickson from Dunvegan who retired in 1910, the second is thought to have been made by one of the McDiarmid weavers in Martintown.

Professional weavers were among the German people who came with the Loyalists to Upper Canada, and more followed from the United States and Germany. Fond of bright colours, these weavers made twill diaper coverlets (Plate 86), some doublecloth, star and diamond (Plate 102), and fancy twills. For show on market days, the fanciest twills went into the making of horse blankets. The twill diaper coverlet was quite popular in the early years, enjoying a brief revival about the middle of the century.

About 1835, the doublecloth coverlet was replaced by a type that took its name from a mechanism fitted to the loom. Called the Jacquard coverlet, it continued to be popular, in particular as a bridal coverlet, until 1900. A Jacquard mechanism was needed to make such a coverlet, and it was quite expensive and needed a high space to operate. Therefore, few professional weavers had one, and those who did also had to acquire the punched, computer-like pattern cards that made the loom function. Some Upper Canadian professional weavers wove their own designs by using sets of cards that they punched themselves rather than the imported kind.

The patterns of the Jacquard coverlets were generally more realistic than earlier types, with flowers, birds, hearts and other motifs being used. Early Jacquard coverlets were dated and had the owner's name worked in a corner, although somewhat later this was replaced by the name of the pattern. These were made by a rather small group of professionally trained weavers working mostly in the Niagara Peninsula and Waterloo County. Many weavers brought their patterns with them from the United

States, and Jacquard coverlets continued to be made in Upper Canada at a later date than in the United States. These later coverlets have a wider range of colours which are harsher, even garish. Plates 104 and 105 show two fine, early Jacquard coverlets which were found in Brant and Oxford counties respectively. Made for Jane Thomson, the Brant County example is dated 1854; the second is also dated 1854. Jacquard coverlets are usually found in the western counties and only seldom in the east, and there were apparently no weavers who had such equipment in the eastern part of the province.

In the old countries, itinerant weavers were known for their amorous tendencies, and the tradition continued into Upper Canada. The following song, collected by Edith Fowke, mentions the names of coverlet patterns and tells us something about the travelling weaver:

> Oh, as I roved out one moonlight night,
> The stars were shining and all things bright.
> I spied a pretty maid by the light of the moon,
> And under her apron she carried a loom.
>
> She says, 'Young man, what trade do you bear?'
> Says I, 'I'm a weaver, I do declare.
> I am a weaver, brisk and free.'
> 'Would you weave upon my loom, kind sir?' said
>   she.
>
> There was Nancy Right and Nancy Rill:
> For them I wove the Diamond Twill;
> Nancy Blue and Nancy Brown:
> For them I wove the Rose and the Crown.[17]

The memory of travelling weavers who came and wove coverlets is persistent throughout the province, but it would have been impossible for them to transport anything but the simplest hand looms, whereas large complicated looms are required to make most coverlets. Only a highly skilled professional weaver had the equipment and the ability to make coverlets such as the Jacquards.

It is probable, however, that the salesmen who travelled about doing simple weaving, perhaps on the farmer's own loom, took orders for the more elaborate coverlets. In some cases at least, it seems likely that a salesman would also take the woman's prepared wools to the master weaver to make a coverlet in the pattern of her choice, but since there are so few Jacquard coverlets found in eastern Upper Canada, it is unlikely that this practice was very common.

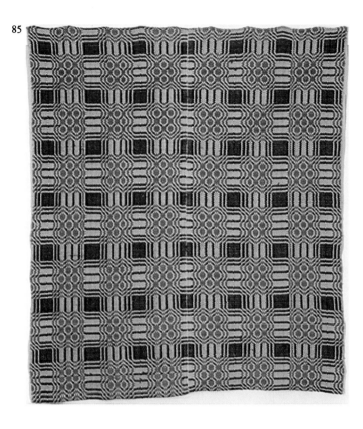

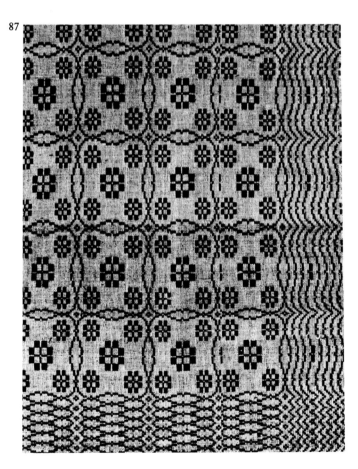

85 Overshot Coverlet: brown and green wool on cotton; Morton, Leeds County, ca. 1850. W. 177 cm, L. 210 cm (70, 83 in.). The pattern reverses in alternate repeats. [P.C.]

86 Twill Diaper Coverlet: detail; banded in blue, red and natural wool; Waterloo County, mid-19th century. W. 166 cm, L. 168 cm (65, 66 in.). The coverlet has been cut down. [P.C.]

87 Summer and Winter Coverlet: detail; indigo blue wool on natural cotton; Ontario, 1st half 19th century. W. 209 cm plus fringes, L. 249 cm plus fringe (82, 98 in.). [R.O.M.]

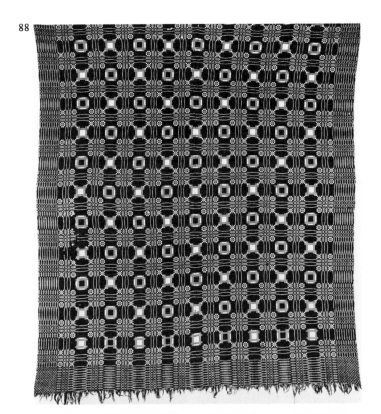

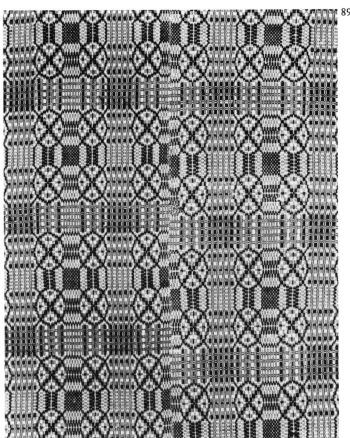

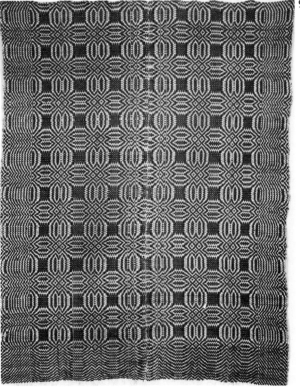

88 Doublecloth Coverlet: indigo blue wool on natural cotton, centre seam; Lincoln County, 1840. W. 178 cm, L. 215 cm (70, 85 in.). [R.O.M.]

89 Freemason's Felicity: coverlet, overshot; dark indigo blue wool on cotton; Lanark County, 3rd quarter 19th century. W. 145 cm, L. 205 cm (57, 81 in.). The pattern does not match at the centre seam, a common problem in homewoven products. Professional weavers predictably matched this seam, because they were more experienced in maintaining an even tension. [P.C.]

90 Nine Roses: coverlet, detail; medium indigo blue wool on cotton warp; handwoven before her marriage by Jane Hamilton, Dundela, Dundas County, ca. 1880. W. 142 cm, L. 185 cm (56, 73 in.). She wove two coverlets, one red, one blue, a traditional practice in the area. Her daughter remembers her mother calling it her rose blanket. [P.C.]

91 Overshot Coverlet: red, green and blue wool on white cotton; handwoven by Peggy McGovern, Irishtown, Grenville County, ca. 1890. W. 155 cm, L. 200 cm (61, 79 in.). The colours here are softer, losing the intensity of those found in earlier coverlets. [P.C.]

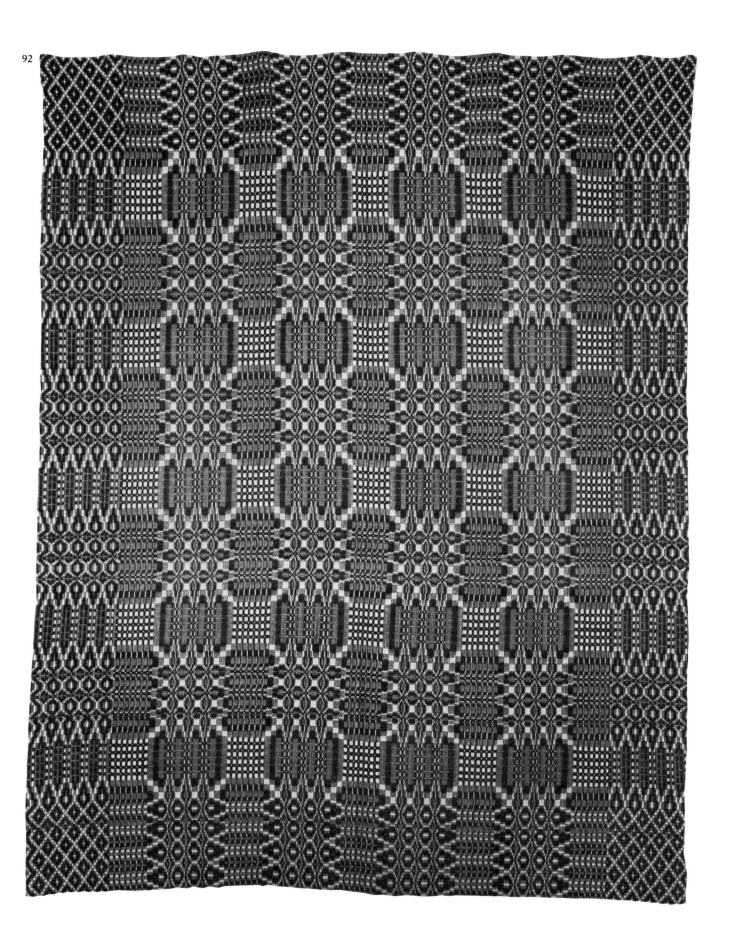

92 Sea Star: coverlet, overshot; red and white; made by John Dickson, a weaver in Dunvegan, 4th quarter 19th century; from the Norman McLeod family, McCrimmon area, Glengarry County. W. 174 cm, L. 225 cm (69, 89 in.). Professionally woven on a wide loom, hence no centre seam; a handsome coverlet. [P.C.]

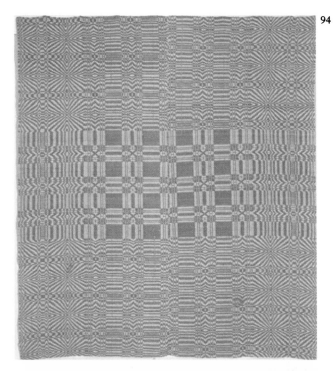

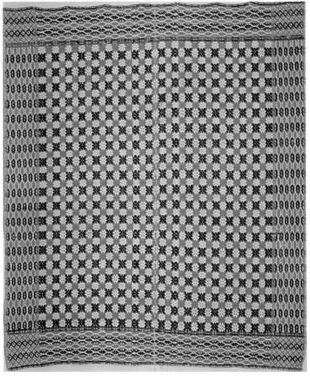

93 Jacquard Coverlet: multicoloured wool on natural white cotton; owned by Elizabeth Dodge, who was married in 1857, Grenville County; ca. 1850. W. 200 cm, L. 212 cm (79, 84 in.). Jacquard weavers are not thought to have been active in this part of the province, and it is possible that Mrs. Dodge, who always lived in the same location, might have been shopping in Watertown when she bought this coverlet. [E.D.]

94 Overshot Coverlet: deep rose and white; made by Mabel Trotter, a local weaver, 4th quarter 19th century; from the Lloyd

Campbell House, near Harlem, Leeds County. W. 177 cm., L. 208 cm (70, 82 in.). [P.C.]

95 Turkey Tracks: coverlet, overshot; red, white and blue; Perth Road, Frontenac County, ca. 1880. W. 145 cm, L. 210 cm (57, 83 in.). [P.C.]

96 Dog's Tracks: coverlet, overshot; orange and indigo; Carleton Place, Lanark County, 3rd quarter 19th century. W. 160 cm, L. 200 cm (63, 79 in.). [P.C.]

97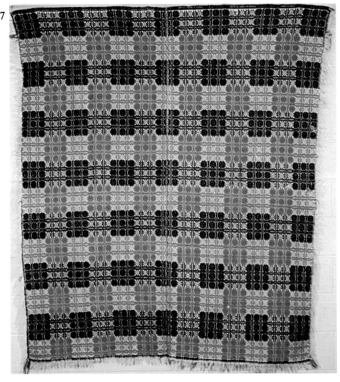

98

99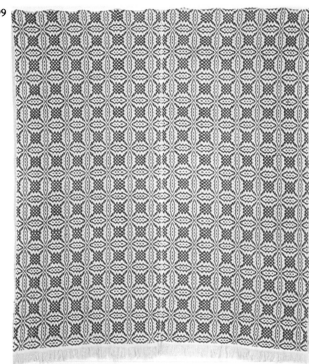

100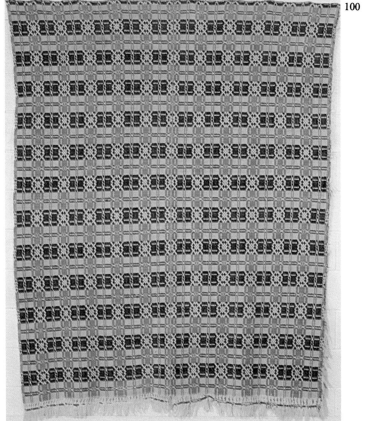

97 Overshot Coverlet: vivid red and indigo blue wool on white cotton; from the family of H. C. Empey, Napanee, Lennox and Addington County, 3rd quarter 19th century. W. 157 cm, L. 182 cm (62, 72 in.). [J.R.P.H.]

98 Jacquard Coverlet: red and white; made by Moses Cherry, Purple Hill, Victoria County, 4th quarter 19th century. W. 190 cm, L. 197 cm (75, 78 in.). Moses Cherry turned out these coverlets in great quantities; the fact that this example has borders on all four sides may indicate it was intended as a table cover. [R.P.P.]

99 Lady of the Lake: coverlet, overshot; handspun, hand-woven, indigo blue wool on natural white cotton; Sexsmith family, Lonsdale area, Hastings County. W. 170 cm, L. 210 cm plus fringe (67, 83 in.). This attractive coverlet with a centre seam appears to be homemade. [P.C.]

100 Overshot Coverlet: orange and indigo blue wool on cotton; from the family of Helen Gillespie, Picton, Prince Edward County, 3rd quarter 19th century. W. 160 cm, L. 200 cm (63, 79 in.). [R.B.]

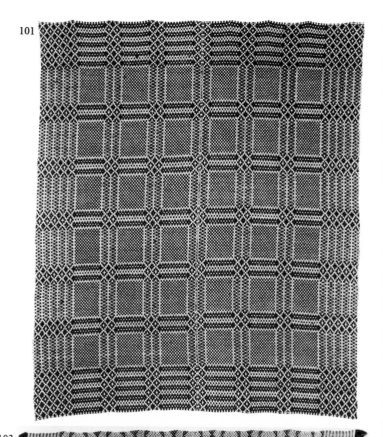

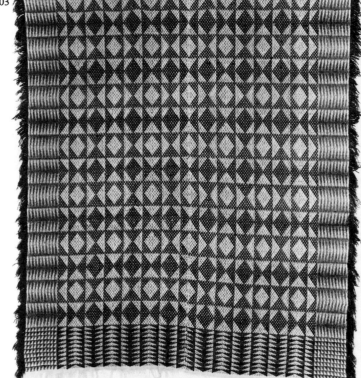

101 Overshot Coverlet: thought to have been made by a weaver in Martintown, Glengarry County, 3rd quarter 19th century; from the McDonald family, Maxville, Glengarry County. W. 166 cm, L. 200 cm (65, 79 in.). This coverlet has an unusual colour combination, black edged with purple on a cream background. Quilts in these colours were used in times of mourning, and possibly this coverlet was as well. [P.C.]

102 Star and Diamond: coverlet; patterned in red, dark blue and olive green wool on a natural white background; Waterloo

County, 3rd quarter 19th century. W. 184 cm plus fringes, L. 225 cm plus fringe (72, 89 in.). [R.O.M.]

103 Star and Diamond: coverlet; fine flame-like border; western counties, early 19th century. W. 186 cm, L. 225 cm (73, 89 in.). [M.J.S.]

104 Jacquard Coverlet: blue and red wool on white cotton, tied doublecloth, centre seam; sparkling colours; Brant County, dated 1854. W. 184 cm, L. 210 cm (72, 83 in.) plus fringe. This coverlet was made for Jane Thomson. [M.L.]

105

105 Jacquard Coverlet: blue, black and red wool on white ground, doublecloth, centre seam; found in Oxford County dated 1854.
W. 185 cm, L. 210 cm plus fringe (73, 83 in.). [M.L.]

106 Jacquard Coverlet: red wool on cotton; found in Listowel, Perth County, 4th quarter 19th century. W. 200 cm, L. 208 cm (79, 82 in.). Presumably the four angels were intended to guard the sleepers from evil during the night. [P.C.]

107 Jacquard Coverlet: rosy red wool on natural white cotton; Waterloo County, dated 1868. W. 171 cm, L. 211 cm (67, 83 in.). Coverlets of this type were made by professional weavers for young women about to be married. [R.B.]

107a Detail. The cartouche reads, "Made by J. Noll and Brothers for Ernestine Herber 1868." The date indicates that this is an early coverlet by the Noll brothers, who worked in Waterloo County during the 4th quarter of the 19th century.

108 Bird of Paradise: coverlet, Jacquard; bands of yellow, lavender, blue and red on natural white cotton; Welland County, ca. 1860. W. 190 cm plus fringe, L. 225 cm plus fringe (75, 89 in.). This coverlet has an unusually wide range of colours. [P.C.]

109

109 Christian Heathen: coverlet, Jacquard; wool on cotton; found in Hastings County, ca. 1850. W. 175 cm plus fringes, L. 192 cm plus fringe (69, 76 in.). The houses at both ends represent Boston, or the Christian country, and the stylized pagodas in the centre represent China, or the heathen country. This pattern was developed in the days when sailing ships went to trade in the Orient. [P.C.]

110

111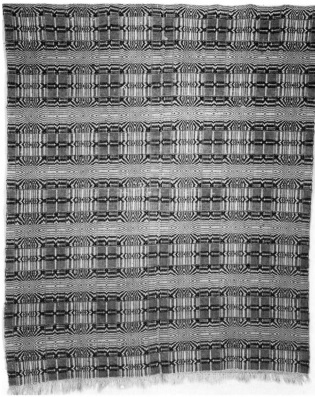

110 Jacquard Coverlet: olive green wool with light blue cotton on natural white cotton; from the Bennett family, Middlesex County, dated 1888. W. 175 cm, L. 200 cm plus fringe (69, 79 in.). This coverlet is somewhat frayed at the ends, and the initials at the top are probably those of the original owner. This is an unusual coverlet with its realistic house design. [P.C.]

111 Sunrise: coverlet, overshot; orange and indigo wool on natural white cotton; from the Roblin family, Prince Edward County, ca. 1850-1860. W. 175 cm, L. 205 cm plus fringe (69, 81 in.). Skilfully woven with a centre seam, this coverlet is probably the work of a local professional weaver. [P.C.]

8 The Fabrics Used in Making Quilts

She'll give me, when she dies,
All that is fitting:
Her poultry and her bees,
And her goose sitting,
A pair of mattress beds,
And a bag full of shreds;
And yet, for all this guedes,
Phillada flouts me!

"Phillada Flouts Me"
Anonymous, 17th century

Selling Canadian homespun cloth; from a watercolour by James Duncan, 1806-1881.

In the very early days, before home cloth making was established, any cloth that the settlers needed had to be bought at the local store. Among the first immigrants to the bush, there would be some enterprising individual who set up a little backwoods store to provide necessities for the settlers who were by no means self-sufficient at the start. The store was part of the man's home, a log shanty like the rest of the buildings in the district, and during the first years he had to combine his business with the tasks of settlement, cutting down trees and breaking soil. The first banker in Perth, Lanark County, for example, left a bell at his house so that his customers could call him from his fields near the river.

Storekeepers found it difficult to obtain stock from their distant sources, and it was not easy to arrange payment for their merchandise. In eastern Ontario, merchants paid for their goods by "bills" arranged through Montreal bankers, and even shipped potash overseas to cover costs. Roderick Mathewson used both methods to supply his Perth store, and in an 1827 letter he wrote to his suppliers, "I will thank you to send some patterns for our winter trade, and if you think a remittance in Potashes will be preferable to bills for my winter supply — have the goodness to say so."[1]

Life was not simple for the storekeeper, who had his finger in many pies and was often required to extend considerable credit to his neighbours. He would set up his counter, possibly only a board across two barrels, and, in some cases, was said to sleep beneath it on a bear skin at night. The storekeeper was an important man in the district: the village provider, father confessor, host and friend to the whole township. He probably knew more about his customers than the local man of the cloth did about his parishioners.

Settler's accounts, such as *Roughing It in the Bush*, tell us that cash was extremely scarce among the people, those who came out from the old country with ready money quickly lost it due to inexperience or misfortune. Only necessities could be bought, but rum, whisky and tobacco were apparently considered in this category, no doubt because they enabled a man to face the long hard days of labour under very trying circumstances. Certainly, these three things were the most common items sold in the early stores and sold in great quantities. A fact we tend to forget, however, is that many pioneer women smoked a pipe, as they still do in the bush of the Yukon and Northwest Territories. In an 1815 *Kingston Gazette* advertisment, John & Finkle, Dry

Goods and Grocers, appealed to this market by offering "ladies twist tobacco."

Large quantities of textiles were also sold, although this is not surprising when one considers how poorly equipped the settlers were to face the cold climate. As soon as possible, farmers began to exchange produce for goods, and the practice of bringing homemade butter to pay the bill at the store continued into the twentieth century. There is a description of a woman going to the store in Peterborough, "carrying a pail of butter on her head, with a basket of butter in one hand and a basket of eggs in the other. She would walk back the same ten miles the same day carrying cloth and other necessities which she had got in exchange."[2] Other arrangements were made, and further west farmers supplied the early forges at Normandale and Tillsonburg with iron ore, working out a credit arrangement for goods.

Reading early account books can be fascinating. In his idle moments, a storekeeper might indulge in philosophical meditations on back pages of his book, recording bits of information important to himself, such as "Harrison Lewis started to school. Recited his first lesson," and, "Feb. 1st took b. white cow to Kids," or, "July 18, had operation on Daisy."[3] One unusual account book has a letter stuck in the back written by a person who calls himself a private investigator: "I was unable to find out where your boy was living, but I gather he is well. Will keep trying."[4]

The storekeeper would often act as the middleman between local weavers and settlers who did not weave. The weaver would take payment in goods from the store, and the storekeeper used the fulled cloth obtained to supplement his imported stocks. The cuttings from articles made with this cloth went directly into quilt patches, along with the usable parts of worn out clothing, and for this reason the kinds of textiles sold in the early stores are very significant in the history of bedding.

One of the earliest surviving account books kept in Upper Canada is that of Samuel Sherwood, who operated a store on the Bay of Quinte about five miles west of Kingston from 1784 to 1791 when he moved to the Belleville area. Sherwood stocked a wide array of fabrics:

> shalon, cloath, striped cotton, brown molten [possibly melton], Scotch sheeting, Russia sheeting, red, brown, green rateen, green base [baize], durant, fustian, Irish linen, gray cloath, flowered flanel, calico, blue strouds, silk trimmings, black lace, Swanskinn, carsemeer [cashmere], hunter's cloth, striped liney wooley [linsey woolsey], muslin and forest cloth.[5]

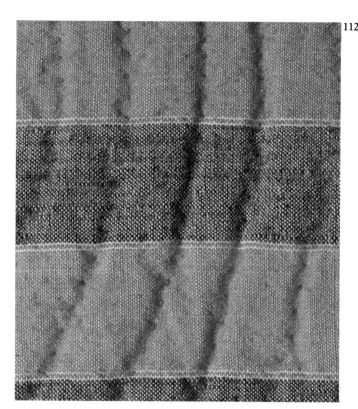

112

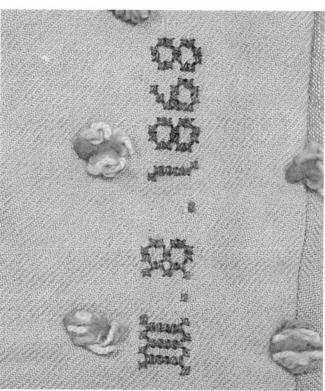

113

112 Wholecloth Quilt: detail of Plate 398; handspun, handwoven wool with cotton warp; banded in rose and brown; made by a member of the Luloff family, Renfrew County, 3rd quarter 19th century. W. 170 cm, L. 175 cm (67, 69 in.). Quilted with homespun yarn in curved lines arranged to form a large diamond in the centre. [R.L.]

113 Nine Patch: quilt, pieced, detail; handwoven wool; Madoc area, Hastings County, dated 1868, a late date for a homespun quilt, but not uncommon in Upper Canada. [C.C.F.C.S.]

114 Log Cabin: quilt back, detail; brilliant red with peacocks and flowers; Frontenac County, ca. 1860. W. 157 cm, L. 180 cm (62, 71 in.). [C.C.F.C.S.]

115 Variable Star: quilt back; handspun, handwoven wool and cotton in red and cream check; Lennox and Addington County, ca. 1850. W. 157 cm, L. 182 cm (62, 72 in.). Quilts were frequently backed with old homespun blankets. [C.C.F.C.S.]

116 Log Cabin: quilt back (see Plate 208); handsome red calico with green and blue stripes and stylized floral designs.

117 Wild Geese Flying: quilt back, detail; early dark blue cotton with white stars; from a Mennonite family, Vineland, Lincoln County, ca. 1850. W. 176 cm, L. 187 cm (69, 74 in.). [C.C.F.C.S.]

Many of these fabrics have names that are no longer familiar to us,[6] but most are heavy and durable, some of thick wool. Sheeting was used both for bedding and for making shirts, frocks and overalls.

An example of the typical sales for a bush store on a single day is recorded in the account book of a general store in Martintown, Glengarry County. The day was December 13, 1830, and the storekeeper, Sheriff McMartin, sold, among other things, ten and a half gallons of whisky, eight and a half pounds of tobacco, ten and a half yards of cotton, two and a quarter yards of apron check and one yard of flushing.[7] Among various items, including the inevitable whisky and tobacco, settlers purchased from David Roblin, Deseronto, Hastings County, in 1838, gingham, fustian, lace, calico, factory cotton, plaid, silk, buckskin, gray cloth and red flannel.[8] In 1845, a general merchant in Kemptville sold cotton, bean cloth, canvas, plaid, cord, sascony, red flannel, moleskin, silk velvet, Orleans, Brown Holland, wadding, quilting and dyes: senna [sienna], and indigo.[9] A Merrickville, Grenville County, merchant offered a wide assortment of fabrics in 1855: broadcloth, ticking, Black Colburg, red flannel, diaper, linen, cambric, print, wadding, gingham stripe, jean, calico, Brown Holland, plaid circassian, cassimere, delane, denham and derry.[10] (The original spellings used in the account books have been retained.) All of these fabrics are typical of those sold in small villages and used in rural areas of Upper Canada during the first half of the nineteenth century; much of it was used to make clothing and household items, but the cuttings and worn out pieces would inevitably make their way into quilts.

Storekeepers kept horses for hire, bulls for service, medicines for the sick, made clothing and mended shoes. Their customers came from considerable distances, often over very bad roads, leaving wives and small children at home to cope with the terrifying emergencies that occurred so often in the bush. These men expected to find seats by the stove where they could relax a bit and catch up with the news. The storekeeper, after all, was in touch with the old country through his suppliers and would have relatively up to date and valuable information to tell.

Roderick Mathewson was such a storekeeper; he was selling dry goods in Perth only four years after it was first settled. He ordered his supplies from Messrs. Watson and Lennox in Glasgow, and they came by ship to Montreal, thence to Perth by boat and wagon. Mathewson carried a surprising quantity and quality of fabrics for a settlement that had been forest primeval less than ten years earlier. The earliest orders for which I have a record were in 1827, and they included large amounts of gray cloth (bleached and unbleached), blue cloth, white and blue cottons, white and purple cottons, threads, prints, calicoes and bombazettes. Mathewson was very active in his trade, and among other fabrics he also ordered moleskins, assortments of calicoes at various prices, tartans, brown drill, blanket, plain Jaconet, muslin, corded muslin, book muslin, plain cambric, linen, white plaiding and fustian.

Before 1820, however, fabrics were scarce in most areas. A Lieutenant Battersley from Montreal wrote Mathewson in 1814 that,

> One can't get a tailor here to make a covering for one's posterior for love or money, I believe I must send to Quebec for the Grey and cotton cloth. There is such a demand for everything that the tradespeople are as saucy as Old Nick.[11]

One suspects that in this particular case part of the scarcity may have arisen from the fact that the tradesmen were too wily to risk their money covering the penniless posterior of a young lieutenant.

Various fabrics were available in limited quantities as early as 1804. An account book for the Clarke Settlement store in Lennox and Addington County lists calico, Irish linen, Bengal Stripes, lace, muslin, gray cloth, along with needles, hanks of thread, papers of pins and knitting needles.[12] By 1826, supplies were easier to come by, so that even Plantagenet, Prescott County, a settlement primarily concerned with lumbering, could stock such textiles as "gray cloth, Holland Bombazette, calico, skeins of thread, sheeting, flushing, linen, flannel, tartain, and skeins of silk."[13] Given the community's major occupation, though, whisky, rum and tobacco ranked very high on the order list.

The earliest quilts in Upper Canada were made from usable pieces of worn out clothing. Useless adult garments were cut down to make clothing for the children, and eventually these, too, wore out. Once again, the garments were ripped apart and the usable portions, such as the piece under the collar and just above the hemline, were sewn together to make a quilt top. This practice continued well into the twentieth century. Canadians did not easily forget the lessons of "Waste not, want not" and "Eat it up, wear it out, and make it do" that were learned early in a pioneer country. Thrift was considered next to godliness in many Upper Canadian households.

Once the top was made, backing had to be found for the quilt. Pieces of cloth, such as worn-out blankets were frequently used, the weaker parts of one overlapping the stronger parts of another. Stuffing must have been a considerable problem in the early days before wool was available. One hears rumours of moss, leaves or milkweed down being used, but I know of no evidence to support this idea. Indeed, vegetable stuffings would soon break down and, in any case, would provide little warmth. Old quilts were used as fillings for newer ones, and they were both quilted together. This was a difficult procedure which resulted in a heavy and even hard end product. Today, tantalizing glimpses of very old quilts can often be seen peeking through ripped seams, but before one yields to the temptation to take a perfectly good quilt apart to find an older one, it should be realized that the older quilt was used as a filler because it was likely worn beyond recognition. Some families had a habit of adding new wholecloth covers to worn quilts, and occasionally it is possible to count as many as eight layers of faded and thin cloth on a single quilt.

Everyone occasionally yields to temptation, however, sometimes with very interesting results. One quilt that came to me without history, except the area in which it was found, was made of wool and had been used as a wrapping blanket for furniture in the truck of a second-hand dealer. It seemed interesting and was old and cheap, so I took it home. Although the quilt was unusually heavy, I decided that it was simply too dirty to leave around the house and popped it into the washing machine. When it came time to remove the quilt from the machine, I regretted the decision, because the quilt was so heavy that I could barely hoist it onto a line strung across the kitchen. Fearing the line would break, I began to investigate and found that there appeared to be several layers of cloth. To relieve the weight, stitches were clipped and cloth removed; first came an entire woollen cloak, complete with braided trim and pockets, then a matching, ankle length skirt, and last a waist and parts of other woollen garments. The pile of cloth on the floor was almost as large as the original quilt. Finally, I found that the original quilt top had colourful homespun blocks, and that no patching was required due to wear. It was a fine discovery, but I was haunted by the thought of a poor old soul so cold in her little frame house that she kept adding layer upon layer of old clothing to her quilt each winter as the fuel grew scarcer and her bones grew colder.

In the early days of settlement, thread was difficult to obtain. It could be purchased at the local store, but frequently this source was miles away over roads that were mere trails in the bush. One hears, occasionally, that thread was made from the bark of certain trees, such as the mousewood, and used as a substi-

tute. This is difficult to prove today, but it seems likely that methods for making such thread could have been learned from the Indians. As early as 1820, the local stores stocked cotton threads of different weights, as well as a kind of thread called "slack." This is a term with which Mrs. Moodie, who brought a good supply of thread over with her, was unfamiliar. She considered it a "Yankee" term, but it was listed in Upper Canadian account books from around 1840 and sold in both ball and spool form. Likely, slack was a word used to describe basting thread which was a weak, cheaper thread sold on large spools. Such threads were pulled out and re-used many times, even in the twentieth century. The various kinds of thread that could be had (they were sold in hanks, skeins and balls) were extremely valuable to the settlers, especially as winter was closing in and bedding necessary. Once flax was grown, though, the settlers were able to make their own thread. This strong linen thread, when found in an early quilt today, is still durable and flexible. Like store-bought thread, it was never plentiful and was precious due to the time and labour it took to make.

Those settlers who had sheep were able to spin woollen threads or yarns. Although woollen thread was not generally considered strong enough or fine enough for sewing, the handwoven quilt in Plate 398 is finely quilted with handspun woollen yarn. It is a very difficult procedure to pull woollen yarn through three layers of stuff and at the same time make fine, even stitches. As a result, quilts were sometimes tied instead of quilted. This was the easiest way to use yarn which, being homemade, did not require the outlay of cash to obtain.

Even though money was scarce for such articles, a certain amount had to be spent to furnish a quilting bee with materials. In 1845, for example, Philary Froom bought from a Kemptville merchant, "8 yards of wading [wadding], 2 dozen threads, 3 thimbles, 4 pounds of candles, and a paper of needles."[14] This money was well spent, since the amount of labour and the quality of the results would far exceed the expense. Unlike other bees, such as logging or barn raising where great amounts of money were spent on whisky and rum and relatively little work done,[15] quilting bees were chaste and productive meetings.

The early quilts made with patches of worn-out clothing consisted of a great assortment of materials: pieces of woollen broadcloth, homespun tweeds, scraps of worn shawls, flannels, cotton prints and plaids. Once the home manufacture of linen and woollen cloth began, homespun cloth was widely used. These were usually pieced quilts, often being

118 Diamonds: quilt; rose and brown homespun and manufactured wool cloth; McMaster family, Leeds County, 19th century. W. 155 cm, L. 220 cm (61, 87 in.). A back has been added in the same pattern to make the quilt reversible. [C.C.F.C.S.]

of the one-patch variety, like the Hit and Miss pattern shown in Plate 396. There were some whole-cloth homespun quilts made, and they consisted of two lengths of material sewn together in the centre and backed with plainer homespun cloth. Some women wove the cloth in blocks or stripes which seem to be imitating patchwork patterns (Plate 412).

Wholecloth homespun quilts were made out of unused material, the traditional way of making quilts in established, old country communities. In an established Upper Canadian community, there was always a backlog of bedding in the family, and a good homespun quilt made of new cloth lasted through several generations.

Quilts made of worn out clothing did not wear as well, even though more time and work went into making them. It was far better to use scraps of new material saved from garment making, for the obvious reason that they were strong and unworn. Such scraps would vary greatly in size, and as none of them could be wasted, great ingenuity was necessary to fit the pattern to the material. Most expert quilt makers would not include used materials in their products,

except in times of economic stress when new cloth was not to be had.

The quilt in Plate 291 was made by the grandmother of a large and busy family in the eighteen nineties. She made several blocks of Eight Point Star, and finished the ends of the quilt in a Hit and Miss pattern. The little girl, who is today an old woman, who helped her grandmother make this quilt, spoke wistfully about it as she stroked the worn cloth softly: "I wonder whose dress that was. I forget now – it was so long ago. Everybody had to have something of theirs in it, you know, nobody could be left out."

Sometimes in a reasonably sound old quilt, one finds a particular material that was used throughout but has disintegrated. Probably, it was the remnants of a garment, well-loved and well-worn, included in the pattern for sentimental reasons. The story is long forgotten, and the cloth, alas, gone before the rest of the quilt.

In the early Log Cabin quilt (Plate 423) made by Jane Armstrong Dawson of Richmond, Carleton County, one finds in each corner, tucked among the brown flannels and serges, a few scraps of white silk brocade, probably from her wedding dress. This was a common practice that has obvious emotional overtones. Memories were woven into many quilts: little Sissy in her red dress the year before she died of scarlet fever, or her brother, Alexander, in his first green suit, and his death two weeks after Sissy. Here is the dress that grandma wore the night she was first kissed by that good-looking scamp whom her father did not like. She never told anyone, but she worked it into her quilt, and through the years it was her little secret, a reminder of when she was young and pretty and desirable.

The making of a quilt was of interest to the community. An old woman recalled the quilt her cousin, Elvira, made many years ago:

It was a log cabin quilt, and Cousin Elvira was making it of a particular type of material, and of certain unusual colours, a small pattern on a dark background, and the reverse for the dark areas of the quilt. Elvira took her blocks around to the neighbours and to the dress-makers searching for suitable pieces in their rag-bags to fit her design. All the little dark scraps had to be of a certain strange colour and pattern. Elvira would make no compromises, nothing else would do for the picture she had in mind. Aunt Maggie and the others watched the quilt grow and they wondered. It was a kind of queer looking thing, but they held their peace and waited. Finally the quilt was finished and the neighbourhood women heaved a collective sigh of relief, for the quilt was a beautiful thing. You would never have believed it, but it was really beautiful with all those dark little pieces gleaned from the whole area.

Grandmothers and aunties would sit by the bedside of a child who was ill and tell the story of the quilt on the bed, or a child would climb into grandma's bed to hear about her quilt. The story was a tale of cousins and aunts who lived in the country far away, and of little children who were dead but not forgotten. It was a way of telling the family traditions, of making the child feel a part of the clan, safe and secure in his or her place in the world.

As early as 1840 in the larger towns, one could buy clothing of fashionable cut or the fabrics with which to make them. According to Susanna Moodie, by 1852 the women in Belleville were "Well dressed... the dress of the higher class is not only cut in the newest French fashion, imported from New York, but is generally of rich and expensive materials."[16] In 1842, C. Kennedy & Co., importers of drygoods in Kingston, advertised their fall stock in the *Kingston Chronicle and Gazette,*

> Which will be found to be large, fashionable and select, in all its inhabitants... among items listed are prints, ginghams, and merinos, Orleans cloth, plain and figured, Delaines, Plaid, spun and embroidered dresses... Black and coloured Satinette... cotton and linen shirtings, and flannels.[17]

These fabrics, or cuttings from dresses made of them, ended up in the rag bag from which materials were chosen for quilts. From all this, it is apparent that a fairly large range of fabrics was available in urban areas at that period.

To supplement the range available in country stores and to prevent the necessity of travelling long distances to buy goods, pedlars soon began to move out into the countryside. The arrival of the pedlar was an exciting event. He was wily enough to plan his appearance at houses where there was a good bill of fare to coincide with mealtimes, because he was traditionally given a meal with the family. The pedlar was still making his rounds on foot when I was a child visiting my great aunt in the country. He walked up the lane bulging with packs strapped to every imaginable part of his body, just as his predecessors had been doing for over a hundred years. My great aunt was an enthusiastic quilter, and the pedlar had special pieces of material tucked in his packs just for her. The bundles were opened one by one and the wares spread over the kitchen. She bought lengths of cottons, spools of thread, needles and pins as her excitement grew. "Och," she would say, "It is really time to start the potatoes," at the same time loath to leave the exciting array of choice bits for her next quilt. Once the pedlar was gone and she had her pieces of cloth, she would keep spreading them out, muttering to herself, planning in her mind the next masterpiece.

Even in areas where it was possible to buy readymade clothing, most people wore homemade. Professional seamstresses moved from home to home, making the year's clothing for the family while they lived with them. The scraps left over were new, unworn and unwashed, and made excellent quilt materials. In a family with many daughters, there would be a great variety to choose from, perhaps for a Log Cabin quilt, since it had the virtue of using up even the tiniest scraps.

A close examination of a Log Cabin quilt will reveal the great wealth and variety of materials used. Tiny pieces are found to be sewn from two or three extremely small scraps. Plate 265 is a fine quilt, a Wild Goose Chase pattern, which was probably made around 1860 using a great range of types of cotton. This particular quilt was not bound and was never used. The materials are bright and unfaded, revealing beautiful cotton print goods in an abundance of colours, and showing just how subtle the colouration was in these early printed cottons.

Dressmakers were allowed to glean cuttings from families who did not save scraps. As a result, there is a type of quilt called a "Dressmaker's" that is very rich in the number of different fabrics used. As materials became easier to obtain and less costly, some quilts were undoubtedly made with materials purchased for the sole purpose of quilt making. This would be the case in particular when the one being made was a "good quilt" to be saved for special occasions.

Nevertheless, women continued to make quilts out of homespun cloth until the last quarter of the nineteenth century. The example in Plate 113 is dated 1868. Almost every household had a large supply of worn flannel or winter sheets that could be cut up for quilting. The material was usually dyed before being used, and, although wool still in the yarn dyes well, flannel sheets will not accept colour so easily. Pieces of splotchy wool in quilts are frequently the remains of such dyed sheets. Often used for quilt backs, flannel sheets would either be dyed or left their natural wool colour. The warm natural brown wool produced by a certain breed of sheep is particularly attractive when used in this way. Dark, striped cotton or flannelette was also popular for backing quilts, but the most common material used was made from bleached and dyed sugar or flour bags sewn together. Unbleached cotton was used as well;

it is an ideal backing that grows softer and whiter with each washing. Good quilts, on the other hand, were backed with a fine quality cotton that was only a little coarser than that used for the front. In very early quilts, the tops were sometimes made of cotton and the backs of homespun linen, an understandable practice for at that time cotton was a rarer and more exotic cloth than homely linen. Almost without fail, Log Cabin quilts were given the compliment of a good and attractive calico or chintz back brightly coloured, of a good weight that was bought especially for the purpose. The occasional quilt has a back made in the same manner as the front so that it is reversible, but this is quite unusual (Plate 118).

Some cotton-topped quilts were given a fine homespun linen or cotton back that was probably made for the purpose. Since it was made on a narrow loom, such a backing usually consisted of three widths of material sewn together by hand. Plates 2, 257 and 283 show quilts of this type which are very large in size. The Wild Goose Chase from Vineland, Lincoln County, is seven by eight feet, while the Cross pattern from Pembroke, Renfrew County, is nine feet wide and over eight feet long, having cut out corners to fit around the bottom posts of a four-post bed that had no footboard. The quilt in Plate 257, on the other hand, was found in Kingston and measures almost eight feet square. These quilts contain no used materials, and they were likely made from scraps as well as fabrics bought for the purpose, because large quantities were needed. They were important quilts and have had good care. The Vineland piece, for example, appears to have seldom been used; it has the initials E. C. worked on the back in a very delicate cross-stitch.

Marriage quilts were often appliquéd, and they usually required larger quantities of cloth of the same pattern than pieced quilts. Because appliquéd versions were made as best quilts, they had a certain aura about them, and, although fewer were made, more have survived for the simple reason that they were seldom used. Most families who had a treasured Star of Bethlehem quilt regarded it in this light, and many have survived as a result. Only an expert seamstress could make a good Star of Bethlehem, and it was an accomplishment of which the maker could be justifiably proud. It is unlikely that any but new materials were used in star quilts, though several have survived that have been made from salvaged materials (Plates 403, 407), no doubt because the maker wished to make the pattern but had only homespun scraps to use. A bold primitive beauty is evident in these quilts; the homespun stars, simple and stark in blue and red against a black sky,

119

create a feeling of the endless night of outer space.

During times of economic stress, such as the depression of the 1930s, people were forced to dip into their rag bags to make quilts, for there was simply no money to buy new material. It has been noted frequently in quilt books that "depression" quilts are in muted colours as a reflection of the sadness and dreariness of the times. This is undoubtedly true, but it should be kept in mind that a woman would have only faded materials with which to work (Plates 120 and 121).

Some people who were naturally thrifty found pleasure in making useful items out of household articles of no further use in their original contexts. Within the principle of "Waste Not, Want Not," it would be considered sinful in many families to buy cloth at the store to make an everyday quilt. Materials were consistently recycled, and such things as sugar and flour bags were saved, bleached and used for all manner of things. Some quilts, such as Beggar's Blocks (Plate 357), were made entirely from bag cloth. When washed, this cloth is soft, strong and easy to dye, unlike flannel. The example shown has the trademark of a brand of oats and flour, Robin Hood and his arrow, still visible on the front of the quilt. As he is rather attractive, Robin may have been left showing in such a prominent position quite deliberately. Sometimes it is possible to read the brand name of the sugar or flour mill which can be of interest in dating or placing the original locale of the quilt maker.

The Love Apple quilt in Plate 318 has been made from a farmer's work smocks and overalls. The colours are faded blues and browns, and some pieces,

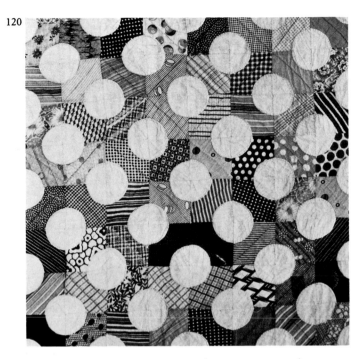

119 Love Apple: quilt, detail of Plate 318; of the unfaded area where a pocket has been removed from a pair of denim overalls.

120 Snowball: quilt, pieced, detail; cotton; subdued colours typical of quilts made in the 1930s; Hay Bay, Lennox and Addington County, ca. 1930. W. 153 cm, L. 192 cm (60, 76 in.). In the 1930s, pattern books showed quilts in light coloured flowery prints; natural looking flowers were favoured for appliquéd quilts. [C.C.F.C.S.]

121 Canadian Conventional Star, or Colonial Flower Garden: quilt, pieced, detail; Lennox and Addington County, ca. 1930.

W. 195 cm, L. 245 cm (77, 97 in.). This pattern is made in the sad colours of the 1930s. [C.C.F.C.S.]

122 Wild Goose Chase: quilt, detail of Plate 265. A colourful variety of unwashed early printed cottons.

123 Log Cabin, Steps to the Courthouse: quilt, pieced, detail; mostly cotton dress goods; Prince Edward County, 3rd quarter 19th century. W. 170 cm, L. 190 cm (67, 75 in.). Log Cabin quilts made use of the tiniest scraps of material. There was a wide variety of dress goods available and in use at this time. [C.C.F.C.S.]

though they have been washed, are stained and some show colour variation where a pocket has been removed (Plate 119). On each patch, a circle of red woollen flannel has been applied in a button hole stitch with red yarn. Similarly, the entire quilt is tied with matching red yarn. The result is amazingly beautiful. The colours are harmonious, blending in shades of earth and sky and set off with brilliant red centres, so that the entire quilt seems to glow. Indeed, it was a labour of love to lavish such painstaking work on such rough material, and one wonders whether it was all that was available, or if this humble cloth was used because it originally belonged to a beloved person. This quilt contrasts strangely with the Love Apple quilt in Plate 317 which is dainty and charming in red, yellow and blue cotton on a white background. The little love apples or tomatoes are slightly stuffed. One can almost smell the freshness of this old-fashioned quilt.

Quilts made from rag bag remnants have a very different quality than those made with "boughten" material. Greater ingenuity had to be used in planning, more daring colour combinations were used, and the result was bolder, more blazing finished items. These quilts were not made in a haphazard or hasty fashion. It took a woman a long time to plan the pattern, but she could not start making it until the outdoor work was over for the year, so while she sat cutting beans for the piccalilli, she had time to plan the quilt in her mind, looking at the yellow beans, the green peppers, the red tomatoes and the differing shades of each blending into the whole, adding just a speck of red pepper to make it come alive. She mulled over patterns as she went about her work, pulling out scraps from the rag bag and smoothing them on her knees while visualizing the pattern that would suit the cloth. She spread the patches on the kitchen table trying them this way and that. Many quilt makers added one or two blocks of a much lighter or brighter colour in what seems to us a haphazard fashion, but what was really intended was the same effect as the red pepper – just a speck to make it come alive (Plates 335, 342). The old-fashioned quilt maker cut her pattern to fit the cloth, and some striking panoramas of colour and design resulted.

In the nineteenth century, making bedding was a never-ending dreary chore. If most women had not found satisfaction in this work, they would not have taken the extra trouble to make their quilts, coverlets and blankets aesthetically pleasing. Women of artistic sensibilities found such creativity stimulating, but, like it or not, they had no choice, for the bedding had to be made.

9 Sets, Borders and Batts

Dreamer of dreams, born out of my due time,
Why should I strive to set the crooked straight?

"The Earthly Paradise, an Apology"
William Morris (1834-1896)

The term "to set" means the act of putting the quilt together, but when used as a noun the set refers to the strips or squares of cloth joining the pieced or appliquéd blocks. Alternately, the blocks can be sewn together edge to edge, as in all-over quilt patterns. In the case of all-over appliqué quilts, the patches are sewn to foundation cloth which is the size of the finished quilt.

All-over pieced quilts, such as the Hit and Miss type, are fairly easy to construct (Plate 324), while designs like Rob Peter to Pay Paul (Plate 372) or Birds in Flight are complicated to assemble. Some are yet more complex, because they must be started in the centre and developed in all four directions.

In Plate 124, the Chimney Sweep blocks are sewn together edge to edge. This same pattern, sewn together with a cross-bar set or lattice strips, can be seen in Plate 126 and, with an intervening block, in Plate 125.

In order to achieve the desired effect, some patterns must be sewn together without a set or intervening block. The Melon Patch in Plate 266 is such a pattern. Usually, there are only two colours used in Jacob's Ladder where the dark and light blocks are sewn together so that the dark areas form a ladder.

A popular method of sewing a quilt together is the cross-bar set, an example of which may be seen in Plate 381 where the dark strips are joined with light squares. In some quilts, the cross-bar set forms a part of the design (Plate 369). The appliquéd example in Plate 297 has the unusual feature of being made in four large blocks joined with a Wild Goose Chase set, but without a border. The result is very striking, and it would seem to reinforce the idea that most quilt makers visualize their quilts as pictures. The Harvest Sun quilt (Plate 250) has a pieced Wild Goose Chase set and border. These examples are fairly complex. The simplest set consists of a plain square placed between each pieced or appliquéd block.

Crazy quilts and Log Cabin quilts are made by sewing the pieces onto a backing or foundation patch as they are made. The resulting blocks are then sewn together to create light and dark areas in the desired pattern.

Elaborate borders were not commonly used in quilts. In general, only the "best" quilt, the one intended for guests or the bride's quilt, had a fine border, although from time to time one finds very good examples with no border at all, or everyday quilts made with a simple border. The most common border consisted of one or more bands of the colours

"Comfort me with apples for I am sick of love." Song of Solomon 2:5

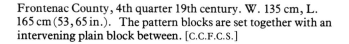

124 Chimney Sweep: quilt, pieced; cotton, shades of lavender with some red on a white background; made by Delila Way (1853-1939), Northumberland County, early 4th quarter 19th century. W. 157 cm, L. 200 cm (62, 79 in.). The blocks in this quilt are sewn edge to edge with no intervening block or strip. [R.B.]

125 Chimney Sweep: quilt, pieced; cotton, red, black and white plaid on a white background; made by Ellen McMullen, Verona,

Frontenac County, 4th quarter 19th century. W. 135 cm, L. 165 cm (53, 65 in.). The pattern blocks are set together with an intervening plain block between. [C.C.F.C.S.]

126 Chimney Sweep: quilt, pieced; cotton flannel and wool broadcloth; blue with black polkadots and black; Sexsmith family, Lonsdale, Hastings County, 1st quarter 19th century. W. 184 cm, L. 240 cm (72, 94 in.). The pattern blocks are sewn together with a cross-bar set or lattice strips. [C.C.F.C.S.]

placed corner to corner. Here, the quilt is put together with alternate blocks of a different colour. The borders are formed using small triangles of contrasting colours. [C.C.F.C.S.]

129 Unnamed Quilt: pieced, nine patch construction; cotton; yellow, green and white; made by Mrs. William Somerville, Balderson, Lanark County, 4th quarter 19th century. W. 155 cm, L. 210 cm (61, 83 in.). [C.C.F.C.S.]

130 Variable Star: quilt, pieced; cotton with handspun, handwoven wool back; browns and pinks, some blue; Miles family, Napanee, Lennox and Addington County, 2nd quarter 19th century. W. 135 cm, L. 172 cm (53, 68 in.). The border on the three sides indicates that this quilt was used on a bed set against a wall. [C.C.F.C.S.]

131 Rose of Sharon: quilt, border detail of Plate 315. The small urns of cherries or grapes are beautifully set into the corners of the border.

132 Rose and Thistle: quilt, border detail of Plate 316. The use of fruits, such as these golden apples and pears, does not happen very often in Upper Canadian quilts.

127 Eight Point Star: quilt, pieced; red and white; Durham County, 20th century. W. 137 cm, L. 170 cm (54, 67 in.). Red and white borders frame the quilt. [S.S.M.]

128 Puss in the Corner: quilt, pieced; cotton; red, yellow and green; Frontenac County, 4th quarter 19th century. W. 183 cm, L. 250 cm (72, 81 in.). The blocks in this pattern are usually

used in the pattern, running around the sides and ends of the quilt. Both pieced and appliquéd versions were given such borders, as in the examples in Plates 127 and 311. Occasionally, these borders are embellished with triangles set in contrasting colours to form a sawtooth (Plate 128) or a dog's tooth (Plate 252).

If a quilt was made to be tucked in at the top and bottom, it seems reasonable that borders would be confined to the sides, but several quilts I have seen, like the one in Plate 129, have borders at the top and bottom only. The reason for this is difficult to explain. Those with borders along one side and across one end only, on the other hand, were intended for use in small bedrooms where the bed stood against one wall but could be seen from an adjacent room (Plate 253). Because most quilts were conceived as pictures, the borders were clearly intended as frames. Elaborately bordered quilts were usually square.

Some appliquéd quilts have attractive borders; the most common are variations of the running vine or festoon. In Plate 135, a Garden Wreath pattern, there is a running vine bearing the same flower as in the wreath. The same pattern may be seen in Plate 134, but with a swag and tassel border, and again in Plate 136 embellished with half flowers set along the edge. All three quilts are in red, green and yellow, and despite the fact that the swag and tassel is very attractive, the running vine seems to make the most harmonious arrangement. In any case, a running vine border, whether pieced or appliquéd, should never be broken, lest it fortell a life or love cut short.

Quilt makers had difficulty with the corners of borders, and some solved the problem by bringing the vines up to small designs inserted in the corners. This may have shortened some lives or ended some loves, but it did result in some charming borders. The Rose of Sharon in Plate 131 has a basket of cherries or grapes in each corner, while the Rose and Thistle in Plate 132 has an exceptionally fine individually designed border with little urns each containing a fruit, a rose and a lily. The rest of this border uses golden apples and red pears or pomegranates. The Rose of Sharon in Plate 314 has a successfully executed running vine border with a flower set into each corner. Both of the embroidered quilts shown in Plates 209 and 239 have running vine borders.

The popularity of the swag and tassel border is pointed out by the Oak Leaf and Reel counterpane in Plate 298, but the stiff little bows or tassels defy gravity in an alarming fashion.

Sometimes, a part of the main design is repeated along the edge of the quilt to form a border, such as in the Starburst in Plate 245, where the points of a star appear as strange little wigwams along the quilt's edge. The Tree of Paradise (Plate 244) has a rather strange border design at the top and bottom of the quilt which probably had some special significance to the maker. Plate 238 shows a French Star that has lively little squiggles in its border that somewhat resemble seahorses and that caused the maker difficulty at the corners. The quilt in Plate 389 has a strikingly handsome chevron border along one side and on part of the other, but it would appear that the maker became weary and finished the design with horizontal bars.

Some quilts were bordered with separate scallops or sawtooth pieces sewn to the edge (Plate 441). Early quilts were frequently trimmed with either netted or crocheted separate fringes, or embellished with lace. This practice fell out of fashion, and unfortunately many such borders were removed at an early date. An example of the crocheted fringe may be seen in Plate 260 where it appears in variegated colours. Before 1860, quilts were often trimmed with gathered frills or flounces of matching material. Occasionally, a plain border acted as a flounce or dust ruffle as in the Cross quilt shown in Plate 2.

There is a type of quilt consisting of a central square or medallion framed with a series of elaborate borders (Plates 272, 273); more simplified versions appear in Plates 376 and 384. Sawtooth and Wild Goose Chase borders were popular in the style of quilt shown in Plate 272, where one of the borders is composed of nine patch blocks sewn end to end, alternating with plain blocks. In the homespun version of this style, the framing borders are long plain strips of cloth in various colours joined by block corners.

The visual impact of certain patterns is stronger without the distraction of a border. The two very striking quilts that appear in Plates 256, and 255 would undoubtedly be toned down if they were hemmed in by a border. The same principle applies to many of the geometric patterns, especially such examples as Rob Peter to Pay Paul (Plate 271), Ocean Waves (Plate 340), Old Brown Goose (Plate 137). Similarly, a border would detract from finely quilted covers that rely on the quilting pattern for visual effect. Nevertheless, a simple border can be used quite effectively, as in the Pineapple quilt reproduced in Plate 368.

Borders were seldom used on a Log Cabin quilt, since the strong visual effect of the Log Cabin unit is weakened when one is used. An example of this may

133 Details of borders found on 19th century Upper Canadian quilts.

133

134

136

135

134 Garden Wreath: quilt, appliquéd; cotton; red, green and white; Harrison family, Wellington, Prince Edward County, ca. 1890. W. 188 cm, L. 191 cm (74, 75 in.). The stuffed leaves and flowers are enclosed by a green and yellow bow knot and hammock border with lightly stuffed tassels. [F.S.H.]

135 Garden Wreath: quilt, appliquéd, all-over shell quilting; cotton; red, green and white; signed and dated "M. F. Murray, 1882," Perth area, Lanark County. W. 145 cm, L. 195 cm (57, 77 in.). The flowers are slightly padded, and the running vine border enhances the pleasant design. [D.C.]

136 Hollyhock Wreath: quilt, appliquéd; cotton; red, green, yellow and white; Athens area, Ontario County, ca. 1860. W. 182 cm, L. 182 cm (72, 72 in.). This pattern, with its diamond-shaped leaves, is early. There is a four heart circle in the centre of each wreath quilted by the grandmother of the former owner. A simple border is formed by placing half flowers along the edge. [C.C.F.C.S.]

be seen in Plate 428, a Straight Furrow pattern, which has a wide red border. The border itself is quite handsome, but its presence reduces the graphic impact of the quilt as a whole.

There were no hard and fast rules concerning borders. As we have seen, there were many traditional kinds that might be used, while some women created their own. Whether they were used or not depended on the maker's judgment, rather than any strictly established procedure.

Sets usually followed convention and borders were largely an expression of individual taste, but batting depended to a great extent on the availability of materials. Once wool was readily obtainable, it was used for the majority of quilts in Upper Canada, since it was not only warmer but cheaper than cotton. To fill a quilt, loose wool could be used, or it could be sent to the mill to be made into a batt.

Many farm women used the wool from their own sheep, but those who didn't keep their own flock were able to buy prepared wool from local mills. The Crazy quilt shown in Plate 429 is filled with wool from the family flock, and the owner can remember helping her grandmother card the wool during the 1920s. This late date shouldn't be surprising; similar quilts were commonly made in the country until at least the 1930s.

Whether the wool was used loose or made into a batt, it had to be thoroughly cleaned and carded to prevent it from smelling when the quilt was warm and to prevent the appearance of small brown spots on the covering fabric that often resulted from improper preparation.

Although a quilt might appear to be all cotton, care must be taken in washing it, because the batt may, in fact, be wool. If it is, the quilt must be washed in tepid water or dry-cleaned. One test to determine the batting material is to hold the quilt up to the light to see if there are any fine wool fibres sticking through the fabric. A wool-filled quilt is light in weight and retains its body since it does not pack down the way cotton does.

Even in the earliest days of settlement, cotton was sometimes used to fill quilts. By 1830, women could buy cotton filling at local stores, where it was called wadding, quiltings, or yards of quiltings. These names probably indicate that it was available both in prepared batts and by the yard. In 1849, the Ontario Wadding Mill, Oswego, New York, was advertising in the *Kingston Chronicle and News* for Canadian agents to sell battings and waddings in the north and west that they manufactured at their wadding mill. It is very probable that most cotton battings used to stuff Upper Canadian quilts were imported from the

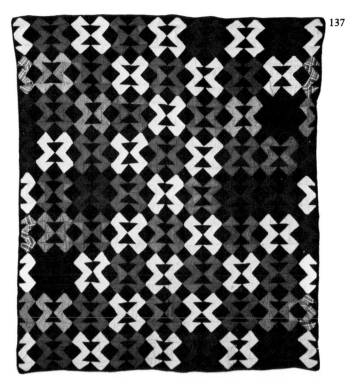

137

138

137 Old Brown Goose: quilt, pieced; cotton; multi-coloured on a dark background; eastern counties, 4th quarter 19th century. W. 160 cm, L. 190 cm (63, 75 in.). This pattern was traditionally done in brown. The blocks are sewn together without an intervening block or set, which results in a lively dancing movement. [C.C.F.C.S.]

138 Wholecloth Quilt: wool and linen, probably handspun and handwoven; gold; Plante family, Renfrew County, ca. 1850. W. 160 cm, L. 185 cm (63, 73 in.). The quilt relies entirely on its quilting design, done with wool in herringbone and spirals, for decorative effect. This is an old-country tradition rarely seen in Upper Canada. [C.C.F.C.S.]

United States during the nineteenth century.

Quilts stuffed with loose wool, especially those made of woollen cloth, were occasionally tied rather than quilted because of the thickness involved. Tying was not always done, however, exemplified by the striped homespun example shown in Plate 398 that is filled with wool and quilted with wool thread in fine sweeping curves, a tremendous undertaking. This particular quilt was made by a member of the Luloff family in Renfrew County. The Luloff women were excellent weavers, and several of their fine, colourful homespun quilts have survived in good condition.

Made of finely spun wool and linen, the whole-cloth quilt pictured in Plate 138 is made with a double layer of homespun woollen cloth and is lightly stuffed with wool. The impact of the quilt is entirely derived from the quilting designs, an old country tradition rarely seen in Upper Canada. The quilting is elaborately done with woollen thread in vertical lines separating rows of small, filled circles or spirals, while in one panel there is a very large repetition of this motif. This unbalanced effect is somewhat unusual and doubtless had some special meaning for the woman who did it.

There is a rule of thumb in the United States that the more seeds to be found in cotton stuffing, the earlier the quilt. Until 1792, when the cotton gin machine was invented, cotton was picked over by hand and more seeds usually remained, although there are exceptions to this rule as some machines didn't do as good a job as some human pickers. In Upper Canada, quilts were being made at a later date than the invention of the cotton gin. It is possible that quilts brought up by the Loyalists may have been filled with unginned cotton, but it is unlikely that many have survived. Occasionally a quilt found here is filled with heavily seeded cotton. I have one which was bought at a local auction by an antique dealer who practically pushed it into my arms. When I washed it, I discovered why he had been so eager to part with it. It was filled with little black specks that startled me so much that I expected the quilt to get up and walk away. An investigation with the scissors revealed that the specks were in fact seeds, indicating that the quilt might be very old. It is an Eight Point Star pattern in a dotted pink and white cotton. The dots have worn through so that they appear as tiny holes. If a quilt like this is found, it is easy to determine whether it contains a great many seeds, for they are quite visible when the quilt is wet.

Some quilts are made with very little stuffing, particularly the elaborately quilted ones since thinner filling is easier to penetrate with a needle. A

139

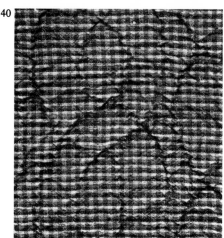

140

141

139 Harvest Sun: quilt, detail of Plate 246. Freehand quilting in trailing vines and baskets of flowers.

140 Hit and Miss: quilt, detail of Plate 378; showing double twisted rope quilting.

141 Harvest Sun: quilt, detail; swirling rosettes on a stippled background. [M.F.F.]

142 Lemon Star: quilting detail of a bird sitting on a woman's hand. [C.C.F.C.S.]

143 Lemon Star: another detail of the same quilt. Each alternate plain block has been finely quilted in a different pattern. This one has four hearts.

144 Snowflake: quilt, detail. The fan, or "dinner plate" quilting shown here was probably the most commonly used

quilting design in Upper Canada. [R.L.]

145 Feathered Star: quilt, detail of Plate 254. A fine example of shell quilting.

146 Feathered Star: quilt, another detail of Plate 254. A rosette on a stippled background.

147 Appliqué: quilting detail showing an unusual goose-eye pattern. The quilt was

made by Althea Spafford, Spaffordton, Frontenac County, 1871. [G.D.]

148 Delectable Mountains: detail of Plate 277; a quilted willow tree.

149 White Quilt: a detail of a beautifully quilted central medallion [R.B.]

150 Peacock: quilt, detail; the quilting is the sole decoration. [C.C.F.C.S.]

certain amount of filling is required, however, to emphasize the pattern and cause the slight relief needed to show the quilting. Experienced quilters know the amounts of stuffing necessary for the various patterns. It was not in keeping with the ethics of the day to skimp on the warmth of the quilt in order to enhance its appearance or make the quilting easier. One had to be practical and thrifty first of all, for what good is a quilt without warmth? Once these requirements were met, though, there was a certain amount of leeway for more artistic expression.

Summer quilts were made with no stuffing (Plate 432), and they would sometimes be backed but not quilted. Appliquéd tops were occasionally finished with hems or bindings and never quilted. In some cases, a quilt was left unfinished by the original maker, someone took a fancy to it, bound the edges and used it as a bedspread. On the other hand, the appliquéd Oak Leaf and Reel in Plate 298 was apparently never intended to be quilted, and hence should really be called a bedspread. The binding is an unusual red twilled cotton that matches the red cotton used in the pattern. If it were not bound when it was made, it is unlikely that the identical material could have been found at a later date. This makes an attractive spread, though one cannot help feeling that it would have been a magnificent quilt.

Plate 149 gives a detail from an all white quilt that is quilted all over in intricate patterns. Apparently, no stuffing was used by the maker, Isabella Forgey Bell of Peterborough County.

The quilts that have survived in the greatest numbers are the lightly stuffed showpieces which were kept for special occasions. The heavily stuffed everyday ones were not valued as highly by the family and were not kept when worn. Nevertheless, more everyday quilts were made during the period than "best" ones, and they frequently show up in quantity at auction sales. These utilitarian quilts are usually well stuffed and often made with woollen cloth. Some of these have no merit other than their ability to keep a body warm, while others are attractive and expressive of the natural taste of the women who made them.

10 Quilt Names

I have fallen in love with American names,
The sharp names that never get fat.

"American Names"
Stephen Vincent Benét (1898-1943)

Star of Bethlehem quilt pattern.

There was a tradition of naming quilts in the old countries that was sanctified by time and resulted in fairly staid descriptive titles varying little from area to area within a country. In contrast, there was a tremendous exuberance in the naming of quilts in the New World. Both in Upper Canada and the United States, quilt names vary tremendously from region to region, and the new one sometimes has little relation to the old. An illustration of this is the Star of Bethlehem; in Texas it is the Star of Texas, while on Amherst Island, a small island in Lake Ontario near Kingston, it is called Amherst Star, yet there is little difference among the basic designs.

The naming of quilts was a folk art in itself. Many reflect rural humour at its best and the uncanny ability of village people to select the right name at the right moment. Old Maid's Ramble, Toad in the Puddle, Swallow in the Path, Duck's Foot in the Mud, Fox and Geese, Devil's Claws, Young Man's Fancy, Crazy Ann, Buzzard's Roost, Corn and Beans, Wild Goose Chase, Hole in the Barn Door, All Tangled Up, House that Jack Built and True Lover's Buggy Wheel are but a few of the apparently never ending picturesque quilt names.

For no apparent reason, one pattern may have several names, each one completely different. Sometimes, they were changed to suit different localities or circumstances, but others, like Topsy, seem to have "just growed." One obvious regional change may be seen in a quilting design called Ocean Waves in the Maritime Provinces and simply Fan quilting in Upper Canada. On the other hand, the Lily pattern might be termed Canada Lily, North Carolina Lily, Lily of the Valley, Meadow Lily, Wood Lily or Day Lily depending on location. Indian Trail is often used as a prime example of a quilt of many names; it might appear as Winding Walk, Rambling Road, Old Maid's Ramble, Storm at Sea, Flying Dutchman, North Wind, Weather Vane, Climbing Rose and a few more.

Quilt names in Upper Canada are similar, generally speaking, to those used in the United States, although we have dropped some of theirs and added a few of our own. Some American names that have political connotations have been changed here. Burgoyne Surrounded, for instance, became simply Homespun in Canada for obvious reasons. Apparently, Canadian women were not sufficiently interested in politics to name quilts for political figures or episodes. If there are any Canadian equivalents to Lincoln's Platform, I do not know of them, but it is never safe to be overly dogmatic about

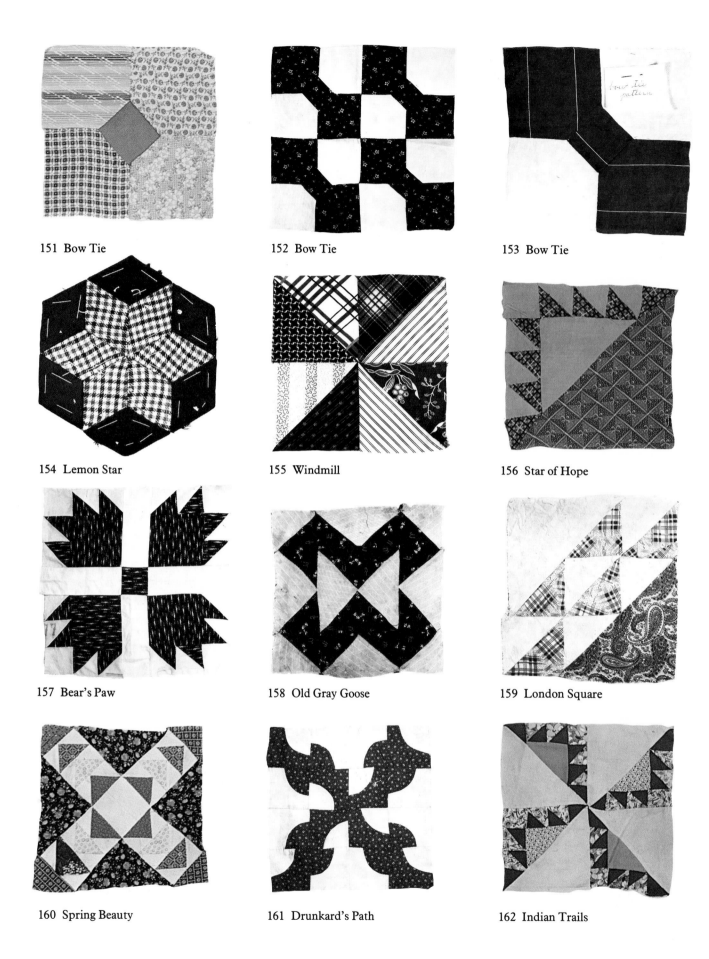

151 Bow Tie

152 Bow Tie

153 Bow Tie

154 Lemon Star

155 Windmill

156 Star of Hope

157 Bear's Paw

158 Old Gray Goose

159 London Square

160 Spring Beauty

161 Drunkard's Path

162 Indian Trails

Mrs. Wood's collection of quilt blocks. [I.W.]

163 Lucinda's Star

164 Goose Tracks

165 Star of Bethlehem

166 Nelson's Victory

167 Delectable Mountains

168 Star of the West

169 Pieced Star

170 Maple Leaf

171 Maple Leaf

172 Basket

173 Nine Patch

174 Log Cabin

175 Mrs. Mary Ellen Wood

quilt names. It is my feeling that the only correct name for a quilt is that given it by the woman who made it. Unfortunately, we seldom know what that name was; surviving members of a family do not remember what Aunt Mary called her quilt, although they may recall when it was made.

When one is talking today to women who did a great deal of quilting in their day, it is surprising how difficult it is to get them to give names to patterns, even common ones. They called their quilts some name or other when they were making them, but did not consider it as important as we do now. Nevertheless, many whimsical names were taken from popular nineteenth century games. They had a pleasing rhythm, and apparently people used them simply because they liked the sound: Jack-in-the-Box, Hands All Around, Puss-in-the-Corner, Lend and Borrow, Pin Wheel, Old Maid's Puzzle, Swing-in-the-Corner, Johnny-Round-the-Corner, Merry Kite and Whirligig.

Before there was electricity in barns, small diamond-shaped openings, surrounded by heavy frames, were cut high in the barn door to let in light. Most of these doors have been replaced by now, but they must have been quite common, judging from the number of quilts called Hole in the Barn Door (Plate 363). This highly descriptive name appears to be scattered throughout Upper Canada, but there are pockets where the same pattern is called Churn Dash and still other areas where it is known as Double

Monkey Wrench. Churn Dash was named after the plunger or dash used in an old-fashioned hand churn (Plate 362), according to an old woman who told me they used the name because the pattern resembled the dash of her mother's churn. In this way, names were changed on whim by people who took the old names rather casually. Pattern books were not common during the early days, the common patterns were known to most people, and they felt quite free to name their quilts as the fancy took them.

In other ways, though, quilt names were thought to be very important. If a young person slept under a quilt whose name might have an adverse effect on the character, the name was changed. One never put a young boy under a Wandering Foot (Plate 328), lest he turn out to be a wanderer, and the quilt would be called instead Turkey Tracks. For the same reason, a Rolling Stone sometimes became Johnny-Round-the-Corner (Plate 342).

The name Chimney Sweep was derived from the shape of the old, multi-flued chimneys that were cleaned by little boys. The practice of using human chimney sweeps and of building chimneys with several flues was becoming uncommon by the time Upper Canadian women were making quilts and gradually the name was changed to Christian Cross or Five Crosses. This might be seen as an example of the exuberance and freedom felt in the New World, for the use of chimney sweeps, who were often no more than seven or eight years old, would probably be seen as Old World oppression by those emigrants whose class had supplied the children. In 1789, the English poet William Blake described such a sweep:

> When my mother died I was very young,
> And my father sold me while yet my tongue,
> Could scarcely cry weep weep weep weep.
> So your chimneys I sweep & in soot I sleep.[1]

It is little wonder that the quilt name was changed to one with more Christian overtones, although it did survive along with Christian Cross, Five Crosses and Courthouse Square to describe the same pattern. The quilt in Plate 348 was called Five Crosses by the woman who made it.

Rob Peter to Pay Paul is a generic name for several patterns in which two colours are used in such a way that it appears that what is cut away can always be used to fill the adjacent block in a reversed colour scheme. It does not quite work out that way because of seam allowances, but that is the general idea (Plates 370, 371, 372, 373). Log Cabin is yet another generic name that includes several patterns or arrangements of the pieces as well as the light and dark areas. The patterns that usually appear are: Pineapple or Windmill Blades, Barn Raising, Straight

Furrow, Steps to the Courthouse, Rail Fence, Light and Dark or Checker Board and Zig Zag or Snake Fence (Plates 413 to 428). Basically, a Log Cabin quilt uses strips or logs to make the quilt pattern. They are usually fastened down on a background with a running stitch and folded over one another to build the pattern, beginning with a small square in the centre of each block. The seams do not show, because each log is turned over and pressed down to hide them.

When one is looking for information about local quilt names, it is well to remember that most women quilting today are using titles found in American quilt books rather than those traditional to their own area. Some American pattern books have been in use in Canada for many years. One example, *Diagrams of Quilt, Sofa, and Cushion Patterns,* found in an Ontario home, was published in 1892 by the Ladies Art Company in St. Louis. It lists four hundred and twenty patterns that one could order by name and number. Upper Canadian women frequently clipped patterns from magazines and newspapers. Many of these were American, such as *Godey's Magazine and Lady's Book;* they published quilt patterns and fashions and were widely read in Canada. *The Family Herald and Weekly Star,* published in Canada, was also widely studied in most rural households for its patterns. By the early twentieth century, it was possible to write away for bundles of remnants accompanied by a booklet of patterns for one or two dollars. One of the most popular pattern books used in Upper Canada was *Aunt Ruth's Book of Patterns.*

It can safely be assumed that in the late nineteenth and early twentieth century only new and fashionable patterns were ordered. The old traditional patterns with their familiar names were easily available closer to home, perhaps from a relative or a neighbour. The Variable Star, Nine Patch, Shoo Fly or Hole in the Barn Door had been made over many years and there was usually someone in the family who could cut out these traditional patterns. Many of these geometric patterns were made by folding a block of cloth and cutting it as folded. Other people used paper patterns or templates, often cut out from cardboard or even tin. It was customary to make a block of a pattern to keep for reference, and some quilters had a collection of blocks, occasionally with the name of the pattern pinned to the block. These are quite rare now, but Plates 151 to 174 show a collection made by Mrs. Wood in Portsmouth Village, Frontenac County, in the late nineteenth century. The old cotton prints give the blocks themselves a certain charm.

With geometric patterns it is often difficult to tell whether the pattern was designed to fit the name or vice versa. I suspect the latter, particularly since there seems to be little doubt that some names were used simply because people liked the sound of them and the pattern had some connotation with the name. Traditionally, Birds Flying is used connotatively; the birds are triangles with the apex of one against the flat side of another. Many patterns, particularly the older geometric ones, employ abstract forms representing natural shapes.

Although it is often difficult to discover the name of a particular everyday quilt, people do seem to know the names of their best quilts. They might vary somewhat, but there is always one name for them in the family. The Princess Feathers (Plate 4) takes its name from a quilting design based on the traditional emblem of the Prince of Wales. It is also called Prince's Feathers, Prince of Wales Feathers, Prince of Wales Plumes and is even known as George Washington's Plumes. The popularity of the design in Upper Canada probably has something to do with the widespread use of the Prince of Wales Feather as a decorative motif in late Neoclassical and Regency furniture during the early nineteenth century. In quilting, the "feathers," either curled at the end or straight, were used in an appliqué pattern for a good quilt.

There are many Rose patterns, all of which are ultimately derived from the Tudor Rose quilting design which had been used for generations. The finely quilted designs in which women took great pride when making a pattern such as this showed to advantage in the traditional, Old World wholecloth quilts, but when patchwork became popular such techniques were no longer as visible. As a result, many of the older designs began to be used as appliqué patterns for good quilts.

The most important of all in the "best" category was the marriage quilt, and many of the names for these were taken from the Bible. Women were religious in the nineteenth century, and their reading was often limited to the Bible and such devotional books as *The Pilgrim's Progress.* They would choose names from these sources that were euphonically pleasing as well as emotionally and religiously significant. The Song of Solomon has provided more names and inspirations for wedding quilts than almost any other source. It is probably the only love poem that a young woman would know, apart from "profane" ballads, and it has the advantage of being one of the most beautiful ever written. No one could take exception to the highly sensual imagery extolling carnal love, since the source was divine inspiration. The

176 Eight Point Star

177 Feathered Star

178 Pot of Tulips

179 Love Apples

180 Log Cabin, Pineapple

181 Hovering Hawks

182 Harvest Sun

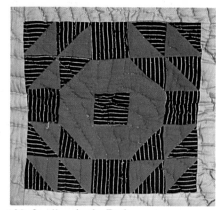

183 Swallow in the Path

184 Old Maid's Ramble

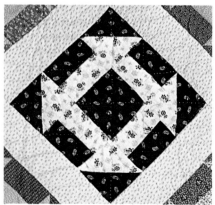

185 Hole in the Barn Door

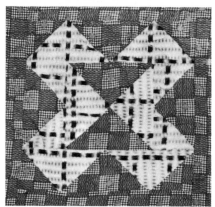

186 Old Brown Goose

187 Bear's Paw

188 Star of Bethlehem

189 Crazy Quilt

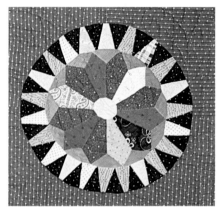

190 Pyrotechnics

191 Jack in the Pulpit

192 Double Hearts and Tulips

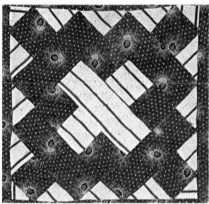

193 Chimney Sweep

194 Pinwheel Star

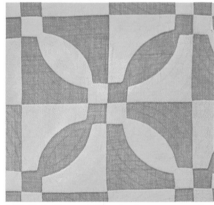

195 Rob Peter to Pay Paul

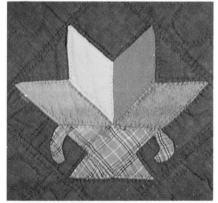

196 Basket of Scraps

197 Lady of the Lake

198 Log Cabin

199 Pieced Pineapple

Rose of Sharon and its many variations is probably the most common pattern for a marriage quilt:

> I am the rose of Sharon, and the lily of the valleys.
> As the lily among thorns, so is my love among the
> daughters.
> As the apple tree among the trees of the wood, so is
> my beloved among the sons.
> I sat down under his shadow with great delight, and
> his fruit was sweet to my taste.[2]

In the portraits of our grandmothers, we see those austere, tight lipped, sober visages and wonder that these were the women who made the Rose of Sharon for their marriage beds, revealing the depth of passion and tenderness that lay beneath those stern countenances and starched bosoms. These were women whose quilts were poems of love in themselves.

Because of the Bible's central place in the nineteenth century household, it is not at all strange that Biblical terms were in common use as quilt names. Cross and Crown, Cross Upon Cross, Hosanna, Jacob's Ladder, Job's Tears, Robbing Peter to Pay Paul, Star of Bethlehem, Star of the East, Tree of Life, World Without End all appear, and there are many others.

Many people came to the new land to seek freedom from the tyrannies of the Old World and to find security in owning their own land, many for the first time. There are parallels for this escape from oppression into a free and fruitful land in the Bible and Bunyan's *Pilgrim's Progress*. Bunyan's hero, Christian, leaves the City of Destruction on a long and dangerous journey to find the promised land, the Delectable Mountains, where he will find happiness. This was a land of plenty, with gardens, orchards, vineyards and fountains of water.[3] The story captured the imaginations of women in nineteenth century Upper Canada, and the Delectable Mountains was a very popular quilt pattern (Plate 277). The parallels are obvious enough. Upper Canadian settlers would rejoice in the opportunity to own their own land, and they were happy despite the hardships they had to endure. Every day they were thankful to their God that their sons would have a better life in the new country.

This secure joy in the face of hardship would have been reinforced by news from the old country where things were not much better than they had been; if anything they were somewhat worse. Alexander Cameron, for example, wrote from Aberfeldy, Scotland, to his brother-in-law, Robert Dewar, in Upper Canada that,

> I consider it good for you that you mustered away so

soon, although with much stress and difficulty, you would be surprised and could not understand the change of the people's minds of both simple and gentry here since you left this place — their [there] is but monkey tricks and turns among the people also gentry with every Tyrannical rule that is rendering decent people giddy headed and giddy faced varying from the rules of Integrity or Charity of good feeling. . . .

On another occasion, Cameron wrote, "We can neither go to the Church or Smithy where their [there] we see a barr for that purpose staring us in our face."[4] There are also injustices about which he fears to write, but he promises that settlers coming over at that time will tell their former neighbours and relatives. Cameron refers to people being put off the land where they had lived for generations, left with neither a place to live nor pasture for the cow.

When the first period of stress had been endured and the newcomers were becoming established on the land, there was an exuberance and joyfulness which began to express itself in the quilts. Freedom from tyranny, land for the boys and no longer the need to sir the Laird of the Castle or touch the forelock to their betters. It went to their heads like wine. The quilts were gay and the colours vivid. Their quilts looked like flags waving on the clothes lines.

Although Mrs. Moodie was very definitely not among the people who had to sir the Laird in the old country, she has left us with an interesting description of the release felt by many Upper Canadian immigrants:

> Here we encountered a boat, just landing a fresh cargo of immigrants from the Emerald Isle. One fellow of gigantic proportions . . . leaped upon the rocks, and flourishing his shilelagh, bounded and capered like a wild goat from his native mountains. "Whurrah! my boys!" he said. "Shure we'll all be Jintlemen."[5]

Indeed, one still hears the expression in Ontario that we are all lairds here.

Remembering the old ways, the women went out to the fields to gather materials to dye their homespuns. They made them bright and cheerful celebrations of the new land; the reds are shouts of joy. The red homespun in Plate 388, Tree Everlasting, is like a flame, and such homespun quilts as those in Plates 379 and 386 were surely made by a jubilant and joyous people, not the sour and dour looking faces that stare at us from the old portraits.

This chapter has dealt with quilt names, yet there is something to be said for those for coverlets, although they are not quite as varied as those for quilts.

200 Austere women such as this made quilts that were poems of love.

simple joy, but it is also true that a conscious effort was sometimes made to draw symbolic elements into the design of a quilt in order to give it much greater significance than a simple bedcover could possibly have.

There is some variation of coverlet pattern names in different parts of the country, but those within a province tend to be constant. It was necessary to have a written draft or pattern to work from when making a coverlet, and these drafts, often hand written on scraps of paper, usually were identified by a pattern name. Dog's Tracks, Turkey Tracks, Freemason's Coat of Arms, Freemason's Felicity, Nine Snowballs, Chariot Wheels and Church Windows are all typical names for overshot coverlets. Most titles are descriptive of the patterns, which consist of endless variations of circles, diamonds and rectangles with many variations on basic designs, although much is due to the imagination of the person who originally named it. Weavers who made Jacquard coverlets are said to have named their patterns after they saw the finished result, especially if they had produced their own variation as was often done. Some names are distinctively Canadian, but most are held in common with the United States, while many have doubtless been lost over the years. Coverlets are often given a generic title based on the type of weaving used; Star and Diamond is one example of this practice.

Quilt names were often based on everyday images, like Hole in the Barn Door, or pious sources, like the Rose of Sharon. Their colouration often revealed

11 Symbolism in Quilts

*She hath a clout of mine
Wrought with blue coventry,
Which she keeps for a sign
Of my fidelity.*

"Phillada Flouts Me"
Anonymous, 17th century

It was noted in Chapter 10 that in the nineteenth century Upper Canadian women were highly religious, drawing inspiration for some quilt names from such works as the Bible and *The Pilgrim's Progress*. This was a kind of Christianity, however, that is no longer with us; it easily accommodated the beliefs in spirits and demons that were held by country people and that had survived through many generations in the older countries. To a large extent, these beliefs were the legacy of older, earth-based religions, and they explained many of the occurrences of everyday life. Surrounding these beliefs were symbols, originally pagan, that were added to those of Christianity; new meanings were overlaid, but the old symbols were never lost.[1]

Natural disasters could wipe out entire families in shockingly short periods of time, and they were often considered the work of malevolent spirits. A great mass of knowledge of how to deal with the spirit world was passed on from generation to generation. The Irish beliefs, for example, in the faery and the banshee were transplanted to Upper Canada with the immigrants, as well as the understanding that neither was necessarily good or bad but placation was required. Tokens or signs were placed on everyday objects, such as the hex signs used on barns in Germanic Pennsylvania and rural Ontario, in order to frighten demons away and encourage the good spirits.

To many country people during the nineteenth century, the very air was filled with the clash of unseen beings battling for the souls of the dying and the newly born. The Scottish practice of burning the bedstead in which someone had died was mentioned in Chapter 3, and it no doubt had less to do with hygiene than it did with the appeasement of the spirits hovering about after death. These beliefs, and indeed this chapter, have nothing to do with the academic study of symbolism, rather they participate in the general knowledge of folk culture which unfortunately has all but died out.

Many of the signs or motifs used were concerned with reproduction, because infants died frequently, and it was extremely important that a woman bear many children. In the old countries, wealth was based to a large extent on the ownership of land; land that was entailed in most families, so that it had to be handed down to a male descendant. No greater disaster could befall an important house than a childless marriage. In humbler homes, children were needed to help with the work and care for the old. Moreover, the life of each member of the clan or family was

Border detail of a quilt made by a woman in the Niagara Peninsula. [Plate 263]

dependent for safety on the protection of the other members.

Given the importance of procreation for the welfare of the family and the belief in a spirit world, the bedstead played an important part in family life, and the bedcover was the natural place to put motifs of procreation, fertility, longevity and immortality. These motifs were deliberately used symbolically, as bridges to reality in which they become overt expressions of an intangible idea in a form that can be recognized. An oak leaf, to take a simple example, may be a symbol of longevity, because the oak tree is strong and endures for centuries.

It is not my purpose to argue the extent to which these symbols were known, especially since even a brief look at country ballads, many of which were sung at home, shows just how aware people were of symbolism in everyday life.

As time went on, people began to have some measure of control over their own destinies, and the need for the safeguards of potent symbols began to lose importance. Once education became universal, young people began to scorn the knowledge passed on to them from their parents and grandparents, and a great cultural inheritance was soon forgotten. A woman in 1900 could read and write, but she had lost a great deal of the folk knowledge that her mother possessed.

By the time Upper Canada was settled, people were beginning to forget the old ways, although superstition still played a large part in their lives. Symbols involving procreation and fertility were still important, but, as the century progressed and sentimental love assumed an importance it did not have in the earlier days of arranged marriages, some of the motifs took on new meanings. By the twentieth century, people had forgotten the original meanings of the designs they still used on their bedcovers. During the nineteenth century, for example, the heart motif was used only on marriage and cradle quilts to indicate love, but today one even sees experienced quilters using the heart motif on quilts intended for the spare beds of middle-aged married women. The original symbol has deteriorated into a pleasing design. Even old women living now probably did not know why they used the old designs, although it is safe to say that their mothers would have.

Symbols were first used as quilting or embroidery designs on counterpanes and quilts made in the Middle Ages. These were wholecloth quilts, and the decoration was achieved by means of the quilted designs, rather than by the patterns and colours as in patchwork quilts. The importance of the quilting designs lessened as patchwork quilts began to be

used commonly, although they survived to some extent in appliqué patterns. The quilting design in Plate 201 is typical of those used in the eighteenth century and earlier. A comparison with Plate 202 shows a similar design (the rose, the starflower and a fruit) used in appliqué on a quilt made about 1890. This same quilt uses another old quilting design, the lily, although it has been stylized to represent a thistle, a symbol of Scottish nationality. The juxtaposition of the rose and the thistle probably symbolized England and Scotland in the quilter's mind.

The most persistently used motifs are those which express the continuity of life passing from generation to generation. Young girls made many quilts, but they were carefully guided and consistently taught by older women who were conscious of passing on the thread of life, as well as traditions, beliefs and mores. One of the first quilts taught a young girl was the Irish Chain. Almost every girl who quilted made a single, double or triple Chain quilt (Plate 203), and the lines meeting, crossing and moving on endlessly represent the chain of life. Yet another design having the same theme is the twisted or braided rope, or lined twist, commonly used in Ontario as a border pattern (Plate 204). The twisted border represents the entwining of two lives forever, and the repeat of this pattern is a small oval within a larger one. In a marriage quilt given me by a great aunt, this symbol is repeated in every block as well as in the border. It is a rather obvious fertility symbol when used in this way. Less romantic souls in the early twentieth century sometimes called this pattern Pumpkin Seed.

Often associated with the lined twist or braided rope, is the phallic symbol of the pine tree with its branches pointing up. Some Pine Tree quilts were made with oversized twisted ropes in vertical lines across the width of the quilt, creating a forceful effect (Plate 205).

A quilting pattern often used with Irish Chain quilts is the swirling rosette, a turning circle representing life with no end. Windmill quilts, of which there is a very large variety, repeat the same message of never-ending life; the windmill blades moving in a ceaseless circle. The same idea is conveyed in a version of a folk song, usually called "The Riddle Song," "A ring when it is turning, it has no end."

A diamond shape has always been considered a symbol of fertility. Large diamonds are still painted on barn doors to ensure productivity within the farm buildings. Early homespun quilts were often made with one large diamond in the centre of a square (Plate 207), and the diamond pattern continued to be used both as a pattern and a unit of a pattern. In most Log Cabin quilts, which were originally for everyday use, the lights and darks were arranged to form large diamonds, or diamonds within diamonds; this repetition, this symbolic doubling, would doubtless add to the potency of the motif. Quilt patterns in which a single block uses a framed central diamond are many: Hole in the Barn Door (Plate 363), Jack in the Pulpit (Plate 352), or King's Crown. The rural Log Cabin quilt is filled with symbolic meanings. The folded strips of cloth represent the logs of the cabin, and the red square in the centre represents the hearth in which the light must never go out. The quilt in Plate 419 was made by a childless woman who made the hearths a dark gray colour, although the rest of the quilt is strangely vivid, perhaps because strong deep colours were traditionally used in Log Cabin quilts.

Understandably, the greatest symbolic repository was not the humble everyday bedcover, but the carefully worked marriage quilt. A marriage quilt showing this tendency appears in Plate 215. The central medallion contains a flowering branch growing out of an urn, an ancient symbol of the renewal of life. The flowers connote fruitfulness and the annual resurgence of growth. The peacocks and butterflies on the branches are symbolic, respectively, of immortality, since it was believed that the flesh of the peacock does not decay, and of the Resurrection of Christ, by extension the resurrection of all men. The latter meaning comes from the emergence of the butterfly from the chrysalis, its apparent tomb. The scalloped circle enclosing the flowering branch with its peacocks and butterflies represents the moon, a common symbol for the female, while the running vine surrounding the circle stands for longevity. The entire frame and its four block corners are symbolic of the world: north, south, east and west. In the final border there are nine patch blocks, since in Christian mythology the number three has to do with the Holy Trinity, and it as well as its multiples are considered mystical. This quilt was made by Frances Mulligan in 1856 in a log house at Hazeldean in Carleton County. The hearts that are quilted throughout show that it was meant to be a marriage quilt. It was made when she was sixteen, but she apparently died before her marriage, for it remained in her father's house.

The general belief that the breaking of a running vine motif could portend an untimely end to life or love was mentioned in Chapter 9. The symbol also has overtly Christian overtones, for in Christian mythology the flowering vine was a vivid metaphor of God and his people, "I am the vine, ye are the branches . . . He that abides in me and I in him, the

same shall bring forth much fruit, for without me ye can do nothing."[2] Pieced quilts often have a running vine border, and in this context it is a symbol of long and fruitful life.

The tree, bush or branch has played an important part in Christian symbolism, but the tree, itself, was worshipped before, and in some areas, after the advent of Christianity. In Britain, the ancient Celts worshipped the oak, and this survived in altered form through the celebrations held around the Maypole. It is well known that the Book of Genesis speaks of both the Tree of Life and The Tree of the Knowledge of Good and Evil:

> Out of the ground made the Lord God to grow every tree that is pleasant to the sight and good for food; the tree of life also in the midst of the garden, and the tree of the knowledge of good and evil.[3]

It was an ancient custom, one which survived into Upper Canada, to plant a green bush in front of the house of a newly married couple, probably to placate the spirits that lived in the trees, who were not necessarily friendly, and to stand for the growth of the marriage over the years. A flowering lily was planted at the corner of a house in Frontenac County at a wedding that took place in the second quarter of the twentieth century, and the plant has been carefully tended throughout the years. It also occasionally happened that one tree would be planted on each side of the doorway, one for each spouse, and when death intervened one of the trees would be cut down. This motif of the fallen tree survives in the symbolism seen on Upper Canadian tombstones and reinforces the idea of the importance that such symbols had.

The flowering bush planted in an urn or basket was the most commonly used tree form in wedding quilts, but there are many related patterns: Pine Tree, Cherry Tree and Birds, Little Beech Tree, Tree Everlasting, Tree of Life, Tree of Paradise and the Tree of Temptation.

It is important to remember that the worship of trees was still a vital part of life in areas of the British Isles, even long after the majority of the people had become Christians:

> There under the shade of an old sacred thorn
> With freedom he sung his loves evening and morn
> He sung with so soft and enchanting a sound
> Thet sylvans and fairies, unseen danced around.[4]

While believing in the Christian religion, small pockets of the population in rural areas in England and the Hebrides still continued to worship trees and other forms of nature.

The Christian symbols used in both classical and folk art are often superimposed on ancient, "pagan"

201
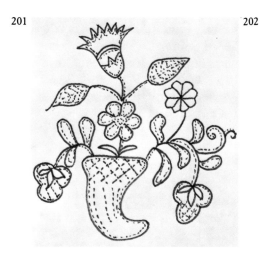

202

203
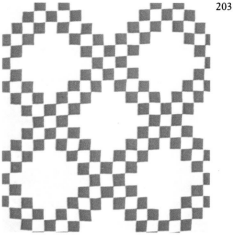

204
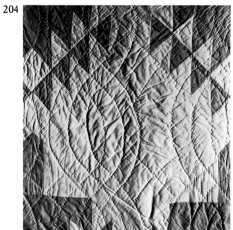

205
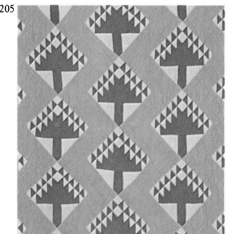

206

207

208
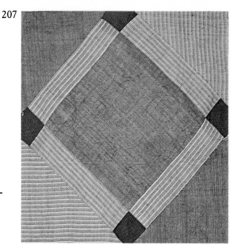

201 A typical quilting design from the eighteenth century.

202 Rose and Thistle: quilt, detail of Plate 316; cotton; made by Eva Richardson, Lindsay, Victoria County, ca. 1900. This little urn, with its rose, starflower (or lily) and a fruit is similar to quilting designs used three centuries earlier. [M.B.T.K.]

203 Double Irish Chain: quilt, pieced, detail; cotton; red on white with polkadot ground; made by Lily Jane McEwen, Lancaster, Glengarry County, ca. 1904. W. 180 cm, L. 232 cm (71, 91 in.). Made during a winter's illness at the age of fourteen, when the maker was staying with her grandmother and aunt who, "got me at the quilt to keep me busy, as I was almost dying of loneliness. Auntie wouldn't let me use the sewing machine." This is a traditional pattern, one that emphasizes the continuity of life. It was used to teach young girls quilt making. [C.M.]

204 Pine Tree: quilt, pieced, detail; Frontenac County, ca. 1880. The Braided Rope quilting pattern symbolizes the entwining of two lives. [C.C.F.C.S.]

205 Pine Tree: quilt, pieced, detail; cotton: green, peach and white; made by

Mrs. William Somerville, Balderson, Lanark County, ca. 1900. W. 150 cm, L. 182 cm (59, 72 in). Quilted in large, vertical braided ropes. [C.C.F.C.S.]

206 Feathered Star: quilt, detail. The turning circle in the Swirling Rosette design represents life without end. [C.C.F.C.S.]

207 Central Diamond: quilt, pieced; homespun in soft muted colours; Walker family, Prince Edward County, mid-19th

century. W. 170 cm, L. 180 cm (67, 71 in.). This simple and forthright format was favoured by early quilt makers. The diamond is a symbol of fertility. [C.C.F.C.S.]

208 Log Cabin, Framed Diamonds: quilt, detail; pieced, silk and wool; Leeds County, 3rd quarter 19th century. W. 172 cm, L. 195 cm (68, 77 in.). Strong double diamonds add potency to the motif. [C.C.F.C.S.]

motifs. A good example of this may be seen in the treatment of the Song of Solomon. The song is filled with symbols that were eventually interpreted as representative of Christ's love for the Church. Yet the symbols are overtly sensual, little different than the sexuality apparent in the motif of the ploughed earth penetrated to receive seed in the Straight Furrow pattern (Plate 216). Both the sensuality and religious overtones of the song appealed to the women of nineteenth century Upper Canada. They took many images from it to use in the making of their marriage quilts in order to express earthly love in sanctified terms:

> My beloved is like a roe or a young
> hart: behold he standeth behind our wall,
> he looketh forth at the windows, shewing
> himself through the lattice.
> My beloved spake, and said unto me,
> Rise up, my love, my fair one, and come
> away.
> For, lo, the winter is past, the rain
> is over and gone;
> The flowers appear on the earth; the
> time of the singing of birds is come, and the
> voice of the turtle is heard in our
> land;
> The fig tree putteth forth her green
> figs, and the vines with the tender grape
> give a good smell. Arise, my love, my fair
> one, and come away....
> My beloved is mine, and I am his:
> he feedeth among the lilies.[5]

The quilt in Plate 316 contains many symbols taken from the entire song: the Rose of Sharon, the lily, the apple, the vine. The maker did not restrict herself, however, including the flowering bush growing from an urn, little trees bearing what appear to be thistles, vines bearing roses, apples, pears and, around the central design, a border of flying birds. The use of Biblical motifs in this way is directly pointed out in an embroidered quilt (Plate 209) where various motifs from the song are selected, and the title of each one is embroidered under it, such as "The Rose of Sharon," "The Cedars of Lebanon" and so on.

This is not meant to indicate that quilts with overtly Christian symbols were absent. The quilt in Plate 386, made of handspun, handwoven materials, has a design of H's and L's which probably stand for "Holy Lord." Such an evocation was intended to keep away evil spirits in much the same way that one makes the sign of the cross at the mention of evil. The same motif was used in the early nineteenth century in the construction of H and L door hinges and for the same reason.

A Sunflower quilt from the Niagara Peninsula has a wide variety of symbols drawn from many sources (Plates 211 to 213). The main body of the quilt is composed of lush sunflowers, each in a block that is contained in a cross-hatch set consisting of diagonal brown and green lines usually considered to represent the ploughed earth. The border is rife with Pennsylvania Duch symbolism, including several hex signs which, when painted on barns, were intended to ward off evil, but, when used on a quilt, were probably intended to ensure fertility. The pinwheel stands for the sun or masculinity and the round circle the moon or femininity. In addition, there are five urns filled with stylized flowers and leaves, their appearance varying in each urn. They include the traditional rose, the star flower, the sheaf of wheat and the oak leaf. Some of the plants bear hearts within hearts, just as most of the emblems have other designs within them. The sides or ends of the quilt have vines bearing the same emblems: the rose, the sheaf of wheat and, in one place, a heart containing an open hand. The open hand is a fairly common motif in bedcovers and often has a heart within the open palm; it is a commonly recognized symbol of friendship.

Birds frequently appear in quilt patterns and quilting designs. In Christianity, the bird is a symbol of the coming of the Holy Ghost, signifying the return of life in springtime as well as the resurrection. During the Middle Ages, it was believed that the swallows buried themselves in the mud in the wintertime and were resurrected in the spring, a renewal of faith being felt when they reappeared. The return of the birds has always been cause for rejoicing, and this is especially true of the swallows. There is an ancient tradition in Scotland that if they cease nesting in the eaves of a house, tragedy will strike within the year, hence the return of the swallows was a matter of great portent. Rural people feel a deep affection for this particular bird, because it nests so close to people. There are at least a dozen swallow patterns among pieced quilts: Swallows-in-the-Window, Swallow's Flight, Chimney Swallows, Flying Swallows, Swallow in the Path, Swallow's Nest, Swallow and so on.

The goose was another popular quilt motif. During the Renaissance, the goose was considered the symbol of providence and vigilance, and people have continued to look on this bird with affection. This is indicated by the number of quilts named after it: Brown Goose, Gray Goose, Goose-in-the-Pond, Goose-in-the-Window, Goose Tracks, Wild Goose Chase, Wild Geese Flying. In this country, we feel exhilarated when the wild geese fly over in spring and fall, since they seem to represent to us freedom from the petty chores of domestic life and the call of the wilderness.

There was a widespread belief among women who made quilts that only God could make a perfect thing. The roots of this belief are very old, going back to the times when people were afraid that the gods would be jealous of their achievements. When a woman was making a quilt which she felt would be perfect, she would deliberately build in a mistake. The error was always in an inconspicuous place, such as at the head or foot of the bed, where it would not detract from the beauty of the quilt, but it was sufficiently obvious that it could not be considered accidental. Most good quilts that I have examined have such a contrived flaw. Plate 218 shows a Feathered Star in yellow and white, finely quilted by an expert needle woman. Careful inspection reveals that in the star in the left hand corner at the bottom two sawtooth pieces have been turned the wrong way. Under no circumstances would the woman who made this quilt have made such an obvious mistake, or have allowed it to remain, if she had, unless it was deliberately done. Such "mistakes" were made only when the woman considered the quilt outstanding.

Symbolism in quilts was not limited to images alone, and the deliberate use of colour to convey meaning is apparent in many instances. Colours were

209 Wholecloth Quilt: embroidered; made by Mary Dickson, Atwood, Perth County, 1897 (the year of her marriage). W. 175 cm, L. 195 cm (69, 77 in.). The central point of interest in this quilt is a basket of brilliantly coloured flowers, done in wool and stuffed with newspaper to create a high relief. This naïve floral arrangement is accompanied by a text reminiscent of a sampler. Surrounding the text and floral arrangement are eight cartouches, each enclosing Biblical flowers and trees with descriptive labels. The motifs and labels are from the Song of Solomon. [M.B.T.K.]

210 Birds in a Tree: quilt, appliquéd; cotton; red, green and white; eastern counties, 3rd quarter 19th century. W. 172 cm, L. 182 cm (68, 72 in.). This is an unusual design – birds, trees and stars with a hammock border. The central tree has a hole in which an object, possibly a nest, can be seen. The quilting lines are so close together that they ripple. [C.C.F.C.S.]

used to set or enhance the mood of a quilt. The intensely violent shades of red and blue in an Indian Hatchet (Plate 411) amplifies its rather ominous mood. The use of white in marriage and cradle quilts indicates purity, while mourning quilts were always made in blacks and grays (Plate 319).

Blue was the colour most commonly used to decorate homemade bedding other than quilts. The colour was obtained from indigo, a vegetable dye derived from the leaves of a plant grown in India since long before the Christian era. The shade of the colour varied with the length of time the material was immersed in the solution. Early coverlets woven by professional weavers were almost always dark indigo blue, and woven coverlets made at home were most often blue, with red being the next most popular colour. Jane Hamilton of Dundela, as mentioned in Chapter 7, made a blue and red coverlet in preparation for her marriage together with blankets with coloured bands to match; these were the traditional colours. Because blue was considered to have powers ensuring the safety of the sleeper, even the thrifty

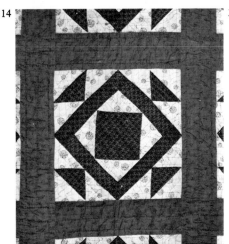

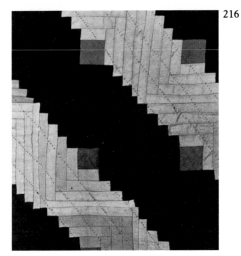

215 Central Medallion: quilt, detail of Plate 272; wool and cotton; browns, yellows and blues; made by Frances Mulligan, Hazledean, Carleton County, 1856. W. 177 cm, L. 187 cm (70, 74 in.). She used motifs usually associated with a marriage quilt: hearts, a flowery branch as well as butterflies and peacocks which are symbolic of immortality. She died at an early age.

216 Log Cabin, Straight Furrow: quilt, detail; woollens in solid colours with prominent red hearths; Golden Lake, Renfrew County, ca. 1920. W. 160 cm., L. 187 cm. (63, 74 in.). This is a primitive, earth-coloured, folksy quilt. [C.C.F.C.S.]

217 Christian Heathen: coverlet, detail of Plate 109.

218 Feathered Star: quilt, detail of Plate 254. In the top segment of the star two triangles have been deliberately misplaced to avoid making the quilt perfect. [C.C.F.C.S.]

211 Sunflower: quilt, border detail of Plate 263. An exceptionally fine appliquéd border on a pieced quilt, which contains Pennsylvania-German motifs such as hex signs, flowers, hearts, etc.

212 Sunflower: quilt, border detail of Plate 263. Hex signs, which appear on barns in Pennsylvania-German areas, are intended to ward off evil spirits and to ensure fertility.

213 Sunflower: quilt, border detail of Plate 263. The circle containing a star probably represents the moon or femininity, and the pinwheel in Plate 212 represents the sun or masculinity.

214 Jack in the Pulpit: quilt, detail of Plate 352. The framed central diamond is a recurrent theme in quilts. The diamond has always been considered a symbol of fertility in rural areas.

housewives of Upper Canada laid out cash to buy indigo dye, rather than use the various substitutes that were available in their fields and gardens that did not provide a satisfactory colour.

Indigo blue quilts were said to have been used a great deal on children's beds, but very few seem to have survived. Possibly, blue has been favoured throughout the years, because it was the colour of the sky when nature was in a peaceful mood. Blue was also associated with faithfulness in love. In the seventeenth century poem, "Phillada Flouts Me," the heroine was given a blue cloth by her lover as a "sign of...fidelity." He threatens to take it away from her and give it to another, if she continues to scorn him. A version of the old Scottish song "A Long Time A-Growing" states that, "around his arm we'll tie a ribbon blue/ And that will be a token that he's married."

It is probable that the patterns of woven coverlets also have symbolic meanings, although they are more rigid than those for quilts. The nature of a quilt allowed greater variation in design, yet both types employed geometric motifs. As in quilt patterns, it is likely that the diamonds and stars indicated fertility, while circles represented either the sun or flowers. Certainly, coverlets made on Jacquard looms gave the weaver greater imagistic range, which resulted in the lavish use of birds, tulips, roses and hearts. Towards the end of the nineteenth century, coverlets became more pictorial rather than symbolic, using deer, squirrels, churches and angels. The Jacquard coverlet in Plate 217 is known as the Christian Heathen coverlet, and the pattern was first made in the days when sailing ships went to trade in the Orient. The houses at one end represent Boston, or Christianity, and the pagodas in the centre represent China, or the heathen country.

Commercially woven coverlets, such as the Marseilles and Bolton counterpanes, continued to use the traditional motifs of earlier homemade ones: stylized stars, trees and flowers. Bolton counterpanes have a chain-like border somewhat similar to the Irish Chain. By the middle of the nineteenth century, however, more realistic looking foliage began to appear in the form of ferns, leaves and flowers. The bedspreads printed in India and imitated in England favoured the flowering branch or tree of life as a pattern. On the other hand, homemade counterpanes like the candlewick variety, which were designed by individual women, are filled with traditional symbols; the pineapple (for hospitality), the star, the open hand of friendship, vines and hearts galore all appear.

Far more than their counterparts in the twentieth century, Upper Canadian women of the nineteenth century lived in a world in which the seasons and the cycles of life dominated their lives. They participated in a traditional and sometimes ancient stock of folk knowledge, including beliefs in spirits and demons. The symbols that they so carefully placed on their quilts were often the same as those used on everyday objects: the furniture, barns and implements that were in constant use. It is still possible today to find these same motifs in the gingerbread and barge boards of rural Ontario homes. These symbols and the beliefs that inspired them were the common property of the whole family, understood and appreciated by all. If the lavish care that these women took in the making of their quilts is a measure of their devotion to their families, the use of protective and emotional symbols in their designs is equally proof of their concern that the family should prosper, the children grow strong and their marriages remain passionate. The images are beautiful, certainly, but they are also indicative of a collective knowledge that has disappeared.

12 Dates, Origins and Styles

O where will be the birds that sing
A hundred years to come?

"A Hundred Years to Come"
Hiram Ladd Spencer (1829-1915)

Dating a quilt is never an easy process, yet there are many clues that can be helpful, some of which unfortunately, have a way of contradicting one another. Generally speaking, it takes first-hand knowledge gained over years of handling many bedcovers of different types and ages, and even then, one can rarely do more than arrive at an approximate date.

If the quilt in question is a family possession, it is advisable to obtain both the married and the maiden names of the maker, together with her birth and death dates, and, where possible, when it was made and where. It makes quite a difference whether grandmother made the quilt at sixteen or sixty. Because these things are easily and quickly forgotten, it is a good idea to write them down on a card attached to the quilt. When actual dates cannot be obtained, it is customary to allow twenty years for each generation. However, many people who arrive at the standard two hundred years have simply added the ages of each generation without recognizing the fact that the generations do overlap.

Occasionally, one finds a date embroidered on the quilt face, where it has been worked into the quilting design, on the back or even on the underside of the top. These documented articles are of great value in dating similar quilts by comparing the materials used, styles and so on.

A quilt's condition is not of much help. Obviously, one made in 1825 that has survived in good shape was seldom used, while another, made only fifteen years ago and used daily by a woman who washes her quilts as often as her sheets, may be in tatters. Nevertheless, a tattered quilt made recently cannot look the same as one in similar condition made over a hundred years ago, due to the types of fabric and thread used.

Patterns and styles can be of some help, because certain patterns were fashionable during rather definite years. A Crazy Quilt made of shiny materials, such as satin or silk, and embroidered with fancy stitching is likely to have been made between 1880 and 1900, although it might be twenty years earlier or later. Most Crazy Quilts were dated, simply because people seemed to like to do this at that period, and this is very helpful in identifying those that do not bear such marks. One would expect that Crazy Quilts would have been made at an early period when cloth was scarce, but people in earlier times preferred to use rectangular shapes even though they had to trim and often piece their scraps to do so.

Bedcovers of handspun, handwoven cloth make

Detail of the Mary Morris quilt made in Elgin, Leeds County in 1825. [Plate 242]

up a large part of Upper Canadian bedding. Experts in weaving can often judge the age of a piece by examining the wool and other threads used in weaving. A linen weft in a coverlet or blanket, for example, indicates that it was probably woven before 1830.

Quilts made before 1860 should contain no machine sewing, even on the undersides of the binding or on the pieces that make up the back. Despite the fact that the sewing machine was invented before this date, it was not commonly used in Upper Canada until later. After this date, many women continued to sew quilts by hand, because it was traditional and one had more control over the small seams. Still, many used the machine in places that did not show to save hours of tedious work and to give added strength. Quilts were frequently rebound at later dates, and those who did the rebinding usually used a machine.

There are other small clues to dating a quilt. Those with flounces about twenty inches deep, with handwoven or netted fringes, or bound with handwoven tapes are likely to have been made in the early part of the nineteenth century. Some women in the later Victorian era added lace edges, narrow frilled flounces and a type of edging called picot. The ap-

pearance of picot can be deceptive, however, because it has been used right into the present century (Plate 440).

Quilts made before 1830 often have handspun, handwoven linen or cotton backs consisting of three strips sewn (whipped) together edge to edge. This was necessary to make up the amount of cloth necessary to back early quilts that might be eight to nine feet square. After 1830, quilts began to be smaller until the middle of the twentieth century when they were made again to fit oversize beds. Covers for cribs, trundle and bunk beds always were made to fit.

Probably the best way to date quilts is by the fabrics used. Therefore, a knowledge of fabric designs and printing techniques is important, and these can be studied in surviving old sample books carried by salesmen, in scrap books containing dated pieces of cloth collected for one reason or another and, of course, in definitely dated quilts. Costumes of various periods may be studied in museums, since the same materials were used in quilts. Even though women did save scraps of cloth for quilting, the contents of the rag bag were under heavy demand and seldom spanned more than ten years of manufactured products.

219

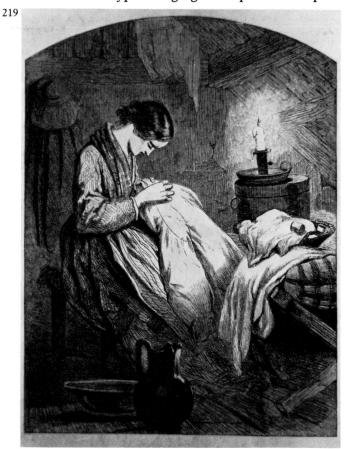

219 The Old Sewing Machine, *Godey's Magazine and Lady's Book*, 1863

220

220 The New Sewing Machine, *Godey's Magazine and Lady's Book*, 1863

A complete study of textiles is too complex to be covered in this book, but a few general observations may be helpful. Canada had no textile industry of her own until well past the middle of the nineteenth century, and all cloth other than homespuns had to be imported from Great Britain or the United States. Cotton material exported from England between 1774 and 1811 was marked with three blue threads in the selvage. Fabrics were printed by wood block until late in the eighteenth century, and the results are not as fine as those produced by the copper plate printing that began about 1780. The copper plate process allowed for a larger repeat and greater detail. Roller printing appeared around 1815 and has been the method used ever since. The steel rollers permitted an even larger repeat, and the hard roller material was capable of even greater detail. It is a rare and exciting event to find a scrap of material printed by copper plate in Upper Canada, and it is very unlikely that wood block examples will turn up.

Certain fabric designs were fashionable at various periods and are indicative of a quilt's age. For example, pillars entwined with flowers were in vogue from 1825 to 1835, while tiny motifs, such as horseshoes and anchors, were popular between 1860 and 1880. Other patterns, such as full-blown flowers, were used continuously throughout the nineteenth century.

Yet another way of dating is by the type of dye used in the cloth. Until the middle of the nineteenth century, both commercial dyes and those made at home were taken from natural products: minerals, plants, woods, insects and shellfish. In 1856, though, a mauve dye was made from coal tar, leading to the development of a whole range of synthetic dyes that produced more standardized colours.

Although indigo was the dye most commonly used at home in the first half of the nineteenth century, others were available. A Kingston retail and wholesale outlet advertised in the *Daily News*, 1852, "DYE STUFFS .... Extract Logwood, Redwood, Fustic, Madder, Sumach . . . Copperas, Alum, etc." (Copperas and alum were mordants used to set the dye.) In rural areas, people continued to make their own dye stuffs and mordants (frequently urine) throughout the nineteenth and into the twentieth century. A woman born in 1893 can remember her mother using onion skins, beet juice, and the barks of trees to colour her wool. Another farm woman born around 1916 recalled:

> I can remember going with mother when I was just a little thing to pick red sumac flowers for Granny to make her red dye. We had to pick the brightest and reddest ones we could find. Other times mother took the horse and wagon into the bush to bring back branches of the butternut trees. Granny prepared her own wool from the fleece of our sheep. She always quilted with pure wool. They used to plunge the fleece into boiling water to kill the ticks. I used to help Granny card the wool. I have one of her quilts somewhere around today; she gave one to each of us girls. She always made striped quilts, one band of plain, one of cretonne, and she always quilted a sort of elongated circle in the middle and around the edges. We have always lived on the same farm since mother's people came over from Ireland a long, long time ago.

Yet another woman from the north of Frontenac County remembers her mother during the 1930s boiling stag horn sumac flowers and butternut branches cut up small to make a purplish-blue dye. The solution was boiled until the right strength was reached when it was tested with small pieces of cloth. Sumac bark was more commonly used in dyeing, and it alone produced a brownish colour. Homespun quilts found in various districts in Upper Canada would indicate that this sumac-butternut dye was fairly commonly used. It was not a very fast colour, however, and one must look at the undersides of the quilt patches to see how vivid it was when new.

When homemade dyes were used to colour the cloth, it is quite difficult to assess the age of the quilt, because the same colours were used over a long period of time. The appearance of synthetic dyes makes it safe to assume that the quilt is no earlier than 1856. The women of Upper Canada continued to make their bedding in the old ways long after new methods became available. As a result, a bedcover made in 1870 may have the appearance of one made a hundred years earlier (Plate 239). While the United States was experiencing a revival of the art of making embroidered bedcovers, in some areas we were still making them in the old styles. We had started later, and the conservative women of Upper Canada liked the tried and true ways.

This conservatism continued as late as 1890, even the sheets and blankets made in that year looked much the same as those made in 1820. The frequent difficulty encountered in dating quilts is further complicated by the diverse origins that affected their design before 1860. After this date quilts tended to reflect fashionable trends rather than the racial origins of the women who made them.

In the period before 1860, there were two main influences affecting our quilt styles, American and European. Settlers coming up from the United States during the late eighteenth and early nineteenth century brought with them the distinctive styles that had been developing in that country during the hundred or more years of settlement. At the same time, immigrants from England, Ireland and Scotland brought their own styles, ones that had not changed very much during the previous century.

Lower Canada seems to have had relatively little effect beyond bordering Upper Canadian counties. One quilt pattern, called the French Star (Plate 238), is said to be completely Canadian in origin; it does not appear in the United States, but it is difficult to tell where it might have originated. The plate illustrates a quilt made in Napanee by a woman whose family came from Ireland.

The styles that came into the province were added to by those that were developed here in response to a different climate and different conditions in general. People of common racial origin tended to live in isolated communities where ethnically based patterns continued to be made over a long period of time, despite the fact that they, too, were being exposed to these altered conditions. The changes in outlook among people who were suddenly free from the relentless domination of European class structures had their effect on designs and colours, particularly in woollen quilts of handwoven cloth.

There are other factors to be considered. Private schools for young ladies, teaching both plain and ornamental needlework, were established as early as the 1820s, even in small towns. This is true of both Protestant and Catholic institutions. Much of this instruction was strictly traditional, but it appears that even the private schools had to adapt to some extent to pioneer conditions. An old gentleman who attended a co-educational private school in Perth, Lanark County, described in a 1905 issue of the *Perth Courier* how, "Mr. Jessop also kept sheep, where I don't know, but I remember the wool we had to tease. I have also a lively recollection of the hooks and eyes we had to cut off, and the old garments to rip." However, many nineteenth century Upper Canadian girls did not go to school; they were taught at home by their mothers how to care for a house and family. At the age of three or four little girls were set at sewing simple quilt blocks such as a four patch or a nine patch. These blocks had to be sewn perfectly or else they were ripped out and resewn until they passed inspection. Such tasks were taken seriously, and both at home and at school children who could not or would not perform them well were punished, even whipped.

By the end of the century, people were not as strict with children. Then, although little girls were still taught to sew at three or four, they were encouraged by starting them on making quilts for their dolls. Even in the 1920s, most little girls made their first quilt blocks before they started to school. Sloppy work was not allowed even then. Only women who began to sew at a very early age and continued to do so routinely could make the fine, even stitches that we see in quilts from the nineteenth century and earlier. Because of changing life styles, very few twentieth century women are able to do the excellent quilting that we find in earlier quilts.

In some households, quilts brought up from the United States with the original settlers have been highly prized up to the present day. Plate 1 shows a magnificent Pineapple quilt brought up from Pennsylvania in 1820 to a farm in Kent County where it remained until it was sold by auction a few years ago. The descendants of the original family told the story of the Pennsylvania woman who stoutly refused to budge from her old home unless her quilt and kitchen cupboard were packed into the already overcrowded wagon.

Another outstanding American quilt (Plate 4) is the Prince of Wales Plumes made by Frances Rowland Stewart in Pittsburgh, Pennsylvania, about 1830 and brought to Upper Canada later in the century. The same colour of green, so dark that it is almost black, appears in both American quilts. These are typical New World examples, using forceful colours with strong designs and displaying a vivacity peculiar to American quilts of the period. While these two have reliable histories telling of their making south of the border, many quilts put together in Upper Canada by descendants of the original settlers have the same features.

There are quilts made in the first fifty or so years of settlement that have a distinctly European flavour. Generally, these differ from their New World counterparts, having a decorated central medallion or square surrounded by frames or borders of patchwork. This medallion may have an appliquéd or embroidered design, or may have been printed for the specific application. Plate 237 shows a quilt by Elizabeth Tett of Newboro, Leeds County, dating from about 1850; it has a printed fabric medallion, which in this case is applied to a foundation cloth with neat button-hole stitches. The body of the quilt is made up of hexagons of beautiful printed cottons imported from Scotland. A few pieces of the cloth retain the stamp of David and Sons, Glasgow.

Upper Canada Village contains a quilt (Plate 240) with an appliquéd square that was made aboard ship by a group of settlers on their way to Grenville County in 1843. It was probably intended for a bride, since it shows a profusion of motifs usually associated with marriage quilts. Other quilts in this tradition (Plates 272, 273) have histories of European

221 Mary Morris Quilt: detail of Plate 242; dated 1825; printed cotton.

222 Variable Star: quilt, detail of quilt dated 1834: copper cylinder printed fabric. [M.F.F.]

223 Variable Star: another detail from the same quilt as Plate 222.

224 Unnamed Quilt: top, detail of hexagons arrayed in rosettes. The top was made, signed and dated "Susan March

1833" (or possibly Susan, March, 1833) in Perth, Lanark County. The entire top is 120 cm (47 in.) wide and 140 cm (55 in.) long, and has been used as a tablecover. It may, in fact, have been made for this purpose. [A.C.M.]

225 Flowering Tree: quilt, fabric detail of Plate 273; ca. 1840.

226 Flowering Tree: another detail of Plate 273.

227 Baby Blocks: quilt, detail of Plate 290; dated 1876-1900; printed cottons.

228 Johnny Round the Corner: quilt, detail; ca. 1880; typical everyday printed cottons of the period. Small printed objects, such as the anchors shown here, were popular between 1860 and 1880. [P.B.]

229 Little House: quilt, detail of Plate 434; ca. 1910; everyday cottons, probably from a little girl's dresses.

230

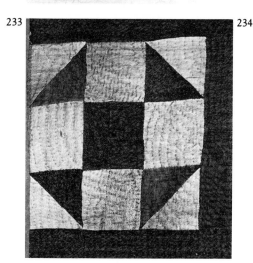

231

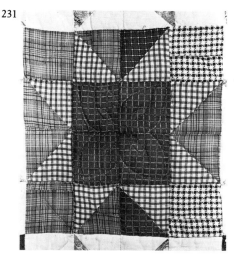

232

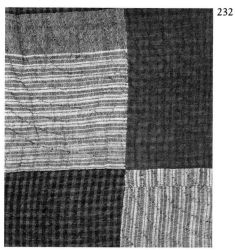

233

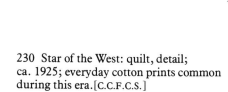

234

235

236

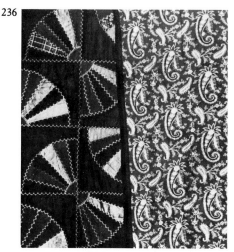

237

230 Star of the West: quilt, detail;
ca. 1925; everyday cotton prints common
during this era.[C.C.F.C.S.]

231 Variable Star: quilt, detail;
McLaughlin family, Port Perry, Ontario
County. Printed cotton dress goods typi-
cal of the 1920s. [C.C.F.C.S.]

232 One Patch: quilt, detail; made by
Switzer family, Moscow, Lennox and
Addington County, 2nd quarter 19th cen-
tury. A fine example of handspun, hand-
woven dress goods made into a quilt.
[C.C.F.C.S.]

233 Shoo Fly: quilt, detail of Plate 385;
handspun, handwoven cloth; ca. 1840.
The purplish colour of this material is
probably the result of a dye concocted
from boiling staghorn sumac flowers and
butternut branches. The unfaded backs of
the patches are a deep, intense colour.

234 Garden Wreath: quilt, detail of Plate
135. Fortunately for us today, quilts were
sometimes signed and dated on the back.

235 Oak Leaf: quilt, appliquéd, detail;
cotton; made by Mrs. Jonas, Bingeman,
Waterloo County, ca. 1873. Mrs. Jonas
was a member of the Swiss-German Men-
nonites, a group that had many fine and
enthusiastic quilt makers. Their patterns
and fabrics were very similar to those used
elsewhere in the province. [N.L.P.]

236 Fan: quilt, pieced, detail; made by
Fanny and Lydia Leis (Swiss-German
Mennonite background), Waterloo
County, ca. 1885. [N.L.P.]

237 Mosaic, or Honeycomb Quilt: detail;
printed cottons; made by Elizabeth Tett,
Newboro, Leeds County, before her marriage in 1850. W. 200 cm, L. 270 cm (79,
106 in.). The hexagons were made with
the aid of a tin template, which has survived. Some of the fine printed cottons are
stamped David and Sons, Glasgow, Scotland. The central medallion, which was
printed especially for quilt making, is
appliquéd in feather stitching to a ground
of cloth. Central medallions of this type
are rare today. [A.C.M.]

backgrounds, although they were undoubtedly produced in Upper Canada. All show a subtlety of colour typical of British quilts. Of course, this style was also made in the United States, but at an earlier period than the settlement of Upper Canada.

The quilts shown in Plates 241 and 242 are of interest not only for their individual appeal, but also because they both have basically the same theme, yet one shows an Old World and one a New World influence. Both were made in early Upper Canada and each portrays a deer hunt.

The first is the creation of Lidia Petch Park and her sister, two Quaker women who lived in a log cabin at Gunn's Hill, near Burgessville in Oxford County during the period 1820 to 1840. The designs are appliquéd to a foundation and embellished with embroidered details some of which are padded. The quilting is exceptionally fine; the stitches that sew down the appliquéd pieces are nearly invisible. The women who made this quilt took great pride in their sewing and would not allow anyone to see their masterpiece until it was finished to the last detail. Although they habitually spun and wove their own cloth and dyed it with vegetable dyes, most of the cloth used here does not appear to be homespun. This remarkable quilt is in the possession of a great-granddaughter of Lidia Petch Park. It has been used and loved for several generations, but recently it has been retired from active use. The Petch sisters also made the Biblical quilt portrayed in Plate 259.

The other illustrated deer hunt quilt was made in 1825 by Mary Morris of Elgin, Leeds County, whose family had come from Ireland around the turn of the century. This quilt is one of the central medallion type with framed borders of beautiful old printed cottons. Mary Morris was born with club feet and, as she could not walk or pursue the normal activities of a young girl, she became a highly skilled needle-woman at an early age. She was only fourteen when this truly remarkable quilt was finished. The central part is embroidered with a flowering tree surrounded by nosegays of delicate flowers. Around this square is a patchwork border of a kind frequently seen in English quilts followed by another frame containing the embroidered deer hunt along with flowers, swastikas and birds. The actual scene is again enclosed in three patchwork borders. This particular hunt was not apt to have taken place in Canada, unlike the Petch scene with its North American Indians, and might have been described to Miss Morris by older members of the family.

The freer form and expression of personal ideas found in the Petch quilt are typical of New World quilts, while the Morris example has been carefully

designed to include the fast moving hunt scene within a traditonal Old World form.

Quilts made by German people in Upper Canada retained strong cultural characteristics. Because most of these people belonged to religious sects such as the Mennonite and Amish, they tended to keep themselves culturally isolated. Most had moved up from Pennsylvania early in the nineteenth century, leaving homes their families had inhabited for almost a hundred years after they had emigrated from the valley of the upper Rhine in Germany and Switzerland. The Rhineland tradition survived in Pennsylvania as it did in Upper Canada, including the symbolic motifs discussed in Chapter 11 on their quilts, barns and home furnishings (Plates 211, 212, 213). Although basic patterns were used, their quilts were known more for their unconventional use of bright colours and the excellence of the workmanship. Tulips, stars, roses and hearts were favourite designs.

The Amish Germans continued to make their traditional wholecloth quilts in one or two colours, or patchwork quilts in the same small-patterned dark prints used for their clothing. Nowadays, the Mennonite and Amish people continue to make quilts with much enthusiasm, but for the most part they are no longer distinguishable from quilts made elsewhere. All Pennsylvania-Germans were not Mennonite or Amish, but it was only these religious groups that seemed to preserve their traditional quilt making ways for any length of time.

European and American influences were strong in Upper Canada, yet the type of quilt made here that should be called unique is made of handwoven wool cloth. Because of the severity of winter here, heavy woollen bedcovers were essential, especially before home heating became efficient. For this reason, the nineteenth century saw the development of a quilt that is distinctly Upper Canadian in style. During the eighteenth century and earlier, homespun quilts were used in Europe and the United States, but they were ceasing to be made about the time Upper Canada was settled. In the older countries, such quilts were predominantly wholecloth, and because blankets were readily available they were not made all that frequently. We were making homespun quilts in Upper Canada when patchwork had become popular. This was expressed in the older countries primarily in cotton rather than homespun. Because even homespun was scarce in the new province, patchwork homespuns were the most economical way of using up small bits of cloth. Patchwork homespun quilts were not made at as late a date in countries other than Upper Canada, and in fact the art of making woollen quilts generally survived longer and was more developed than elsewhere. Patchwork examples were still being made, for example, when patterns became livelier, hence the beautiful and striking pieces shown in this book.

Homespun quilts are most common in areas settled by the Scots, but they do turn up in other regions. In the Wilno area of Renfrew County, there is a distinctive type of homespun quilt, and in German areas quilts of this kind were created in much the same way as in Pennsylvania.

In my opinion, homespuns are the most interesting style of Upper Canadian quilts. They were never intended to be fashionable, rather they are truly the reflection of the spirits and traditions of the people, affected neither by stylish trends nor the influence of neighbours. By the 1860s, the mingling of the people had resulted in the mixing of many ethnic traditions. By this time, too, magazines and newspapers, mostly from other countries, were influencing the population at large. Nevertheless, there were still pockets in the country where small isolated groups of people of common origin continued to work in their accustomed ways, making their cloth and bedcovers as their mothers and grandmothers had done before them.

In her book *Patchwork*[1], Averil Colby states that there is evidence that homespun woollens were made into rough patchwork quilts in Scotland from the middle of the eighteenth century, although very little is known of them now. The first Scottish people were already emigrating to the United States and, to a lesser extent, to Lower Canada about that time, while by the latter part of the century they were coming directly to Upper Canada. It is probable that they brought this homespun tradition to the upper province, and here it flourished. There are many examples of homespun quilts still to be found in Ontario today. Many of these were made at a fairly late date, yet early ones are still around despite the ravages of time, wear and neglect. Homespun quilts tended to stay at home, since a woman who was marrying usually took her fine cotton ones with her and left the old homespuns behind. These everyday quilts are most often found in homes inhabited by Scottish people, and it is safe to say that they were made there.

Despite the fact that homespun quilts were intended to be utilitarian, there is considerable diversity among patterns. Some might have been used for "good", or at least for more important rooms, such as the pieced and appliquéd Daisy and Basket pattern (Plate 404), that required a great deal of care to make. Most, however, are the early central

medallion type or those made in old and traditional patterns. Many of these are quite elaborate.

The earliest homespun quilts used geometric forms, the square or the diamond, the rectangle or the triangle, employed in large blocks. The most common pattern consists of a large central square or diamond surrounded by one or two borders, each one of which has blocks of a different colour in the corners (Plate 375). Because these large patches and long borders were frequently made up of small bits of cloth, often flannel sheets showing different amounts of wear, the dye would not take to the same degree over the entire block. This resulted in subtle variances of colour that today are very attractive, causing an effect like that of shifting light across a surface.

Another simple form is shown in Plate 377 which is made up of an olive green square in the centre and a soft orange-red border with bars of the same green set in at the ends. This particular style is quite similar to that used by the Amish in the United States, although those made south of the border may be of a later date and are usually quilted with more elaborate designs. In general, the style is similar to the central medallion quilts made of cotton or linen in England and Ireland, and it is interesting to note that the same women who made early homespun quilts in the central square or diamond patterns also created them in cotton. Still, in some families it is difficult to ascertain whether a quilt was made by a mother or a daughter. The homespun quilts in Plates 377 and 384 were produced by the Urquart sisters or their mother in Dunvegan, Glengarry County; they are the creators of the cotton quilt shown in Plate 280.

Some wholecloth homespun quilts were made of cloth woven expressly for the purpose of making a bedcover. These are not common, though, except in one area of Renfrew County to be discussed later, yet they were occasionally made in Scottish households in various counties.

Checked or striped materials were worked into homespun quilt designs. The example in Plate 392 contains bits of twenty-six different types of homespun, as if the woman who made the quilt was making a sampler of her homespuns.

There are several Hit and Miss patterns which were made up of rectangular pieces of cloth of assorted sizes and colours. The quilt in Plate 396 is made of dark pieces of cloth, some of which are heavy wool, while cleverly placed orange rectangles enliven the design. In most cases, the rectangles have been trimmed to the same size and are sorted for colour, some pieces probably having been dyed to achieve the desired result. In Plate 395, the coloured squares have been arranged to form an effect like amberina glass. This was a type of glass quite popular in the nineteenth century that varies in colour from amber to ruby. The quilt was likely made to imitate this subtle colour shift, since the squares start at one edge in a vivid red, gradually fade through orange to amber, and then back again to red. The quilt is toned down by the use of black in every alternate square and in the border. Another interesting effect is achieved quite simply by the use of a contrasting set separating the squares of cloth (Plate 381).

Long strips of vividly coloured homespun were used to make striped quilts (Plate 382). The triangle was used frequently in a sawtooth pattern, a forerunner of the Flying Bird patterns. There are homespun quilts made in Nine Patch, Variable Star, Snake Fence, Jacob's Ladder, Tree Everlasting, Indian Hatchet, Eight Point Star and even Star of Bethlehem. A noteworthy example is the Star quilt (Plate 391) from Lansdowne in Leeds County that consists of a pinkish brown star extending from edge to edge on a dark brown background. The star is made by using a square for the centre and large triangles to form the points as in the Variable Star pattern. The result is a homespun quilt striking for its subtlety and simplicity.

Plate 399 shows a quilt made of pieces of assorted heavy woollen cloth combined with orange-red homespun assembled in a variation of the Geometric Star pattern. The star in this pattern resembles a cross with notched ends, but in this particular variation of it the two points of the cross that form one arm have been inverted, so that it does not look like a cross. Such an effective change in the basic pattern resulted in two black squares near the centre of the quilt. This variation on a theme was made by a woman who was a member of the Church of Scotland and who did not hold the Catholic Church in great esteem. Under no circumstances would she have allowed anything resembling a Catholic cross in her home, and it is quite likely that she reversed the pattern specifically to avoid the possibility. Like many homespun quilts, this example was made with a central square and borders, the "cross" being in the central square.

Most homespun quilts were quilted in fan patterns or in diagonal lines. Over all, even though the designs have been carefully arranged to give the greatest visual impact, there has been little attempt to make them into anything other than useful everyday quilts. No time was spent on the actual quilting other than to insure a firm and adequate attachment.

There are a few elaborate patterns made from pieces of heavy cloth and scraps of homespun, all used materials. Plates 252 and 407 portray Star of Bethlehem quilts made up of diamonds in red and black or red, black and blue. The star in Plate 252 was created by using very heavy and crude materials with dog's tooth borders on each end, but the result is quite handsome. Plate 407 shows a lively Star quilt composed of assorted wools, some being parts of coat material. One might think that the maker had the Biblical verse in her mind, "the Morning Stars sang together, and all the sons of God shouted for joy."[2]

There are homespun quilts that have been designed and executed with great care and artistry. One of these, a Harvest Sun, of homespun, home-dyed cloth is nothing short of spectacular (Plate 400). The background is rusty red and the points of the suns are enclosed in black circles. The back is of homespun as well, but the binding has been done by machine, probably at a later date. The intricate pattern is closely quilted in a fan design. Made on Scugog Island, Ontario County, this beautiful quilt is one of the finest homespuns I have ever seen.

The Orange Peel quilt illustrated in Plate 401 is made of wool, possibly homespun, but of such fine, light quality that it is difficult to be certain. The quilting is finely done in a herringbone pattern, except around and inside the crescents that form the pattern which have been echo quilted. A four-heart design has been quilted between each unit of the pattern, while the border is quilted with running vines, double hearts, single hearts and tulips. This quilt, which comes from the Niagara district, was probably made by a woman of German descent.

Another woollen quilt from the same area (Plate 404) was made with great delicacy. Its colours are rose and black with cream coloured pieced baskets and yellow daisies that have been appliquéd. The quilting is in herringbone lines on the triangles with diagonal lines on the background and curved lines around the basket handles. The quilt back is rose homespun.

The three quilts just mentioned are of a different order than many homespun quilts, since the quilters have successfully attempted to make a finer creation than was usual. Matching cloth was used, while in most examples the material does not necessarily match in texture or colour. Even so, striking results were often accomplished by the use of varying materials and colours. Exciting arrangements and daring colour combinations were used in these less formal quilts to achieve dramatic effects.

A very charming and successful quilt is composed of scraps of various materials including homespuns (Plate 389), some of which were in very short supply when it was made. This quilt is exciting in both design and colour, and has a quality that may be called "folk art." It was probably made for a child by a grandmother, a suspicion that arises from the fact that the stitches are wavering and uneven although the design is quite sophisticated. Each block is a different pattern and each one is named for something dear to the heart of a child: Windmill, Sugar Cone, Grandmother's Cross, Baby Blocks, Old Gray Goose, Wild Goose Chase and Tree of Paradise. There is a large Tree of Paradise in the central area, above which is a block with a black background containing a large H – possibly signifying heaven. Most of the blocks, including this tree, were not only pieced individually, but also pieced into the background rather than appliquéd onto a foundation cloth, probably because cloth was in short supply. Fruits and stars are appliquéd at random, and there is a spectacular chevron border in bright colours: red plaids, whites and floral blacks. The chevron border extends along one side and about a third of the way down the other, when it changes to horizontal stripes. The quilt came from a log house in Martintown, Glengarry County, where a branch of the McMartin family has lived since the area was settled during the last twenty years of the eighteenth century.

There is a very interesting and probably unique group of homespun quilts originating in the Wilno area of Renfrew County. Most of them are whole-cloth and have been made by members of a group of Polish people who first came to Upper Canada in the middle of the nineteenth century. They deliberately kept themselves culturally isolated from the rest of the country, and they continued to practice the crafts they had brought with them from the old country. Not only their bedcovers, but also their furniture[3] bear the unique Wilno stamp.

Many of the women of this group were expert weavers, who continued to make bedding and cloth for clothing until much later than was common in the rest of Upper Canada. These women appear to have woven cloth in striped and checked patterns specifically for making wholecloth quilts, while others were constructed of finely woven homespun blocks. All of them were backed with plain homespun cloth.

Although it would seem that most of these quilts were composed of cloth woven for the purpose, there is evidence that bedcovers were made from the wide, gaily striped homespun skirts when they had fallen out of fashion. The skirts were taken apart at the seams and used with a backing and binding to make bedcovers that were tied with bright tufts of homespun yarn rather than quilted. Often no filling was used. The opening placket of the skirt can frequently be seen and the marks of sewing where the hem was ripped out and the waistband removed. The quilts that were not tied were quilted in close firm rows using homespun yarn.

Many of these delightful quilts were made by the women of the Luloff family, of whom there were several generations of weavers. The degree to which the old traditions survived in the Wilno area can be illustrated by the report of an antique hunter who entered a Luloff house in search of a find. One of the women of the house was busily picking apart the seams of a homespun petticoat to make a bedcover. This scene took place less than two years ago. It is understandable that the women would be doing this since the colours in these old homespuns are intense and vivid, making bedcovers of considerable charm.

As we have seen, our quilt designs came from the United States or the old European countries of Scotland, Ireland, England, Germany and Poland. Those from the United States included a strong German element, because of the many German immigrants who came north to settle in the Niagara Peninsula and Waterloo County. These people had a well-developed folk culture that tended to remain homogenous. There was, as well, some French-Canadian influence, particularly in the County of Glengarry since it borders Lower Canada. By 1860, everyone was influencing everyone else, except in a few isolated rural communities like Wilno, the Gaelic speaking Highlander sections in the back townships of Glengarry, and small groups of German people in southern Ontario who remained isolated for religious reasons. In addition, the circulation of magazines and needlework books from the United States profoundly affected our quilt patterns and names. Only in these isolated rural areas did people continue to make traditional styles, and by the end of the nineteenth century even these people had stopped making the heavy woollen quilts that had retained some of the very early features.

It is interesting to inspect several quilts made by the same woman. Often they have a recognizable style, so that one can frequently pick them out before their provenance is known. For example, the same woman, who lived in nineteenth century Prince Edward County, made the quilts shown in Plates 264, 323 and 424. These are beautiful quilts handsomely made by a woman who had a flair for colour. Nellie Silver, who was making quilts in the early twentieth century, used shades of blue-violets, lavenders, grays and so on. Her quilts were widely dispersed at an auction, but they can often be picked out by their colour combinations. It is often impossible to identify a specific maker, but quilts made by a family group do occasionally show the same type of identifiable style. A family in the Kingston area made a series of quilts that show a fondness for deep, intense colours; one of them is dated 1880.

The Hit and Miss pattern was always used for utility quilts, even though most of the one-patch quilts that have survived have been trimmed to shape and sorted for colour. Crazy quilts were made in large quantities from 1890 to 1920. These were made both in a practical utilitarian style and as ornamental throws decorated with silk and embroidery. The Crazy quilt reached the zenith of its popularity near the end of the nineteenth century.

Delectable Mountains was a favoured pattern during the period 1840 to 1860. Red and white quilts were fashionable around 1890 — both as good and everyday quilts. Many of the red and white appliquéd examples were made at this time. Appliquéd quilts were made for "good" into the twentieth century, the most popular nineteenth century pattern probably being the Rose of Sharon. A pieced pattern that was frequently used for the same purpose was the Star of Bethlehem or a variation of it.

During the nineteenth century and the first quarter of the twentieth, Upper Canadian women continued to make the simple, traditional patterns for their everyday quilts. These included Irish Chain, Nine Patch, Fox and Geese, Old Maid's Puzzle, Hovering Hawks, Jacob's Ladder, Bear's Paw, Wild Birds Flying, Wild Goose Chase, Five Crosses, Hole in the Barn Door, Shoo Fly, and Swallow's Nest, as well as variations of these and other family patterns. Log Cabin quilts were commonly made, changing from utilitarian quilts in the earlier years to elaborate throws in later years. Several dated Log Cabin quilts were created in the 1860 to 1890 period, although the style continued to appear until the 1920s. Probably the earliest Log Cabin shown in this book is in Plate 414; it was made by Phoebe Anne Saylor of Bloomfield, Prince Edward County before her marriage in 1862.

Upper Canadian quilts are, for the most part, those of farmers and other rural workers. Even the bedcovers of wealthy Upper Canadians were made by settlers in a raw, new land.

238

238 French Star: quilt, pieced and appliquéd; cotton; pumpkin yellow and white; made by Elizabeth Fennel (1823 - 1894), the great-grandmother of the former owner, Napanee, Lennox and Addington County, 2nd quarter 19th century. W. 192 cm, L. 196 cm (75, 77 in.). The charming little squiggles on the border have the appearance of seahorses. [C.C.F.C.S.]

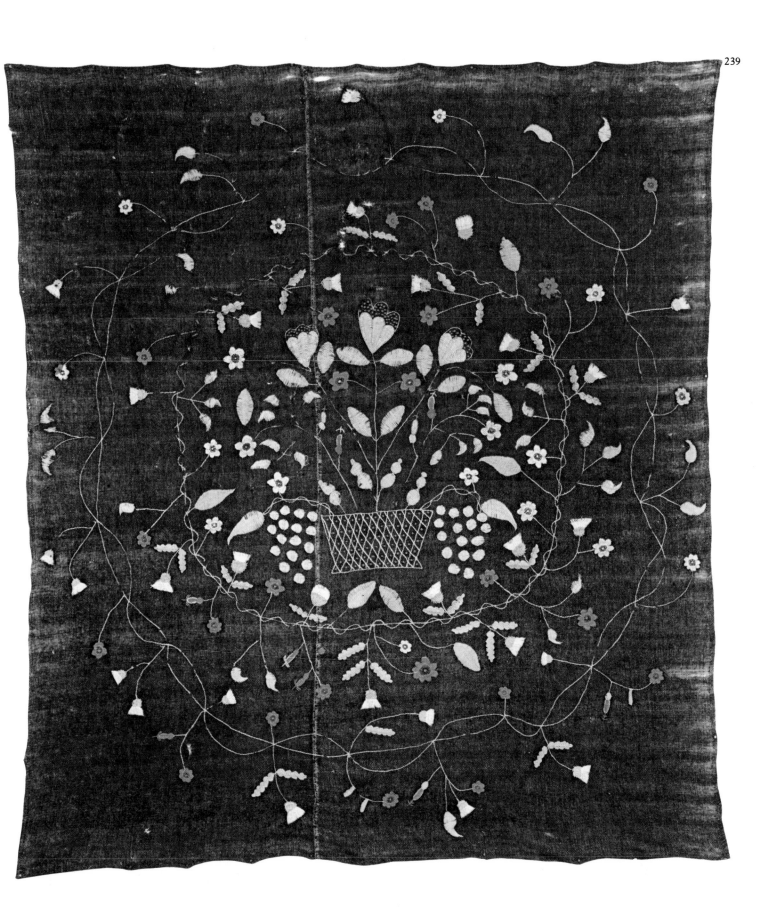

239

239 Embroidered Quilt: wool, probably handspun and woven in three widths sewn together; made by Elsie McCullock, Grand Valley, Dufferin County, ca. 1870. W. 180 cm, L. 200 cm (71, 79 in.). The woman who made this beautiful quilt was also a folk painter, and her work shows the same delicacy in both media. This quilt bears a striking resemblance to examples made in the United States a hundred years earlier. [C.H.]

240

240 Irish Ship Quilt: pieced and appliquéd; printed cottons; mostly reds and blues on a white ground; made during a family's 1843 emigration voyage from Northern Ireland, a journey that terminated in Oxford Township, Grenville County. W. 190 cm, L. 210 cm (75, 83 in.). The quilt has a central medallion with several borders of hearts, shamrocks and flying geese. This was probably a marriage quilt "kept for good." [U.C.V.]

241

241 Appliquéd Quilt: cotton; multicoloured on a white background; made by Mrs. Lidia Petch Park and her sister at Gunn's Hill, Oxford County, ca. 1840. W. 167 cm, L. 197 cm (66, 78 in.). The quilt depicts a lively pioneer scene with Indians on horseback hunting in the woods near a house with a picket fence, flower beds and grape arbours. Birds, flowers, trees and running dogs abound. The Indians, birds, flowers, even the finials on the gate posts and the door knobs, are stuffed. Details, such as the deer's antlers, the Indian head-dresses and the spots on the dogs, are embroidered. This is a quilt of exceptional interest. [M.L.]

242

242 Mary Morris Quilt: embroidered, central medallion type; printed cotton, with borders or frames; made by Mary Morris (at the age of fourteen), Elgin area, Leeds County, 1825. W. 185 cm, L. 200 cm (73, 79 in.). Mary Morris was born in 1811 with a physical handicap that prevented her from walking. As a result, she became a skilled needlewoman at an early age. This beautiful example of her work has been carefully preserved by relatives, and it has been suggested that the running horses and dogs express her yearning for freedom of movement. The quilt is backed with handspun linen, contains little or no stuffing and is finely quilted. This quilt was made very shortly after immigration, and European influences are visible in its making.
[C.C.F.C.S.]

242a

242a Detail of flowering branches, birds, peacocks and swastikas; probably all have been used symbolically.

Epilogue

The quilt was an intimate part of family life. The children snuggled beneath the lions, zebras and elephants of the Circus quilt on their bed. It became soft and worn, but the bright red animals remained as vivid and familiar as the family cat. Many of us slept as children warm and secure during frigid winter nights in unheated bedrooms under quilts made by our mothers and grandmothers. Every morning we smoothed out the Cat's Cradles and the Irish Chains and folded the heavy wool comforters on the blanket boxes ready for the next night's onslaught. In spring, the clothes lines all over the village blossomed with multi-coloured quilts.

It was pleasant to sleep under quilts made by loving and familiar hands. Under these homemade covers a child felt safe and comforted. The good spirits evoked by love and devotion safeguarded us from the dark and evil demons of the night. Love went into the making of these quilts. Young women dreamed of fine husbands as they made their marriage quilts and thought of the time when they would be together beneath them. A cradle quilt was prepared with love and faith by mothers and friends for the anticipated baby who would lie wrapped in its folds as safe as in the womb. An aged grandmother expressed her feeling for a favourite grandchild by making a quilt to keep him safe and warm; perhaps it might be an Old Brown Goose so that the lullaby she sang him would stay close by throughout the night.

It is sad to come to the end of an ancient tradition. Women no longer make quilts as part of their daily routine to keep their families comfortable. People still make quilts and some are very beautiful, but they have become too precious to sleep under, wear out and throw away. The era of the everyday quilt is past and gone forever. Quilts even look different now. Made with synthetic materials and puffy batts, they are more like comforters in appearance. Quilt makers who have not held a needle for years have started in again to make quilts to sell, and corners are cut, easy patterns are sought. Women who come from long lines of quilt makers refer in all innocence to quilts that were made "before." Before, that is, they were made to sell.

Of course, there is a hard core of women who are continuing to make quilts for their own satisfaction as well as to sell, and they work with the utmost care and integrity. They are genuinely interested in maintaining high standards of quilt making. But it is different now; quilts are worth money. Only the brashest among us will curl up with a book on top of a quilt, old or new. Nonetheless, quilts were meant to be used, and those that are faded and worn a bit are still appealing to the eye. The colours of the little pieces of prints run into each other, achieving a new harmony. New quilts can never emulate the subtlety of colour that is acquired through age and use with the slight yellowing of the whites and the faint softening of the bright colours.

For some women quilt making was a release of pent up artistic feeling that had no other outlet. These were the women who created the masterpieces, even though they might be merely everyday quilts. The woman who made the Snake Fence in Plate 322 was an artist painting with her needle, thread and scraps of cloth the beauty she saw from her window of a snake fence crossing a snowy field in the late afternoon when colours lay on the snow.

Year after year some women exhibited their best quilts at country fairs. The prize money, trifling though it may have been, was very important to many, since they had absolutely no other source of income even to buy thread. This was the case in particular for unmarried women living at a relative's house. Quilts that won prizes were treasured over the years folded away in the bottom drawer to be shown to visitors and relatives.

On the other hand, there were acres of quilts made in Upper Canada that, although they did keep one warm, have not one redeeming feature for the eye. I have seen a farmhouse where there were close to fifty quilts either in use or stored for future use, and not one of them was anything other than some pieces of dull coloured cloth sewn together as they came to hand. No attempt had been made to make them attractive.

A great many women made quilts simply because they had to keep their families warm. They took no pride in their work and did not enjoy it. The same applied to women who had to prepare the yarn and weave it into blankets. Many doubtless felt like the woman in the old verse,

> The weary pund, the weary pund.
> The weary pund of tow.
> I think my wife will end her life
> Before she spin her tow.

Every day was the same, "The cardin o't, the spinnin o't, the warpin o't, the winnin o't," from dawn to dusk.

I was told the story of a dying woman who asked that her loom be brought out of the shed onto the lawn beneath her bedroom window where she could see it. There she insisted that it be broken up and burned before her eyes. She said it was the only way she could ensure that no other woman would have to put in the hours of tedious labour that she had on that loom. There were many women like this one who were compelled by circumstances to spend their lives in hard labour for which they were unsuited. They worked like slaves tied by the bonds of love for their husbands and children.

Women in more fortunate circumstances in the nineteenth century who did not like to weave or sew could pay to have it done for them. Even then church groups quilted to order. Expert quilters will often say that one cannot get a fine quilt if many hands have worked on it, but many people were satisfied by the results. Catalogues advertising quilt patterns would also supply the pieces of a quilt top already cut out and ready to be assembled in one's choice of colour, or they would supply the top all made up. I would suspect, however, that a woman at that time who would order a made-up quilt would keep it a deep, dark secret.

Despite all these things, the majority of women who made quilts enjoyed it. Quilting bees were fun and a great excuse for a good gossip. It was a happy life for most women. The owner of the quilt in Plate 277 can remember the quiet pleasure of her mother and the hired girl when they sat down of an evening to work on the current quilt. All the women who made quilts in the nineteenth century were not skilled needlewomen. Many had a fine eye for design, but their stitches were wobbly and their attention to detail left much to be desired. As long as a woman had a needle and a few rags, though, she could make herself a masterpiece, and a surprising number of women did just that from the most unlikely looking materials. Out of the crudest little log shanties came beautiful, gaily coloured quilts fit for a queen. One can see them yet on farmers' clothes lines, flying high over the mud, the hens and the discarded machinery, "and I will make thee beds of roses and a thousand fragrant posies."[1]

A Gallery
of Traditional
Quilts

243

243 Star of Bethlehem: quilt, pieced; cotton with a vivid star in deep strong colours; made by Elizabeth Dodge, Mainsville, Grenville County, 4th quarter 19th century. W. 166 cm, L. 193 cm (65, 76 in.). The corners are elaborately quilted with double-wake robins in vine rosettes, large daisies, hearts, leaves and a willow tree; no two corners are alike. [E.D.]

244

245

246

247

244 Tree of Paradise: quilt, pieced; cotton; red and white; made by Millie South, Lennox and Addington County, ca. 1900. W. 170 cm, L. 217 cm (67, 85 in.). Four large Trees of Paradise are arranged to form a large star, an unusual graphic design. Arched church doors are quilted along the borders. [C.C.F.C.S.]

245 Starburst: quilt, pieced; cotton; red, yellow and green stars on a white ground; made by Mrs. William Neilson, Kingston, Frontenac County, ca. 1840. W. 170 cm, L. 190 cm (67, 75 in.). The rays of the star have been quilted. This piece has been passed down from mother to daughter for several generations. [C.C.F.C.S.]

246 Harvest Sun: quilt, pieced; cotton; made by Mrs. Welbank, Picton, Prince Edward County, 4th quarter 19th century. W. 145 cm, L. 195 cm (57, 77 in.). The finely quilted white background sets off the seven traditional suns. There is a basket in each corner overflowing with flowers and vines, which trail between the harvest suns. [C.C.F.C.S.]

247 Feathered Star: quilt, pieced; cotton; red and white; Switzerville, Lennox and Addington County, 3rd quarter 19th century. W. 180 cm, L. 195 cm (71, 77 in.). The blocks are placed so that they almost touch, an effective design. [C.C.F.C.S.]

248

250

2:

248 Star of Bethlehem: quilt, pieced; printed cotton; Riddle Road, Dundas County, 4th quarter 19th century. W. 155 cm, L. 180 cm (61, 71 in.). The combination of the well-organized, coloured prints of the stars and the polkadot background gives this quilt a fresh, cheery look. [C.C.F.C.S.]

249 Star of Bethlehem: quilt, pieced; cotton; red, yellow, black and white on a dark blue background; western counties, 4th quarter 19th century. W. 172 cm, L. 190 cm (68, 75 in.). The dark blue is an effective background for the colourful star. The baskets and small stars are appliquéd. [R.P.P.]

250 Harvest Sun: quilt, pieced; Wild Goose Chase set and border; cotton; red and white; made by Amelia Crozier, Napanee, Lennox and Addington County, 4th quarter 19th century. W. 147 cm, L. 190 cm (58, 75 in.). At the time of the harvest sun, the wild geese begin to fly south. [C.C.F.C.S.]

251 Star of Bethlehem: quilt, pieced; cotton; Kingston, Frontenac County, 4th quarter 19th century. W. 187 cm, L. 200 cm (74, 79 in.). The single large star is made from plain cottons in blazing colours; the plain areas are quilted in hearts. [C.C.F.C.S.]

252

253

252 Star of Bethlehem: quilt, pieced; wool, some cotton; red and black; Young family, Hastings County, 1st quarter 20th century. W. 115 cm, L. 175 cm (45, 69 in.). This small quilt has a strong visual impact. The dog's tooth border reminds one of a Navaho rug. [C.C.F.C.S.]

253 Variable Star: quilt, pieced; cotton, handspun, handwoven back; printed woolens and cottons in shades of browns and greens; Lennox and Addington County, 2nd quarter 19th century. W. 162 cm, L. 180 cm (64, 71 in.). This quilt was intended to be used on a bed in a corner; note the single block corner with a star pattern. [C.C.F.C.S.]

254 Feathered Star: quilt, pieced; cotton; yellow and white; Ola Ross family, Cornwall, Stormont County, 3rd quarter 19th century. W. 170 cm, L. 202 cm (67, 79 in.). The border has yellow piping, and the quilting is done in large double rosettes and a shell pattern. The star in the bottom left-hand corner has two triangles deliberately misplaced to avoid making the quilt perfect. [C.C.F.C.S.]

255

255 Blazing Sun or Sunburst: quilt, pieced; cotton; red, white and blue; Kemptville area, Grenville County, 3rd quarter 19th century. W. 175 cm, L. 175 cm (70, 70 in.). One large exuberant sun fills the entire quilt. The individual diamonds, which make up the sun are unusually large, 30 cm x 30 cm (12 in.). [P.S.]

256

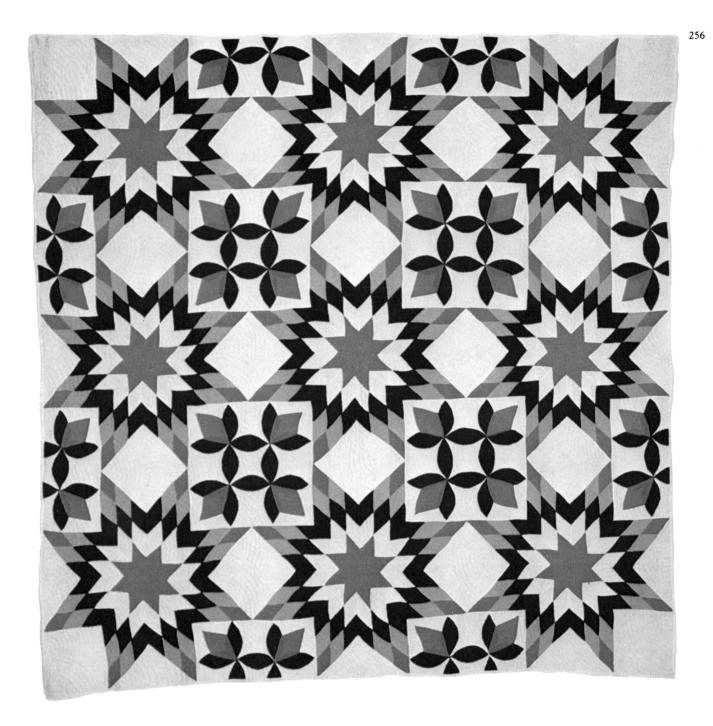

256 Harvest Sun and Dutch Tulip: quilt, pieced; cotton; made by Elizabeth Aikey (Plate 75), Potter's Settlement (near Tweed), Hastings County, ca. 1860. W. 177 cm, L. 177 cm (70, 70 in.). Made by the great-grandmother of Ann Davison. [J.D.]

257

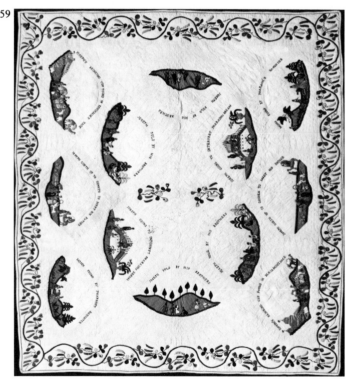

258

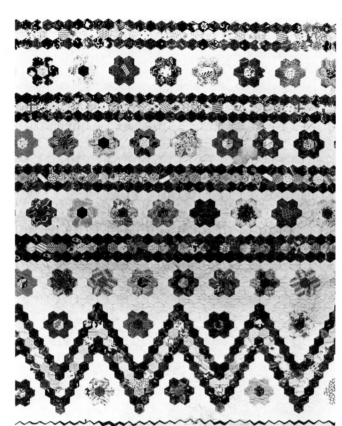

259

259

257 Unknown Pattern: quilt, pieced; cotton; Kingston, Frontenac County, 1st quarter 19th century. W. 227 cm, L. 230 cm (89, 90 in.). This is a large, early quilt made from delicately coloured cotton prints. [J.J.B.]

258 Mosaic: quilt, detail; printed, multicoloured cottons; made by the Sinkler sisters (Eleanor, Margaret, Elizabeth and Agnes), Brockville, Leeds County, ca. 1850. The pattern papers are still in the backs of the hexagons, and the colours of the cottons used are exceptionally beautiful. The entire quilt measures 220 cm (87 in.) wide and 350 cm (138 in.) long, unusually long, especially for the width. [A.C.M.]

259 Joseph Quilt: appliquéd; white cotton, using a wide variety of material scraps, both cottons and woollens; western counties, ca. 1860. W. 171 cm, L. 196 cm (67, 77 in.). The quilt has a field with six scenes from the life of Joseph, each one of which is used twice, and each one of which has a title above it. The borders take the form of trailing vines and perennial pea. The quilt is lightly padded and quilted in ray triangles around the scenes with trailing vines between. [R.O.M.]

259a Detail of Joseph coming to interpret Pharaoh's dream.

261

260 Embroidered Quilt: pieced; wool; dark shades of gray and brown with brightly coloured design and trim; found in the Ottawa area, Carleton County, 3rd quarter 19th century. W. 160 cm, L. 199 cm (63, 78 in.). The flowers are hooked in a raised design, and "L. You" (Love You?) is embroidered in one square. This quilt is reminiscent of the bed rugs used in the 18th and early 19th centuries. The designs of bed rugs were worked with needles, not hooked. Inventories indicate that bed rugs were used in Canada to a limited extent, although none seem to have survived. [N.M.M.]

261 Log Cabin: cradle quilt, pieced; multicoloured on brown background; Lanark County, 3rd quarter 19th century. W. 37 cm, L. 72 cm (15, 28 in.). Cradle quilts were not tucked in and were usually small. Like their larger models, Log Cabin cradle quilts are particularly appealing. [C.C.F.C.S.]

262

262 Maple Leaf and Rose: quilt, pieced and appliquéd; Newcastle area, Durham County, 3rd quarter 19th century. W. 160 cm, L. 215 cm (63, 85 in.). A well-designed piece quilted in hearts and roses. [C.C.F.C.S.]

263 Sunflower: quilt top, pieced; cotton with appliquéd border; Niagara Peninsula, 3rd quarter 19th century. W. 212 cm, L. 212 cm (83, 83 in.). The border does not relate in some ways to the entire design, but it has a magnificent array of vines, urns, hex symbols, tulips, hearts and sheaves of wheat. Notice the heart with the open hand in it, a commonly recognized symbol of friendship. The other symbols are intended to ward off evil and ensure fertility. [R.P.P.]

264

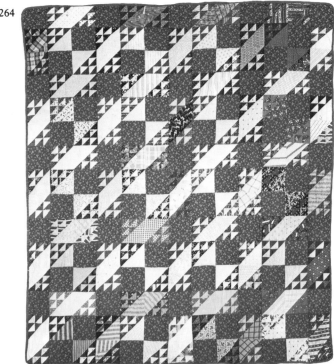

265

266

267

264 Birds in the Air: quilt, pieced; cotton; multicoloured, red predominant; Bloomfield, Prince Edward County, 4th quarter 19th century. W. 165 cm, L. 187 cm (65, 74 in.). The skilful arrangement of colour and shape give the illusion of swift movement. [C.C.F.C.S.]

265 Wild Goose Chase: quilt, pieced; cotton, eastern counties, ca. 1860. W. 175 cm, L. 205 cm (69, 81 in.). This quilt has a colourful variety of unwashed early printed cottons; it was never bound. [C.C.F.C.S.]

266 Melon Patch: quilt, pieced; cotton; faded pumpkin yellow and white; Newboro, Leeds County, 3rd quarter 19th century. W. 185 cm, L. 185 cm (73, 73 in.). All lines are curved, both in the pattern and quilting. The curved lines, which are difficult to seam together, have tiny seam allowances. [C.C.F.C.S.]

267 Tree of Paradise: quilt, pieced; cotton; red and white; Prince Edward County, 4th quarter 19th century. W. 160 cm, L. 193 cm (63, 76 in.). The Tree of Paradise is one of the most attractive quilt designs of the 19th century. [C.C.F.C.S.]

268

270

269

271

190 cm (63, 75 in.). A star has been pieced and then appliquéd in the plain area of the quilt's centre. [M.S.W.]

270 Snail's Trail, or Monkey Wrench: quilt, pieced; cotton; pumpkin yellow and white; Prescott, Grenville County, 3rd quarter 19th century. W. 169 cm, L. 250 cm (67, 98 in.). A charming early quilt, this example shows an interesting repetition of an angular form in the border. [C.C.F.C.S.]

271 Rob Peter to Pay Paul: quilt, pieced; cotton; green and orange; Lennox and Addington County, 19th century. W. 195 cm, L. 205 cm (77, 81 in.). The three patch construction is unusual. [C.C.F.C.S.]

268 Missouri Puzzle: quilt, pieced; cotton; green and white; Kingston area, Frontenac County, 1860-1880. W. 170 cm, L. 212 cm (68, 85 in.). Double hearts are quilted in the plain blocks. The quilt has never been washed, and the original blue chalk marks for the quilting designs are still evident. [C.C.F.C.S.]

269 Quilt: pieced and appliquéd; shades of brown on cream background; made by Mary Ann Moulton from a paisley woollen shawl, Thamesville area, Kent County, ca. 1850. W. 160 cm, L.

272

272 Central Medallion: quilt; wool and cotton; made by Frances Mulligan, Hazeldean, Carleton County, 1856. W. 177 cm, L. 187 cm (70, 74 in.). Frances Mulligan made this quilt at the age of sixteen. She used motifs usually associated with a marriage quilt: hearts, a flowering branch, etc. She died at an early age. [C.C.F.C.S.]

273

273 Flowering Tree: quilt, appliquéd and pieced; cotton; made by Miss Battey, Ontario County, ca. 1840. W. 195 cm, L. 222 cm (77, 87 in.). Elaborate borders frame the central medallion, which contains the flowering tree. The printed cotton fabrics in this quilt are beautiful. [R.L.]

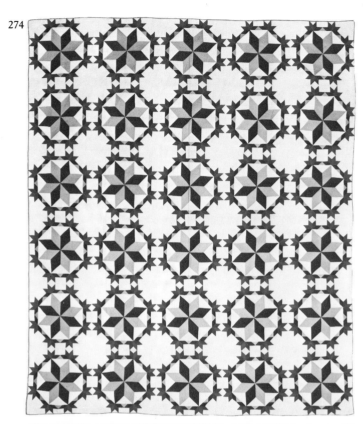

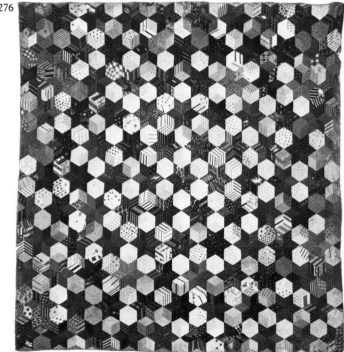

274 Pin Wheel Star: quilt, pieced, design variant; cotton; pumpkin yellow and dark blue on a white background; made by the Phoenix family, Durham County, ca. 1890. W. 182 cm, L. 220 cm (72, 87 in.). An example of meticulous design and execution. [S.S.M]

275   Block and Star: quilt, pieced; wool and cotton; purple, brown, white and black with touches of pink; Young family, Hastings County, 1st quarter 20th century. W. 185 cm, L. 194 cm (73, 76 in.). [C.C.F.C.S.]

276 Baby Blocks and Stars: quilt, pieced; cotton; multi-coloured; Uxbridge area, Ontario County, 3rd quarter 19th century. W. 200 cm, L. 225 cm (79, 89 in.). [C.C.F.C.S.]

277 Delectable Mountains: quilt, pieced; cotton; red and white; made by Elizabeth Dodge, Mainsville, Grenville County, 4th quarter 19th century. W. 153 cm, L. 194 cm (60, 76 in.). Elizabeth's daughter remembers the quiet pleasure shared by her mother and the hired girl sitting down to quilt "when the snow was blowing." The quilting in this example is exceptionally fine. [E.D.]

278 Delectable Mountains: quilt, pieced; printed red and white cotton on a white background with blue polka dots; Matheson family, Mitchell, Perth County, 2nd quarter 19th century. W. 200 cm, L. 205 cm (79, 81 in.). [M.L.]

279 Combination of Patterns: quilt, pieced; cotton; lavender, pink and blue; eastern counties, 3rd quarter 19th century. W. 150 cm, L. 170 cm (59, 67 in.). A Geometric Star contains an Indian Hatchet and is surrounded by borders of Sawtooth and Streaks of Lightning. In the border, there is another little Indian Hatchet set beside a house. Possibly, this quilt tells the story of a massacre. [C.C.F.C.S.]

280 Feathered Square and Diamond: quilt, pieced; cotton; red and white; Urquart family, Dunvegan, Glengarry County, 1st quarter 20th century. W. 174 cm, L. 180 cm (69, 71 in.). This early style of quilt making is found in both wool and cotton in Glengarry County. [C.C.F.C.S.]

281 Delectable Mountains: quilt, pieced square in square format; cotton; rosy red and blue on a white background; made by Hannah McAndrew, Newboyne, Saskatchewan, 4th quarter 19th century. W. 170 cm, L. 175 cm (67, 69 in.). This is one of five of her quilts that were in use at the cottage of her grandson in Lanark County. There is a richness achieved here through the use of fabrics that look older than the quilt. [C.C.F.C.S.]

282

282 Delectable Mountains: quilt, pieced; printed cottons; reds, greens and browns; made by Elizabeth Hannah McAndrew, Newboyne, Saskatchewan, 4th quarter 19th century. W. 157 cm, L. 180 cm (62, 71 in.).Found in Lanark County at the home of her
grandson. [C.C.F.C.S.]

283

283 Wild Goose Chase: quilt, pieced; cotton, an excellent selection of early prints; Vineland, Lincoln County, ca. 1820-1840. W. 200 cm, L. 232 cm (79, 91 in.). The initials E. C. are worked in cross-stitch on the back. [C.C.F.C.S.].

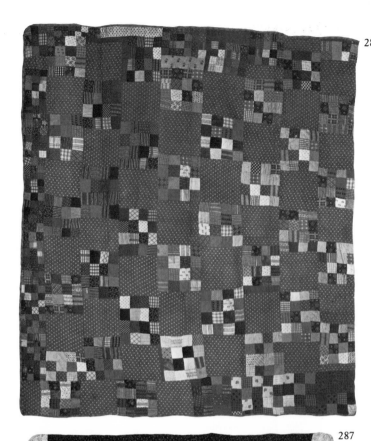

284 Variable Star: quilt, pieced; wool, some cotton; Centreville, **Lennox and Addington County, 4th quarter 19th century. W. 160 cm, L. 181 cm (63, 72 in.).** [C.C.F.C.S.]

285 Four Patch: quilt, pieced; cotton; Lanark County, 3rd quarter 19th century. W. 175 cm, L. 200 cm (69, 79 in.). The maker ran out of material for the set and became somewhat disorganized, but the small, brightly coloured patches of old material result in a most attractive quilt. [C.C.F.C.S.]

286 Nine Patch: quilt, pieced; printed cotton with a homespun wool back; multicoloured, blues and red predominant; Frontenac County, 3rd quarter 19th century. W. 140 cm, L. 170 cm (55, 67 in.). [C.C.F.C.S.]

287 Nine Patch: crib quilt, pieced; cotton; multicoloured; Carleton County, 4th quarter 19th century. W. 110 cm, L. 140 cm (43, 55 in.). [C.C.F.C.S.]

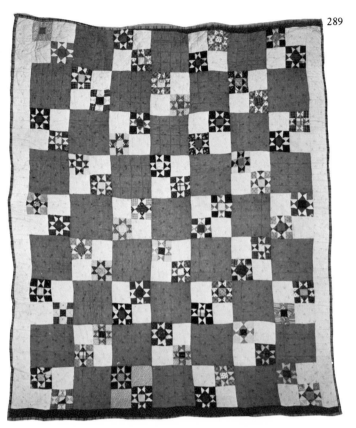

288 Variable Star: quilt, pieced, pattern variant; cotton; multi-coloured; Lennox and Addington County, ca. 1900. W. 162 cm, L. 192 cm (64, 75 in.). [C.C.F.C.S.]

289 Variable Star: quilt, pieced; cotton; Hastings County, 4th quarter 19th century. W. 157 cm, L. 185 cm (62, 73 in.). Sixty-four tiny twinkling stars contrast with the soft, peaceful mulberry colour in the alternate blocks. [C.C.F.C.S.]

290

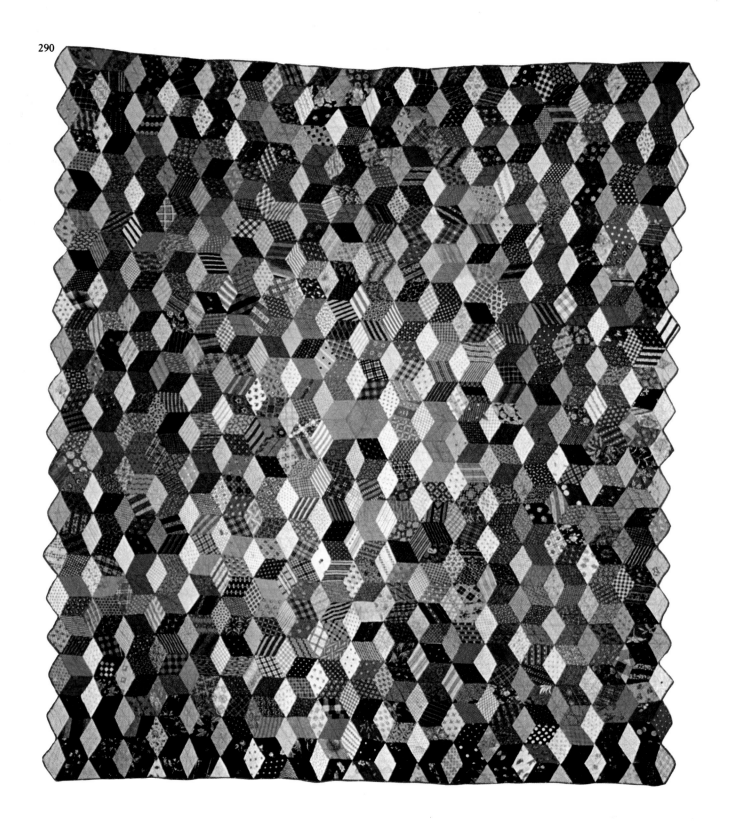

290 Baby Blocks: quilt, one of a pair; printed cottons; Merkley, Williamsburg, Dundas County, 1876. W. 190 cm, L. 222 cm (75, 87 in.). There are two dates on the quilt, 1876 and 1900, which probably indicate the date the top was made and the date of quilting. The colours are beautiful and the workmanship excellent. [P.C.]

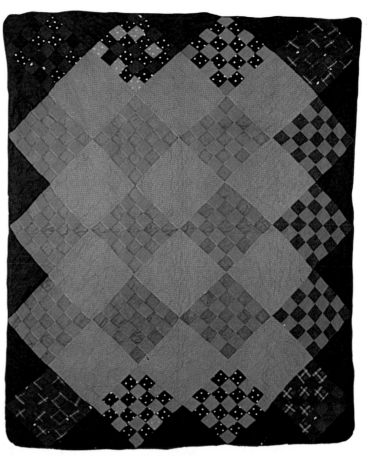

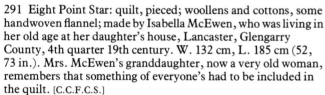

291 Eight Point Star: quilt, pieced; woollens and cottons, some handwoven flannel; made by Isabella McEwen, who was living in her old age at her daughter's house, Lancaster, Glengarry County, 4th quarter 19th century. W. 132 cm, L. 185 cm (52, 73 in.). Mrs. McEwen's granddaughter, now a very old woman, remembers that something of everyone's had to be included in the quilt. [C.C.F.C.S.]

292 Five Patch: quilt, pieced; cottons and wools; Kingston area, Frontenac County, 4th quarter 19th century. W. 174 cm, L. 217 cm (68, 85 in.). The blocks have been arranged in a cruciform pattern, and the dark colours have been enlivened by a few bright squares. A warm quilt for everyday use, this example has been carefully quilted allover in a shell pattern. [C.C.F.C.S.]

293

294

295

296

293 Double Heart: quilt, appliquéd; cotton; red and white; Smith family, Perth, Lanark County, 3rd quarter 19th century. W. 202 cm, L. 215 cm (80, 85 in.). The quilt is decorated with an edging made from folded, handwoven linen tape. The entire design has been arranged in a naïve and charming manner. [T.F.]

294 Double Hearts and Tulips: quilt, appliquéd; cotton; red and white; Jewell family, Orono, Durham County, 1865-1870. W. 180 cm, L. 180 cm (71, 71 in.). This finely constructed quilt was made by two Jewell sisters for a third, who married and moved to the West in 1871. [J.B.]

295 Free-Form Design: quilt, appliquéd; cotton; red and white; Napanee, Lennox and Addington County, 1st quarter 20th century. W. 142 cm, L. 165 cm (56, 65 in.). The red designs were made by cutting folded papers into patterns. This quilt designer was almost carried away in her enthusiasm. [C.C.F.C.S.]

296 Double Hearts and Tulips: quilt, appliquéd; cotton; red and white; made by Sarah Anne Polk, Portland, Leeds County, 4th quarter 19th century. W. 170 cm, L. 225 cm (67, 88 in.). [C.C.F.C.S.]

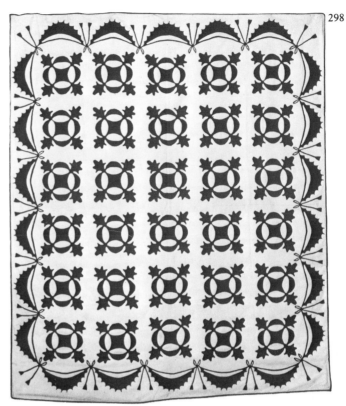

298

300

297 Stylized Urn and Oak: quilt, appliquéd; cotton; red and white; Hastings County, 4th quarter 19th century. W. 160 cm, L. 190 cm (63, 75 in.). This unusual design consists of four blocks separated by an inside set of Wild Goose Chase. [R.B.]

298 Oak Leaf and Reel: unquilted counterpane, appliquéd; bow knot and hammock border; red and white cotton; Niagara Peninsula, 19th century. W. 162 cm, L. 195 cm (65, 78 in.). [R.P.P.]

299 Carpenter's Wheel: quilt, appliquéd; cotton; red and white; Bowmanville, Durham County, 1st quarter 20th century. W. 182 cm, L. 212 cm (72, 83 in.). [R.A.B.]

300 Bow Tie: quilt, pieced; cotton; red and white; made by Mrs. Clyde, Odessa, Lennox and Addington County, 20th century. W. 175 cm, L. 185 cm (69, 73 in.). [C.C.F.C.S.]

301

301 Double Hearts and Tulips: quilt, appliquéd; cotton; Hallowell family, Newtonville, Durham County, 4th quarter 19th century. W. 177 cm, L. 205 cm (70, 81 in.). The central square with large double heart and tulip is surrounded by blocks of tulips. Notice the one upside down tulip in the bottom row, probably a deliberate "error" to avoid offending the spirits. [C.B.]

302

302 Old Rose of Sharon: quilt, appliquéd; cotton; Oxford County, 2nd quarter 19th century. W. 215 cm, L. 215 cm (85, 85 in.). The lush roses and the tulip border are symbolic, perhaps, of the fruitful area in which the quilt was made; it is a good example of the type of quilt beloved by people of Pennsylvania-German descent. [M.L.]

303

304

305

306

303 Album Quilt: pieced; cotton, composed of various patterns; red and white; western counties, 4th quarter 19th century. W. 157 cm, L. 205 cm (62, 81 in.). [P.C.]

304 Wagon Wheels: quilt, appliquéd; cotton; red and white; made by Mrs. Beaubien, Amherst Island, Lennox and Addington County, 1st quarter 19th century. W. 157 cm, L. 200 cm (62, 79 in.). [C.C.F.C.S.]

305 Peony: quilt, appliquéd; cotton; red and buff on a white background; Prince Edward County, 3rd quarter 19th century. W. 155 cm, L. 204 cm (61, 80 in.). The peony form is used as a quilting pattern in the alternate plain blocks. This quilt was made for a bed that could be seen from one side only, probably in a slip-bedroom. [C.C.F.C.S.]

306 Full Blown Tulip: quilt, pieced; cotton; yellow, buff and red on a white background; Lanark County, 4th quarter 19th century. W. 152 cm, L. 190 cm (60, 75 in.). An intricate pattern because of the curved lines. [C.C.F.C.S.]

307

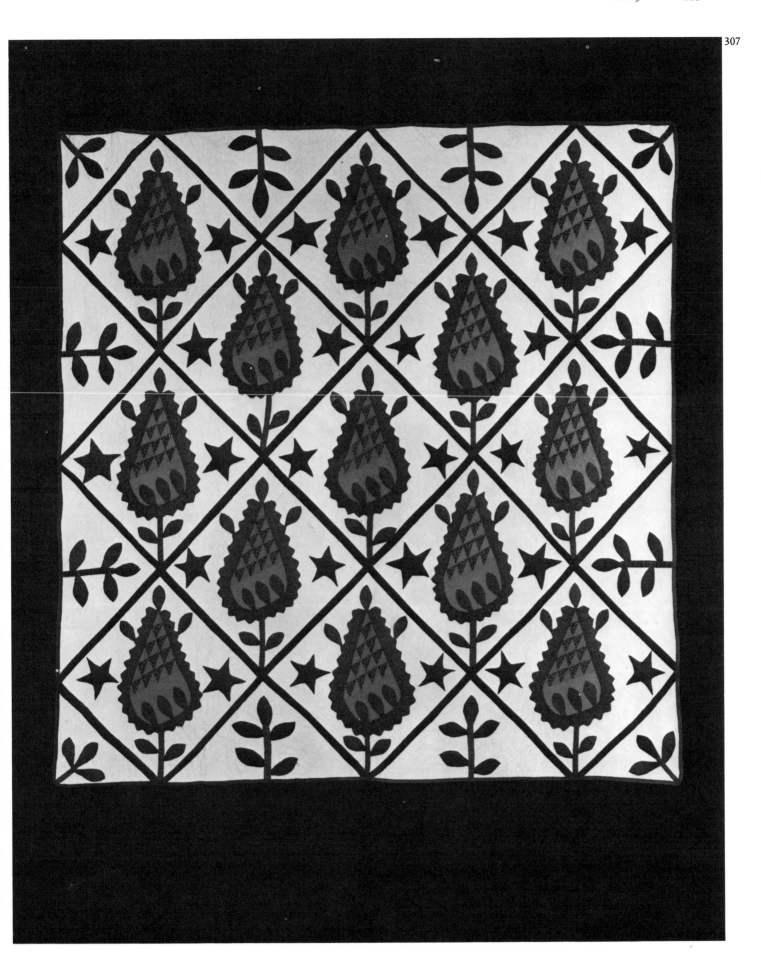

307 Pineapple: quilt, pieced and appliquéd; cotton; yellow and green on a white background, red stars; Woodville, Victoria County, 4th quarter 19th century. W. 167 cm, L. 177 cm (66, 70 in.). In the 19th century, the pineapple was recognized as a symbol of hospitality and was used on guest bed quilts. [C.B.]

308

308 Rose Quilt: appliquéd; cotton; made by Eliza Gillespie for her daughter, Martha, Wolfe Island, Frontenac County, ca. 1860. W. 163 cm, L. 221 cm (64, 87 in.). This beautiful quilt is still a treasured possession of the family, whose women are all expert quilters. [H.H.]

309

309 Rose of Sharon: quilt, appliquéd; cotton; Carleton Place, Lanark County, 3rd quarter 19th century. W. 155 cm, L. 217 cm (61, 85 in.). This folksy, lively version of a traditional pattern has been recently quilted. [C.C.F.C.S.]

310

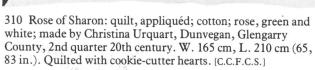

311

312

313

310 Rose of Sharon: quilt, appliquéd; cotton; rose, green and white; made by Christina Urquart, Dunvegan, Glengarry County, 2nd quarter 20th century. W. 165 cm, L. 210 cm (65, 83 in.). Quilted with cookie-cutter hearts. [C.C.F.C.S.]

311 Conventional Tulip: quilt, appliquéd; cotton; mauve, yellow and white; Egor family, Kingston, Frontenac County, 1st quarter 20th century. W. 170 cm, L. 202 cm (67, 80 in.). The tulip design is quilted in the alternate plain blocks. [C.C.F.C.S.]

312 Fleur de Lis, or Tulip: quilt, appliquéd; cotton; red and white; made by Christina Urquart, Dunvegan, Glengarry

County, 1st quarter 19th century. W. 157 cm, L. 198 cm (62, 78 in.). The flowers face one way as though the quilt was made for a wall bed, or one in a slip-bedroom. The tulips look like stylized lilies and may be the result of French-Canadian influence in Glengarry County. [C.C.F.C.S.]

313 Tulip Wreath: quilt, appliquéd; cotton; green and red on a white background; Niagara Peninsula, 4th quarter 19th century. W. 167 cm., L. 217 cm (66, 85 in.). A most attractive design with great curves and flourishes. [R.O.]

314

315

316

314 Rose of Sharon: quilt, appliquéd; cotton; red, green and yellow on white; Carleton Place area, Lanark County, 3rd quarter 19th century. W. 163 cm, L. 180 cm (64, 71 in.). [P.B.]

315 Rose of Sharon: quilt, appliquéd, pattern variant; cotton; rose and yellow on a white background; Cecil Wilson family, Durham County, 3rd quarter 19th century. W. 170 cm, L. 192 cm (67, 76 in.). This quilt has attractive small urns of cherries in the corners; it is beautifully quilted with lines .64 cm (¼ in.) apart. [R.P.P.]

316 Rose and Thistle: quilt, appliquéd; cotton; red, green and yellow on a white background; made by Eva Richardson, Lindsay, Victoria County, ca. 1900. W. 190 cm, L. 190 cm (75, 75 in.). The quilt maker has used a cheerful profusion of motifs, and the quilt may, in fact, be earlier than 1900; it is initialed "M." [M.B.T.K.]

317

317 Love Apple: quilt, appliquéd; cotton; Grenville County, 3rd quarter 19th century. W. 152 cm, L. 210 cm (60, 83 in.). The red tomatoes are stuffed. [P.S.]

318

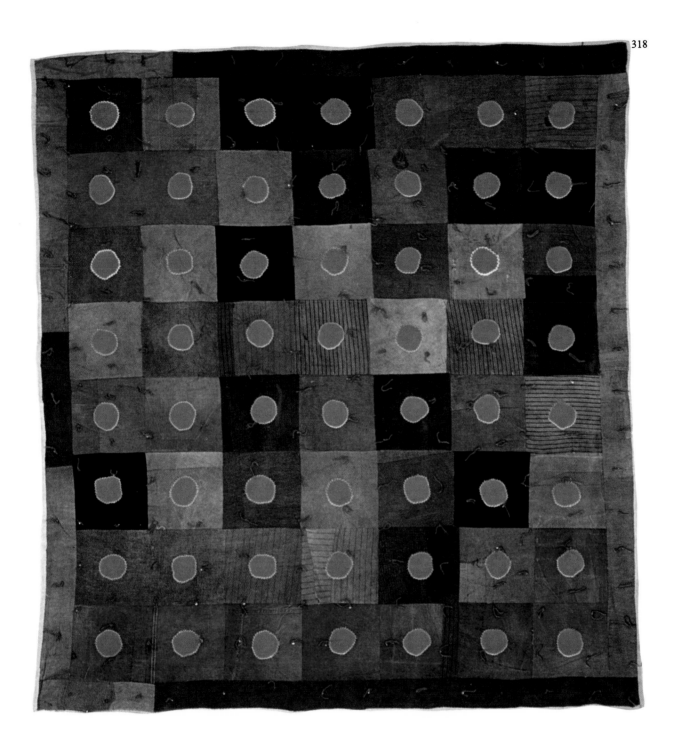

318 Love Apple: quilt, appliquéd; denim work clothing and red flannel; Enterprise, Lennox and Addington County, probably 20th century. W. 175 cm, L. 195 cm (69, 77 in.). This is a surprisingly beautiful quilt made from very humble cloth. [C.C.F.C.S.]

319 Chained Five Patch, or Double Irish Chain: quilt, pieced; wool and linen; Napanee, Lennox and Addington County, 19th century. W. 190 cm, L. 206 cm (75, 81 in.). The blacks and grays used here probably indicate that this is a mourning quilt. [C.C.F.C.S.]

320 Puss in the Corner: quilt, pieced; red floral print and white cotton; made by Ellen McMullen, Verona, Frontenac County, 1st quarter 20th century, quilted at a later date. W. 180 cm, L. 200 cm (71, 79 in.). [C.C.F.C.S.]

321

321 Embroidered Quilt: embroidered with Berlin wool on Henrietta cloth; multicoloured on a light brown background; initialed "B.M.," Lindsay, Victoria County, 3rd quarter 19th century. W. 182 cm, L. 205 cm (72, 81 in.). A wide variety of naturalistic and symbolic motifs are used here. [U.C.V.]

322

322 Snake Fence: quilt, pieced; cotton; Beaubien family, Amherst Island, Lennox and Addington County, 4th quarter 19th century. W. 175 cm, L. 205 cm (69, 81 in.). The colours are those of snow along a snake fence in winter. [C.C.F.C.S.]

323 Flower Pot: quilt, pieced; cotton; Prince Edward County, 3rd quarter 19th century. W. 157 cm, L. 200 cm (62, 79 in.). This is one of a group of quilts made by a woman skilled in the use of colour. [C.C.F.C.S.]

324

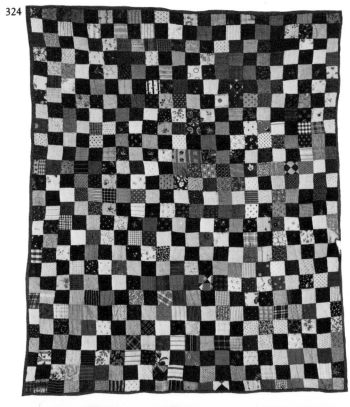

325

326

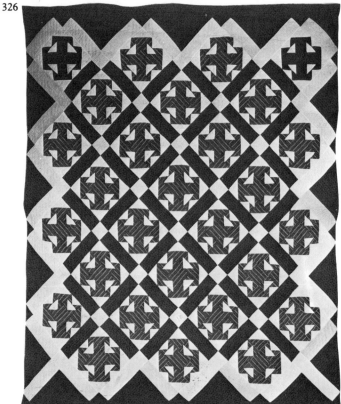

327

324 Hit and Miss: quilt, pieced; cotton; multicoloured; Lanark County, 4th quarter 19th century. W. 150 cm, L. 180 cm (59, 71 in.). An exceptional number of attractive, early printed cottons are used here, including some pieces printed in patchwork designs. [C.C.F.C.S.]

325 World Without End: quilt, pieced, design variant; rose and white cotton; made by Mrs. Charleston, Wellington, Prince Edward County, 4th quarter 19th century. W. 167 cm, L. 232 cm (66, 91 in.). Stars within stars, diamonds within diamonds, world without end. [C.C.F.C.S.]

326 Double T: quilt, pieced; cotton, made in various shades of red combined with white; Blackwell family, Wellington, Prince Edward County, 4th quarter 19th century. W. 172 cm, L. 215 cm (68, 85 in.). [C.C.F.C.S.]

327 Indian Trail: quilt, pieced; cotton; pink, yellow, white and dark blue on a white background; McNab family, White Lake, Renfrew County, 4th quarter 19th century. W. 145 cm, L. 180 cm (57, 71 in.). [C.C.F.C.S.]

328

329

330

331

328 Turkey Tracks, or Wandering Foot: quilt, pieced; cotton; brown and green on a white background; Prince Edward County, 19th century. W. 160 cm, L. 215 cm (63, 85 in.). [U.C.V.]

329 Thousands of Triangles: quilt, pieced; printed cottons; made by a Merkley, Williamsburg, Dundas County, 4th quarter 19th century. W. 159 cm, L. 206 cm (63, 81 in.). Small cuttings from other quilts were saved to make this type of quilt. [P.C.]

330 Birds in Flight: quilt, pieced; cotton; Frontenac County,

4th quarter 19th century. W. 155 cm, L. 184 cm (61, 72 in.). The stylized birds are placed in diagonal rows across the quilt, larger and spaced more widely in the centre as the birds approach and smaller and closer together in the far corners as they fade away. [C.C.F.C.S.]

331 Maple Leaf: quilt, pieced; cotton; olive green and white; made by Elizabeth Dodge, Mainsville, Grenville County, 4th quarter 19th century. W. 152 cm, L. 202 cm (60, 80 in.). This pattern is considered to be of Canadian origin. [E.D.]

332

332 Eight Point Star: quilt, pieced; cotton; Uxbridge area, Ontario County, 1st quarter 19th century. W. 170 cm, L. 200 cm (67, 79 in.).
Many quilt makers painted pictures with their needle and cloth. Here, the stars are placed edge to edge, and the overall effect is that of a
forest floor in autumn. [C.C.F.C.S.]

333

333 Hole in the Barn Door: quilt, pieced; wool and flannelette; made by Mrs. Donald Ferguson, Beachburg, Renfrew County, 4th quarter 19th century. W. 155 cm, L. 180 cm (61, 71 in.). Deep, intense colours were favoured by this quilt maker. [C.C.F.C.S.]

334

335

336

337

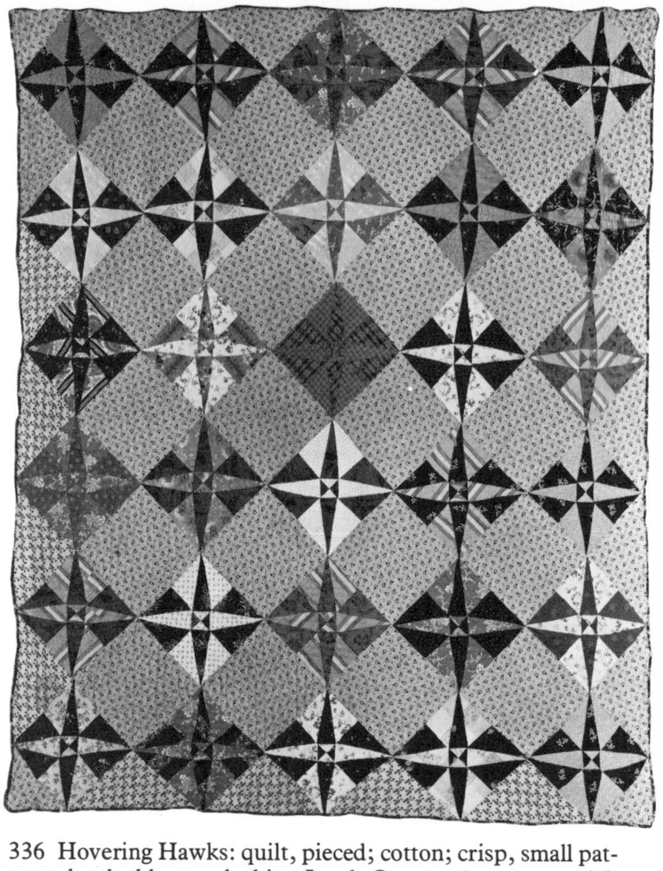

334 Star Puzzle: quilt, pieced; cotton; made by Nellie Silver, Odessa, Lennox and Addington County, 20th century. W. 157 cm, L. 187 cm (62, 74 in.). There is a fascinating play of colours here; the entire quilt is made of different shades and tones of blues, lavenders and mauves. [C.C.F.C.S.]

335 Stepping Stones: quilt, pieced; cotton; Carnahan family, Scotch Corners, Lanark County, 4th quarter 19th century. W. 170 cm, L. 220 cm (67, 87 in.). The bright red block among the muted blues, browns and blacks has been added "for spice." [C.C.F.C.S.]

336 Hovering Hawks: quilt, pieced; cotton; crisp, small patterned reds, blues and white; Leeds County, 1st quarter 19th century. W. 152 cm, L. 187 cm (60, 74 in.). There is one red triangle in the centre of each block, a device which effectively lightens and unites the pattern. [C.C.F.C.S.]

337 Crossed Canoes: quilt, pieced; printed cottons; made by a Merkley, Williamsburg, Dundas County, 4th quarter 19th century. W. 170 cm, L. 206 cm (67, 81 in.). The Merkleys made most of the patterns fashionable at the time. [P.C.]

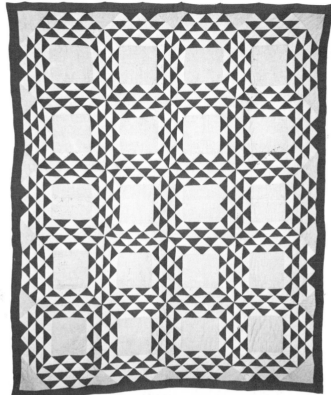

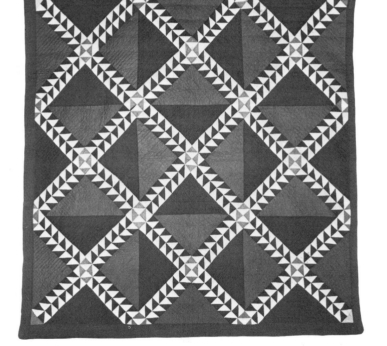

338 Bear's Paw: quilt, pieced; cotton; striped red and black on white; made by Sarah Anne Polk, Portland, Leeds County, 4th quarter 19th century. W. 162 cm, L. 195 cm (64, 77 in.). [C.C.F.C.S.]

339 Ocean Waves: quilt, pieced; red and buff cotton; Lansdowne, Leeds County, early 20th century. W. 165 cm, L. 197 cm (65, 78 in.). The small triangles running in different directions give the restless effect of ocean waves. Women tended to make patterns that reflected what they saw every day. The

woman who made this quilt lived along the shore of the St. Lawrence River. [C.C.F.C.S.]

340 Ocean Waves: quilt, pieced; cotton; multicoloured; made by Miss Scinda Reynolds Hope, Goodwood, Ontario County, ca. 1900. W. 177 cm, L. 205 cm (70, 81 in.). [S.R.H.]

341 Lady of the Lake: quilt, pieced; red, green and white cotton; made by Mrs. Allison, Wellington, Prince Edward County, 1st quarter 19th century. W. 180 cm, L. 185 cm (71, 73 in.). The vivid, restless surface of this quilt symbolizes the lake. [C.C.F.C.S.]

342

342 Johnny-Round-the-Corner, or Rolling Stones: quilt, pieced; cotton; Lennox and Addington County, ca. 1900. W. 145 cm, L. 162 cm (57, 64 in.). This is a vivid quilt with an unusual amount of black used, which is relieved by the rather startling use of white in a few blocks. [R.P.P.]

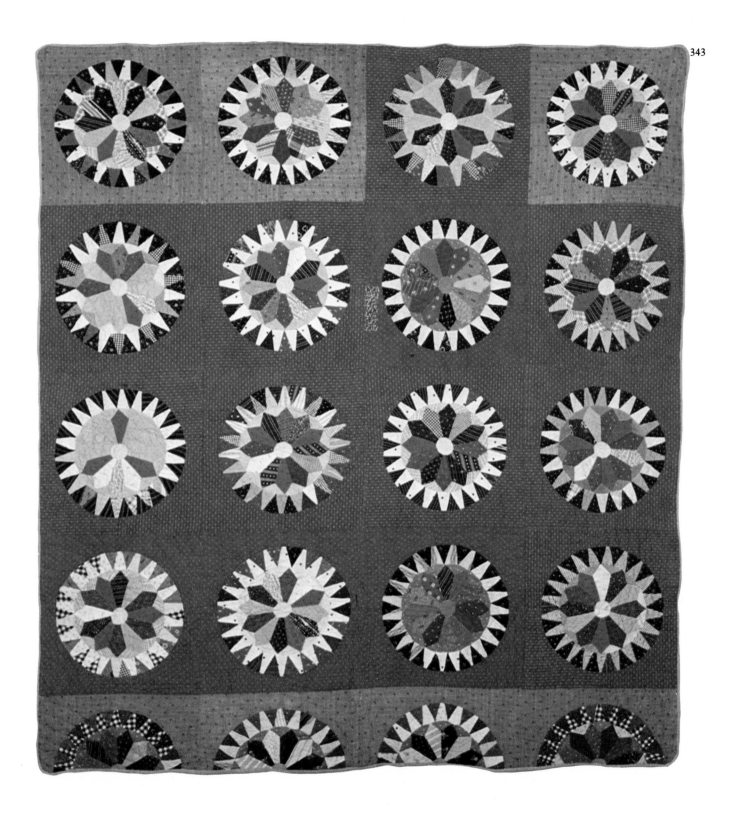

343

343 Pyrotechnics: quilt, pieced; cotton; Wilton, Lennox and Addington County, 3rd quarter 19th century. W. 162 cm, L. 180 cm (64, 71 in.). This is a country quilt in an intricate pattern. [C.C.F.C.S.]

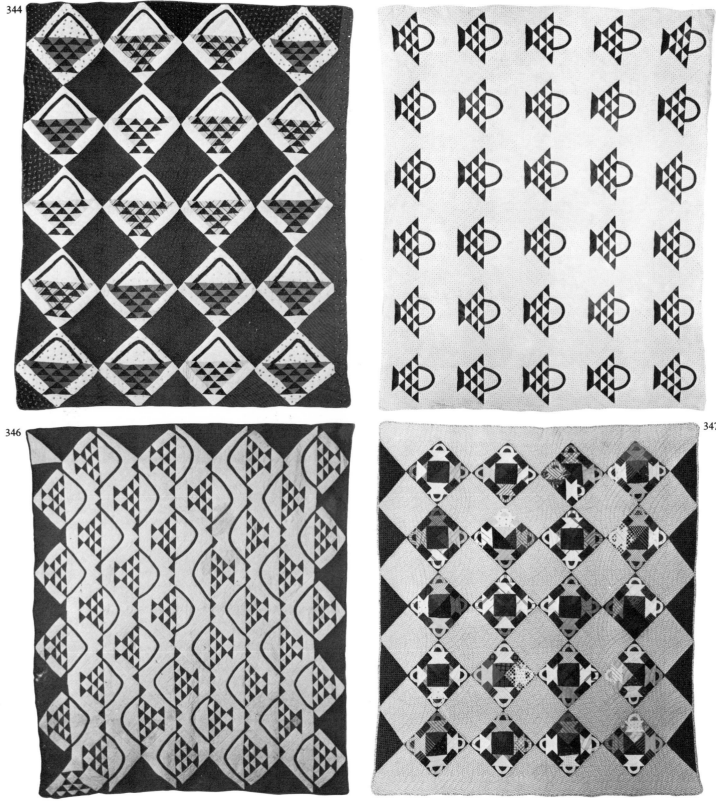

344 Cherry Baskets: quilt, pieced with an appliquéd handle; wool and cotton; Kingston area, Frontenac County, 3rd quarter 19th century. W. 162 cm, L. 200 cm (64, 79 in.). An unusually colourful basket quilt. [C.C.F.C.S.]

345 Cherry Baskets: quilt, pieced with appliquéd handles; made by Emma Van Alstyne, Napanee, Lennox and Addington County, 1st quarter 20th century. W. 155 cm, L. 190 cm (61, 75 in.). More than one generation in this family produced fine quilt makers. [C.C.F.C.S.]

346 Baskets: quilt, pieced with appliquéd handles; pumpkin yellow and white; made by Delilah Way, Northumberland County, ca. 1850. W. 168 cm, L. 187 cm (66, 74 in.). The baskets are stylized, and the handles form scalloped designs across the quilt. [R.B.]

347 Four Baskets: quilt, pieced with appliquéd handles; cotton prints; shades of blue and red predominate; Gananoque, Leeds County, 1st quarter 20th century. W. 154 cm, L. 182 cm (61, 72 in.). The arrangement of the baskets is unusual. [C.C.F.C.S.]

348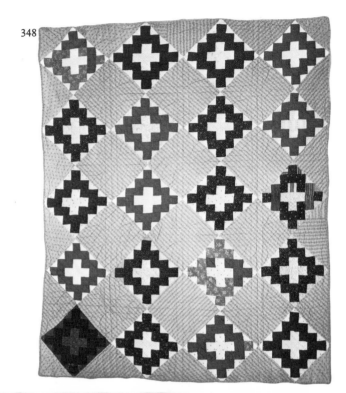

349

50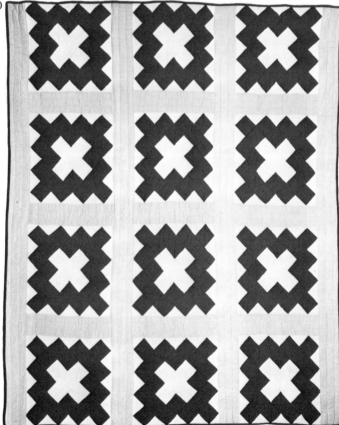

351

348 Five Crosses: quilt, pieced; cotton; Leeds County, 3rd quarter 19th century. W. 160 cm, L. 200 cm (63, 79 in.). Dark, printed crosses on a white print with pink flowered alternate blocks. [C.C.F.C.S.]

349 Chimney Sweep: quilt, pieced; cotton; Amey family, Bath, Lennox and Addington County, 4th quarter 19th century. W. 157 cm, L. 231 cm (62, 91 in.). The pattern looks like the top of an old-fashioned chimney. [C.C.F.C.S.]

350 Chimney Sweep: quilt, pieced; cotton; red, white and yellow; Frontenac County, 4th quarter 19th century. W. 158 cm, L. 200 cm (62, 79 in.). This is a startlingly vivid use of colour for a bedspread. [C.C.F.C.S.]

351 Old Maid's Puzzle: quilt, pieced; cotton; multicoloured; Leeds County, 4th quarter 19th century. W. 167 cm, L. 182 cm (66, 72 in.). Made for everyday use, this quilt is a fine example of the tremendous appeal of 19th century geometric patterns. [C.C.F.C.S.]

352

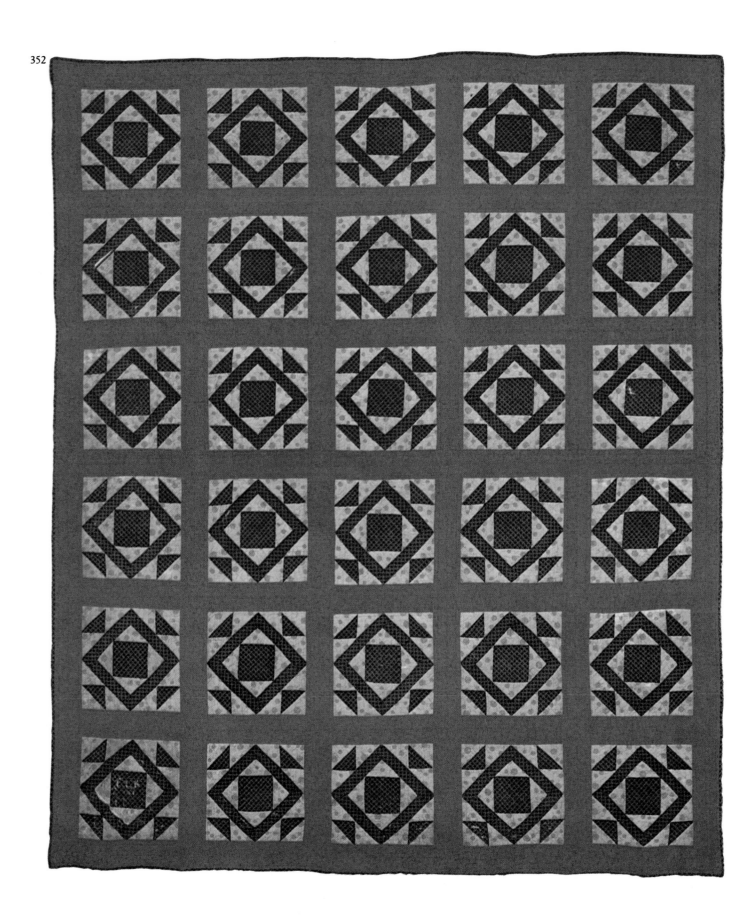

352 Jack in the Pulpit, or Toad in the Puddle: quilt, pieced; cotton; Lennox and Addington County, ca. 1860. W. 170 cm, L. 207 cm (67, 82 in.). A medley of red cottons and a buff background. [C.C.F.C.S.]

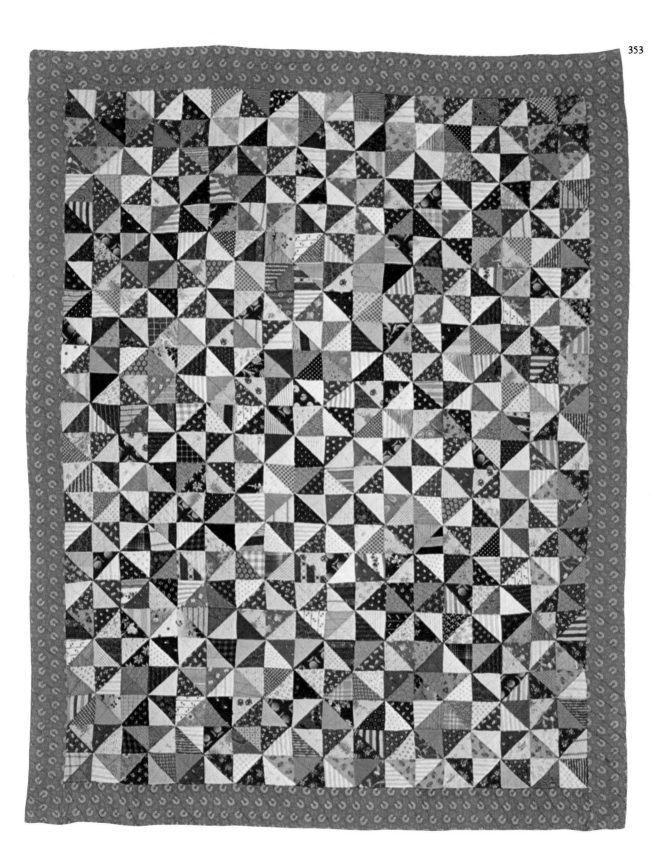

353 Windmill, or Broken Dishes: quilt, pieced; cotton; Wellington, Prince Edward County, ca. 1880. W. 162 cm, L. 210 cm (64, 83 in.). This is a colourful quilt with a lively, briskly moving surface. [C.C.F.C.S.]

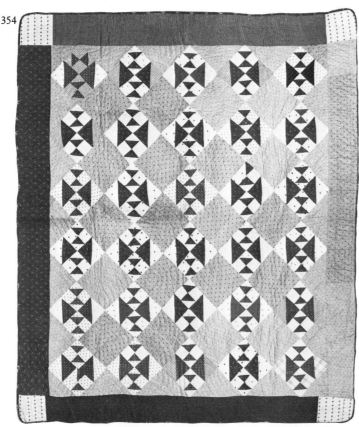

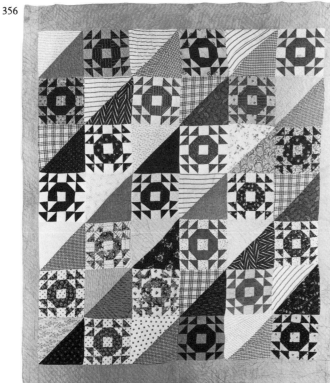

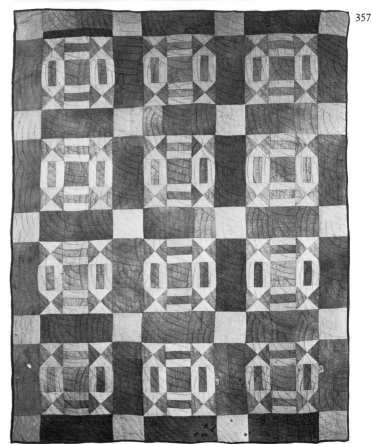

354 Crosses and Losses: quilt, pieced; cotton; Kingston, Frontenac County, 1860-1880. W. 165 cm, L. 192 cm (65, 75 in.). Block corners are used here as in the early central medallion quilts. [C.C.F.C.S.]

355 Cat's Cradle: quilt, pieced; cotton; dark blue and white; McKendry family, South Gower, Grenville County, 4th quarter 19th century. W. 152 cm, L. 167 cm (60, 66 in.). [C.C.F.C.S.]

356 Swallow in the Path: quilt, pieced; cotton; made by a

Merkley, Williamsburg, Dundas County, 4th quarter 19th century. W. 170 cm, L. 260 cm (67, 102 in.). A vivacious arrangement of lights and darks, although all the colours are muted. [P.C.]

357 Beggar's Blocks: quilt, pieced, design variant; cotton; rose and yellow; Belleville area, Hastings County, 1st quarter 20th century. W. 163 cm, L. 207 cm (64, 82 in.). The quilt has been made from bleached and dyed flour or sugar bags. [C.C.F.C.S.]

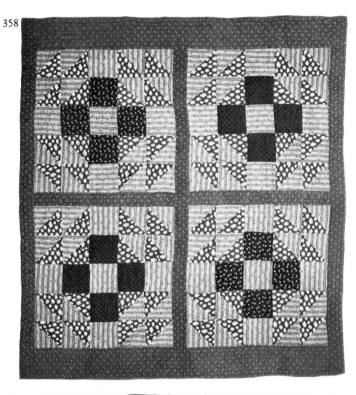

358 Swallow in the Path: quilt, pieced; cotton; reds and blues; made by Mrs. Ferguson, Beachburg, Renfrew County, 20th century. W. 170 cm, L. 185 cm (67, 73 in.). The entire quilt is composed of four large blocks. [C.C.F.C.S.]

359 Windmill: quilt, pieced; glazed cotton; deep pink and dark blue; made by Mrs. Ferguson, Beachburg, Renfrew County, 1st quarter 20th century. W. 182 cm, L. 190 cm (72, 75 in.). The four large blocks making up this quilt are unusual, their appearance almost unrelated to the function of a bedcover, however, the result is dramatic. [C.C.F.C.S.]

360 Eternal Triangle: quilt, pieced; cotton; Carnahan family, Scotch Corners, Lanark County, 4th quarter 19th century. W. 170 cm, L. 220 cm (69, 87 in.). Blue and white printed cotton on an unbleached cotton ground. This is an everyday quilt of great charm and delicacy. [C.C.F.C.S.]

361 Tree Everlasting: quilt, pieced; cotton; red and white; Sydenham area, Frontenac County, 4th quarter 19th century. W. 185 cm, L. 212 cm (73, 83 in.). [C.C.F.C.S.]

362 Churn Dash: quilt, pieced; cotton; red and white; Mustard family, Elgin, Leeds County, 4th quarter 19th century. W. 162 cm, L. 200 cm (64, 79 in.). [C.C.F.C.S.]

363 Hole in the Barn Door: quilt, pieced; cotton; made in a Mennonite family, Vineland area, Lincoln County, 4th quarter 19th century. W. 158 cm, L. 198 cm (62, 78 in.). This pattern, a popular one in the 19th century, was named for the small, heavily framed window cut into the barn door. [C.C.F.C.S.]

364 Mixed Ts: quilt, pieced; cotton; Carnahan family, Scotch Corners, Lanark County, 4th quarter 19th century. W. 160 cm, L. 190 cm (63, 75 in.). The simple repetition of an everyday object creates an interesting pattern. [C.C.F.C.S.]

365 Bourgoyne Surrounded, or Homespun: quilt, pieced; indigo blue and unbleached white cotton; Glengarry County, 4th quarter 19th century. W. 157 cm, L. 170 cm (62, 67 in.). This is a utility quilt. [C.C.F.C.S.]

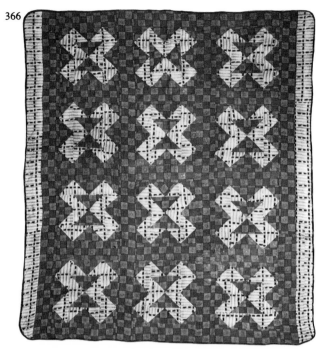

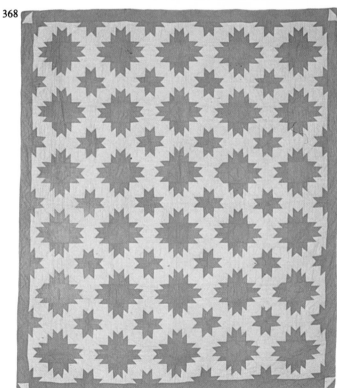

366 The Old Brown Goose: quilt, pieced; cotton; made by Elizabeth Hannah McAndrew, Newboyne, Saskatchewan, 4th quarter 19th century. W. 173 cm, L. 197 cm (68, 77 in.). Used for many years at the home of her grandson near Christie Lake, Lanark County. Although this pattern derives its name from the lullaby "The Old Gray Goose," it was usually made in brown, a more pleasing colour for bedding. [C.C.F.C.S.]

367 Four Patch: quilt, pieced; design variant; printed cottons; made by Mrs. Hubble, Stirling, Hastings County, ca. 1900. W. 148 cm, L. 187 cm (58, 74 in.). Each block consists of four units, and each unit is composed of sixteen squares separated by red and white sawtooth strips. The blocks are joined by red and white lattice strips in a Wild Goose Chase pattern. [C.C.F.C.S.]

368 Pineapple: quilt, pieced; cotton; green and white; made by Jane Sears King, Elginburg, Frontenac County, 1st quarter 20th century. W. 180 cm, L. 220 cm (71, 87 in.). This is an attractive quilt showing the effective use of a simple border, yet it is a complicated pattern, called Pineapple by the family. [A.S.]

369 The Jennie Quilt: cotton, pieced; made by Jennie Covey (1886-1906) using the samples from a sample book given to her by an uncle who was a salesman. W. 163 cm, L. 198 cm (64, 78 in.). The top was finished and quilted by Ila Wood and her mother-in-law in Kingston, Frontenac County. This quilt followed the time-honoured tradition of handing a quilt down to a member of the family in each generation bearing the same Christian name as the maker. [I.W.]

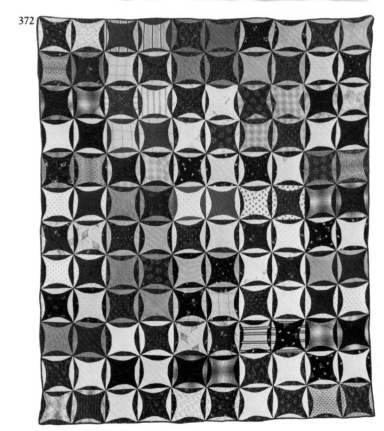

370 Rob Peter to Pay Paul, or Wheel of Mystery: quilt, pieced; cotton; red and white; Leeds County, 4th quarter 19th century. W. 170 cm, L. 225 cm (67, 89 in.). Large circles form within the total pattern of smaller circles. [C.C.F.C.S.]

371 Rob Peter to Pay Paul, or Wheel of Mystery: quilt, pieced, design variant; red and white cotton; Frontenac County, early 20th century. W. 165 cm, L. 187 cm (65, 74 in.). [C.C.F.C.S.]

372 Rob Peter to Pay Paul, or Orange Peel: quilt, pieced; cotton; made by a Merkley, Williamsburg, Dundas County, 4th quarter 19th century. W. 159 cm, L. 206 cm (63, 81 in.). The colours are dark and restrained, but two bright red blocks are set in the centre with two rose ones elsewhere. The whole surface is kept moving by the repeated black patches, while the red and rose areas break up the monotony. [P.C.]

373 Rob Peter to Pay Paul, or Drunkard's Path: quilt, pieced; cotton; red and white; Smith's Falls, Lanark County, 1st quarter 19th century. W. 167 cm, L. 190 cm (66, 75 in.). [C.C.F.C.S.]

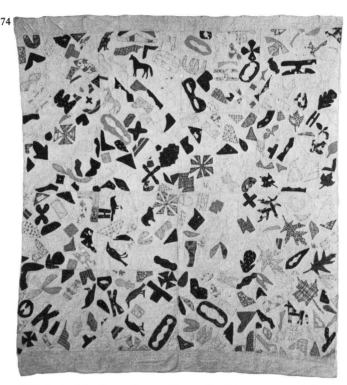

374 End of the Scrap Bag: quilt, appliquéd; cotton; made by Jean Horn, Utica, Ontario County, 1889. W. 160 cm, L. 180 cm (63, 71 in.). Small scraps left at the bottom of the rag bag were cut into designs dictated by the shape of the scrap and appliquéd to a foundation sheet. The figures are small: horses, leaves, dogs, masks, letters, etc. The designs used here are similar to those in a much more elaborate quilt made in England during the 19th

century and illustrated in Averil Colby's *Patchwork*. This quilt was made by an aunt of the present owner. [I.D.]

374a Detail. As some fabrics have faded more than others, some details stand out; there is a great profusion of small shapes. This type of quilt was fun to make.

375

375 Central Square in a Diamond: quilt, pieced; handspun, handwoven wool; Leeds County, 2nd quarter 19th century. W. 152 cm, L. 195 cm (60, 77 in.). This was a common format in early homespun quilts found throughout the eastern counties, although this example is particularly powerful. [C.C.F.C.S.]

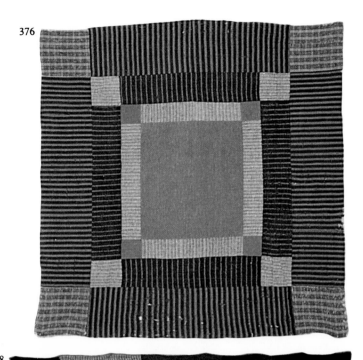

376 Central Square: quilt top, pieced; handspun, handwoven wool (used materials); Farquharson family, Renfrew County, 3rd quarter 19th century. W. 140 cm, L. 140 cm (55, 55 in.). Each border is wider than the previous one, and the orange colour is carried outward from the centre to the edges. [P.C.]

377 Central Square with Bars: quilt, pieced; handspun, handwoven wool; Urquart family, Dunvegan, Glengarry County, 4th quarter 19th century. W. 155 cm, L. 162 cm (61, 64 in.). This machine quilted example has been made of left-overs. [C.C.F.C.S.]

378 Hit and Miss: quilt, pieced; handspun, handwoven wool; Wilno area, Renfrew County, 4th quarter 19th century. W. 142 cm, L. 185 cm (56, 73 in.). The arrangement of the bright orange and blue checked patches in contrast with the black in this wild Hit and Miss pattern is reminiscent of the painted furniture from the Wilno area. [C.C.F.C.S.]

379 Stripes: quilt, pieced; handspun, handwoven wool; vivid, almost luminous red; Glengarry County, 3rd quarter 19th century. W. 150 cm, L. 172 cm (59, 68 in.). [C.C.F.C.S.]

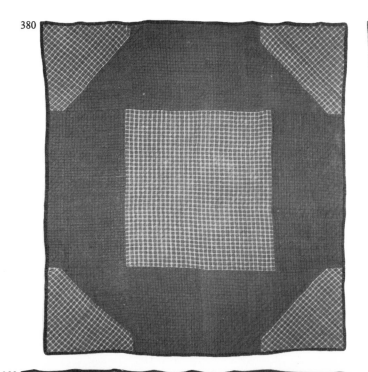

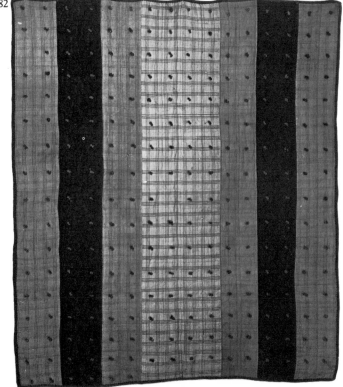

380 Central Square in a Diamond: quilt, pieced; handspun, handwoven wool; Kingston area, Frontenac County, 3rd quarter 19th century. W. 175 cm, L. 185 cm (69, 73 in.). This is a simple, early design using blue and red check, blue predominating. [J.M.]

381 One Patch: quilt, pieced; wool, some handspun, handwoven; made by Mrs. Adam Ritchie, Perth Road, Frontenac County, 3rd quarter 19th century. W. 162 cm, L. 192 cm (64, 76 in.). A cross-bar set of dark brown rectangles joined by light squares sharply delineates the quilt. [N.R.]

382 Stripes: quilt, pieced; handspun, handwoven wool; rose, buff and black; Ilderton, Middlesex County. W. 167 cm, L.

195 cm (66, 77 in.). Made in a traditional manner with seven stripes. [P.B.]

383 Diamonds, or Snake Fence: quilt, pieced; handspun, handwoven wool with a cotton weft; rose and black with one light gray area; English family, Hastings County, 3rd quarter 19th century. W. 142 cm, L. 185 cm (56, 73 in.). [C.C.F.C.S.]

384

384 Central Square with Borders: quilt, pieced; handspun, handwoven cloth; deep grays on rose; Urquart family, Dunvegan,
Glengarry County, 4th quarter 19th century. W. 171 cm, L. 181 cm (67, 71 in.). The contrasting block corners in the borders or frames
make an interesting allover design. [C.C.F.C.S.]

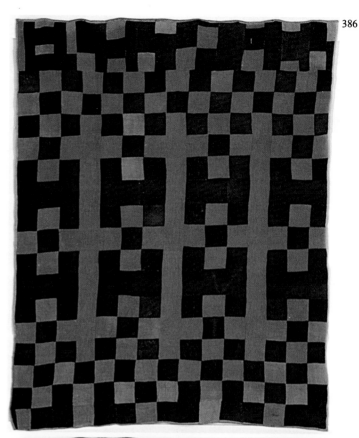

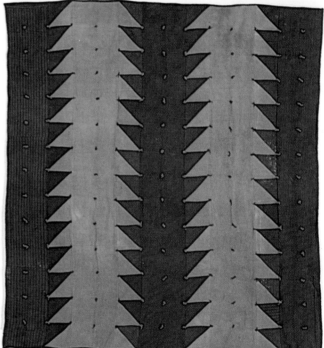

orange red and black; Tamworth area, Lennox and Addington County, 2nd quarter 19th century. W. 162 cm, L. 205 cm (64, 81 in.). The H and L undoubtedly stand for Holy Lord and are intended to protect the sleeping person. [C.C.F.C.S.]

385 Shoo-Fly: quilt; pieced; handspun, handwoven wool on cotton; purplish red and brown; Centreville, Lennox and Addington County, 2nd quarter 19th century. W. 165 cm, L. 192 cm (65, 76 in.). The same splotchy purple dye was used for many homespun quilts and is said to have been made from sumac flowers and butternut branches. Originally the colour would have been brilliant. [C.C.F.C.S.]

386 H-L: quilt; pieced; handspun, handwoven wool; vivid

387 Nine Patch: quilt, pieced; handspun, handwoven wool; purplish blue with red plaid blocks; Tamworth, Lennox and Addington County. W. 177 cm, L. 220 cm (70, 87 in.). [C.C.F.C.S.]

388 Tree Everlasting: quilt, pieced; handspun, handwoven wool, possibly some commercial woollens; from a Mennonite family, Jordan Station area, Lincoln County, 3rd quarter 19th century. W. 165 cm, L. 180 cm (65, 71 in.). [C.C.F.C.S.]

389

389 Album Quilt: pieced and appliquéd; wool, some handspun, handwoven pieces; from the Sandy McMartin family, Martintown, Glengarry County, 2nd quarter 19th century. W. 160 cm, L. 165 cm (63, 65 in.). The quilt has blocks of various patterns showing symbols dear to the heart of a child: Tree of Paradise, Windmills, Sugar Cone, Old Gray Goose, and Wild Goose Chase. A large H stands above the Tree of Paradise, presumably indicating heaven. A handsome chevron border goes up one side and partly down the other. This quilt is bright and lively, and has that indefinable quality of folk art. [C.C.F.C.S.]

390

391

392

393

century. W. 167 cm, L. 192 cm (66, 75 in.). The pink star on a brown background gives this quilt a dramatic simplicity. [C.C.F.C.S.]

390 World Without End: quilt, pieced; handspun, handwoven wool; red and dark green; Tamworth area, Lennox and Addington County, 3rd quarter 19th century. W. 147 cm, L. 194 cm (58, 76 in.). This pattern creates an illusion, because it is made up of two separate patterns combined in such a way that when the quilt is viewed from one angle large stars appear, while from another angle diamonds, triangles and squares emerge. [C.C.F.C.S.]

391 Variable Star: quilt, pieced; handspun, handwoven wool with cotton weft; Lansdowne, Leeds County, 3rd quarter 19th

392 Bars: quilt, pieced; handspun, handwoven wool, arranged like bricks with strips between the rows; Glengarry County, 3rd quarter 19th century. W. 145 cm, L. 180 cm (57, 71 in.). Aside from the interesting design, this important quilt contains a sampler of twenty-six different colours and patterns of handwoven cloth. [P.C.]

393 Snake Fence: quilt, pieced; handspun, handwoven wool; blues, grays and orange; Schermerhorn family, made by Millie South or her mother, Forest Mills Road, Lennox and Addington County, 3rd quarter 19th century. W. 152 cm, L. 170 cm (60, 67 in.). [C.C.F.C.S.]

394

394 Central Square with Frames: quilt; manufactured and homewoven woollens; browns and blacks with lighter colours in the central blocks; Lonsdale area, Hastings County, 3rd quarter 19th century. W. 166 cm, L. 190 cm (65, 75 in.). The central square is made up of nine patch blocks alternating with plain ones. The striking sawtooth outer border echoes the colours of the inner border. [C.C.F.C.S.]

395

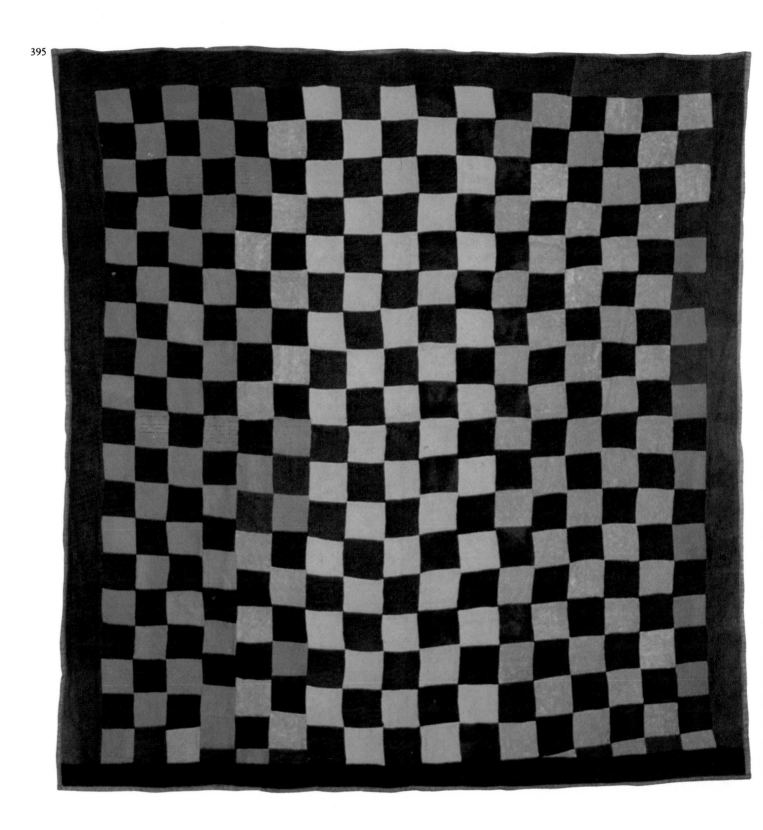

395 Amberina: quilt, one patch; handspun, handwoven wool; Sterling family, Markham area, York County, 3rd quarter 19th century. W. 165 cm, L. 168 cm (65, 66 in.). The patches are arranged in a colour scheme suggestive of amberina glass, a type of art glass popular in the nineteenth century that varies in colour from amber to ruby. [C.C.F.C.S.]

396

396 Hit and Miss: quilt, pieced; wool with some handwoven patches; Urquart family, Dunvegan, Glengarry County, 3rd quarter 19th century. W. 140 cm, L. 175 cm (55, 69 in.). The colours on the front are dark with a few vivid patches; the back is a startling rose handwoven flannel, probably a dyed blanket. [C.C.F.C.S.]

397 Clay's Choice: quilt, pieced; red and black wool (manufactured and homespun); Hastings County, 4th quarter 19th century. W. 173 cm, L. 195 cm (68, 77 in.). This is one of the numerous windmill patterns. [C.C.F.C.S.]

399 Geometric Star: quilt, pieced; wool, some homespun patches; orange red with blacks and grays; handwoven by Annie McGregor (great-great-grandmother of the present owner), Glengarry County, 3rd quarter 19th century. W. 163 cm, L. 167 cm (64, 66 in.). Colour is used sparsely but effectively here. [J.M.]

400 Harvest Sun: quilt, pieced; handspun, handwoven wool with a cotton weft; rusty red and black; Scugog Island, Ontario County, 3rd quarter 19th century. W. 172 cm, L. 217 cm (68, 85 in.). [S.S.M.]

401 Orange Peel: quilt, pieced; thin wool, possibly handwoven; blue on an orange background; Niagara Peninsula, ca. 1840. W. 180 cm, L. 192 cm (71, 76 in.). The quilting follows the lines of the pattern, and the border is quilted in hearts, tulips and vines. [U.C.V.]

398 Wholecloth Quilt: handspun, handwoven wool; orange and gray stripes; Luloff family, Renfrew County, 3rd quarter 19th century. W. 170 cm, L. 177 cm (67, 70 in.). Quilted in sweeping curves arranged to form a large diamond in the centre. The back is made from homespun wool, and the filling is loose wool. The entire quilt is quilted with homespun yarn, a tremendous undertaking. [R.L.]

402

402 Stripes: quilt, pieced; wool; Durham County, 4th quarter 19th century. W. 162 cm, L. 200 cm (64, 79 in.). [S.S.M.]

403 Star of Bethlehem: quilt, pieced; wool; glowing reds and blues against a black sky; Ontario County, 4th quarter 19th century. W. 157 cm, L. 210 cm (62, 83 in.). [S.S.M.]

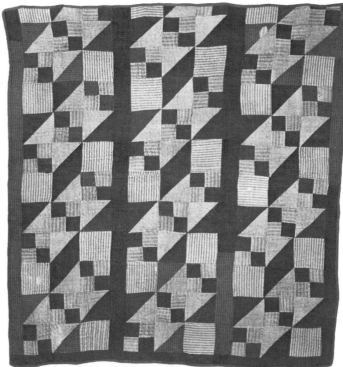

404 Basket and Daisy (four petals): quilt, pieced and appliquéd; handspun, handwoven wool; rose and black; Kitchener, Waterloo County, 3rd quarter 19th century. W. 175 cm, L. 197 cm (69, 78 in.). Both the flowers and basket handles are appliquéd, and the quilting is done in closely spaced lines echoing the pattern. This is an exceptionally fine quilt. [R.P.P.]

405 Jacob's Ladder, Stepping Stones, or The Tail of Benjamin's Kite: quilt, pieced; handwoven wool; roses and browns; Elgin, Leeds County, 4th quarter 19th century. W. 160 cm, L. 170 cm (63, 67 in.). A complicated pattern for a homespun quilt. [C.C.F.C.S.]

406 Eight Point Star: quilt, pieced; homespun, handwoven

wool on cotton; orange, black and lime green; Uxbridge area, Ontario County, 3rd quarter 19th century. W. 155 cm, L. 190 cm (61, 75 in.). An example of firm and close quilting. [M.J.S.]

407 Star of Bethlehem: quilt, pieced; assorted woollens; Durham County, 4th quarter 19th century. W. 157 cm, L. 212 cm (62, 83 in.). In spite of the fact that this quilt is composed of discarded coats and other heavy materials, a lively and vivacious result was achieved. [C.C.F.C.S.]

408 Star of Bethlehem: quilt, pieced; wool (some homespun); reds, blacks and grays; Durham County, ca. 1860. W. 160 cm, L. 180 cm (63, 71 in.). This is a country quilt, made of used materials, but very successful. The black triangles joining the red points are dramatic touches. [P.B.]

409 Orange Peel: quilt, pieced; homespun, handwoven wool in soft coloured plaids; Richmond family, Slash Road, near Napanee, Lennox and Addington County, 4th quarter 19th century. W. 180 cm, L. 190 cm (71, 75 in.). [C.C.F.C.S]

410 Flyfoot, or Catch Me If You Can: quilt, pieced; wool and handwoven flannel; made by Jane Armstrong, Richmond, Carleton County, 4th quarter 19th century. W. 150 cm, L. 165 cm (59, 65 in.). The pattern is in dark colours with a rose set and background; a few blocks have light backgrounds for accent. [C.C.F.C.S.]

411

411 Indian Hatchet: quilt, pieced; handspun, handwoven wool; Winchester area, Dundas County, 3rd quarter 19th century. W. 155 cm, L. 190 cm (61, 75 in.). An atmosphere of foreboding is created by the ominous colours. [C.C.F.C.S.]

412

412 Wholecloth Quilt: handspun, handwoven wool; Luloff family, Golden Lake area, Renfrew County, 3rd quarter 19th century. W. 170 cm, L. 195 cm (67, 77 in.). Woven in large checks that look like patchwork. [C.C.F.C.S.]

413

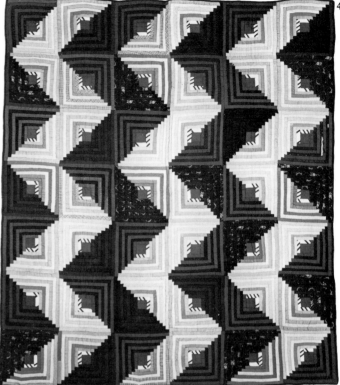

414

415

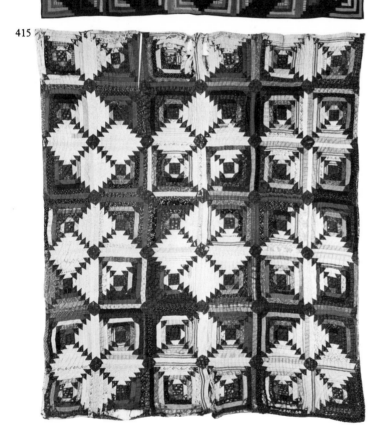

416

413 Log Cabin, Barn Raising: quilt, pieced; assorted fabrics; multicoloured; made by Mrs. Lebadoff, Oshawa, Ontario County, 1920. W. 182 cm, L. 197 cm (72, 78 in.). Mrs. Lebadoff was a Mennonite of Russian origin who lived in Manitoba before coming to Oshawa. [R.L.]

414 Log Cabin, Zig-Zag: quilt, pieced; cotton, wool and silk; multicoloured; made by Phoebe Ann Saylor, Bloomfield, Prince Edward County, before her marriage in 1862 when she was seventeen, signed "P. A. S." in red wool embroidery. W. 171 cm, L. 202 cm (67, 80 in.). [P.E.C.M.]

415 Log Cabin, Wild Goose Chase: quilt, pieced and appliquéd;

cotton; Hartington, Frontenac County, 3rd quarter 19th century. W. 145 cm, L. 167 cm (57, 66 in.). Small triangles of red cotton are sewn across the corners of the squares formed by the logs, an unusual pattern. [C.C.F.C.S.]

416 Log Cabin, Steps to the Courthouse: quilt, pieced; wool and linen; black, gray and red; Lennox and Addington County, ca. 1860. W. 167 cm, L. 208 cm (66, 82 in.). The pattern is a variant of the Log Cabin type, similar in overall effect but different in construction. Nevertheless, most old quilters agree that any quilt using "logs" or narrow strips of folded cloth is a Log Cabin. [C.C.F.C.S.]

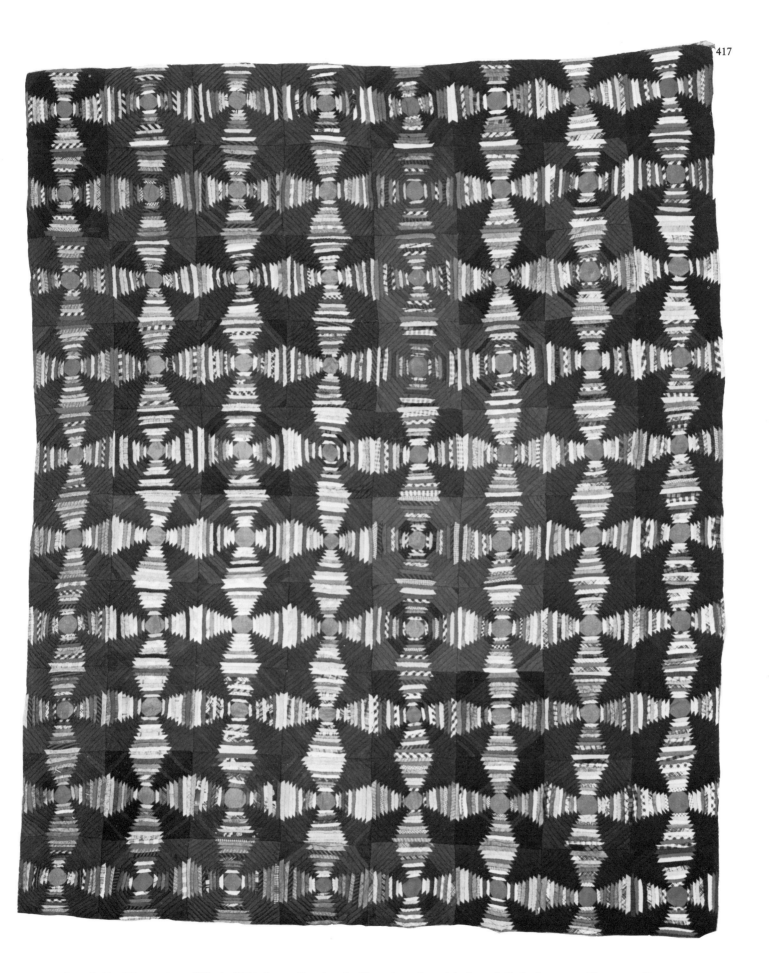

417

417 Log Cabin, Pineapple, or Windmill Blades: quilt, pieced; silk and wool; multicoloured; Sydenham area, Frontenac County, ca. 1890. W. 145 cm, L. 175 cm (57, 69 in.). The use of miniature ''logs'' must have required infinite patience. [C.C.F.C.S.]

418

418   Log Cabin, Pineapple, or Windmill Blades: quilt, pieced; wool and cotton; made by Amelia Crozier, Napanee, Lennox and Addington County, 1st quarter 20th century. W. 160 cm, L. 187 cm (63, 74 in.). [C.C.F.C.S.]

419

419 Log Cabin, Chevron: quilt, pieced; cotton; Verona, Frontenac County, ca. 1900. W. 165 cm, L. 167 cm (65, 66 in.). Each strip radiating out from the gray centres of the blocks is a brighter colour. The last strip is a vivid orange. In this strange quilt, the hearths are cold, and the brightly coloured roads lead away from home. [C.C.F.C.S.]

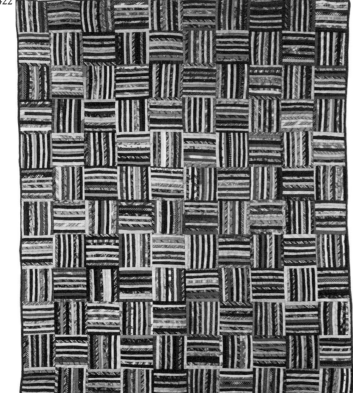

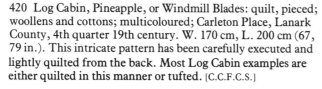

420 Log Cabin, Pineapple, or Windmill Blades: quilt, pieced; woollens and cottons; multicoloured; Carleton Place, Lanark County, 4th quarter 19th century. W. 170 cm, L. 200 cm (67, 79 in.). This intricate pattern has been carefully executed and lightly quilted from the back. Most Log Cabin examples are either quilted in this manner or tufted. [C.C.F.C.S.]

421 Log Cabin, Chevron, or "V" Pattern: quilt, pieced; wool, silk and cotton; multicoloured, red predominant; made by Mrs. Spencer, Kingston, Frontenac County, ca. 1860. W. 140 cm, L. 192 cm (55, 76 in.). This is an unusually vivid and sparkling quilt. [C.C.F.C.S.]

422 Log Cabin, Fence Rails: quilt, pieced; silk and cotton; Sydenham area, Frontenac County, 4th quarter 19th century. W. 155 cm, L. 180 cm (61, 71 in.). The strong yellow log in each block draws the entire design together. [C.C.F.C.S.]

423 Log Cabin, Barn Raising: quilt, pieced; wool; browns with touches of white; made by Jane Armstrong Dawson, Richmond, Carleton County, 3rd quarter 19th century. W. 155 cm, L. 167 cm (61, 66 in.). The few scraps of white silk brocade are probably cuttings from a wedding dress. Scraps from wedding dresses and marriage suits were used in many quilts. [C.C.F.C.S.]

424

425

426

427

424 Log Cabin, Barn Raising: quilt, pieced; homespun wool and cotton; a flat surface dotted with red hearths; Bloomfield, Prince Edward County, ca. 1860. W. 157 cm, L. 200 cm (62, 79 in.). There are several different patterns of Log Cabin quilts; the name depends upon the way the light and dark areas are arranged. [C.C.F.C.S.]

425 Log Cabin, Light and Dark, or Sawlog: quilt, pieced; cotton and wool; made in Hastings County, on the back is written: "for Harvey Hills made by Gramma in her 82nd year in the year 1893". W. 180 cm, L. 202 cm (71, 79 in.). [C.C.F.C.S.]

426 Log Cabin, Light and Dark: quilt, pieced; silk and wool; Sydenham area, Frontenac County, 3rd quarter 19th century, tied and backed at a later date. W. 172 cm, L. 185 cm (68, 73 in.). [C.C.F.C.S.]

427 Log Cabin, Straight Furrow: quilt, pieced; wools, velvets, prints and plaids; Leeds County, 3rd quarter 19th century. W. 152 cm, L. 185 cm (60, 73 in.). This is a crisp looking quilt with a large red hearth and narrow logs. [C.C.F.C.S.]

428

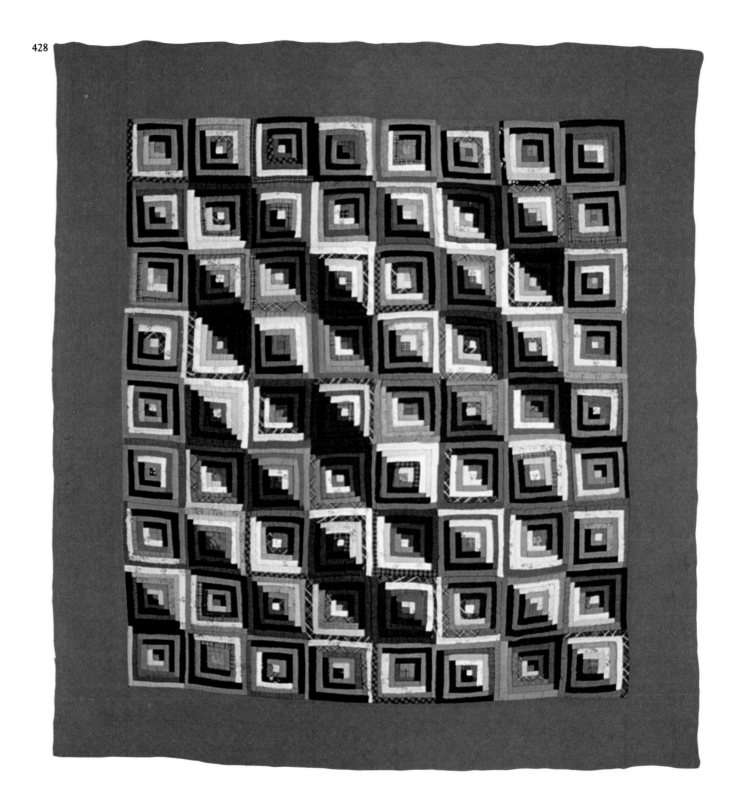

428 Log Cabin, Straight Furrow: quilt, pieced; assorted materials, mostly wools; Durham County, 1st quarter 20th century. W. 180 cm, L. 200 cm (71, 79 in.). This is a handsome quilt, but its wide, red woollen border reduces the graphic impact of the quilt as a whole. [C.C.F.C.S.]

429 Crazy Quilt: pieced; silks, cottons, and wools, fans arranged to form half wheels; made by Mrs. Adam Ritchie, Perth Road, Frontenac County, ca. 1925. W. 157 cm, L. 210 cm (62, 83 in.). The present owner, the maker's granddaughter, can remember helping to card the wool from the family flock of sheep that was used for the filling. [N.R.]

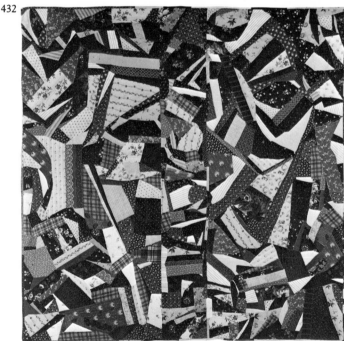

430 Fannie's Fan: quilt, pieced; wool; made by Miss Scinda Reynolds Hope, Stouffville, York County, ca. 1900. W. 162 cm, L. 197 cm (64, 78 in.). Fannie's Fan was one of the patterns popular during the period in which a familiar object was repeated to form the design. [R.Y.]

431 Crazy Throw: quilt, pieced; silks and satins; multicoloured; Hastings County, ca. 1900. W. 135 cm, L. 140 cm (53, 55 in.). This is a presentation quilt; the blocks have been embroidered by various friends. There is a great variety of motifs used: sheaves of wheat, a little dog begging, birds, flowers, garden rakes and a chair embroidered in silk threads. [C.C.F.C.S.]

432 Crazy Quilt: printed cottons; multicoloured; Carleton Place, Lanark County, 4th quarter 19th century. W. 186 cm, L. 188 cm (73, 74 in.). A lightweight summer quilt, backed, quilted, but unstuffed. [C.C.F.C.S.]

433 Friendship, or Name Quilt: white cotton with red embroidery; Wilton area, Lennox and Addington County, ca. 1920. W. 151 cm, L. 189 cm (59, 74 in.). This type of quilt was usually made by a church group; names were collected and then embroidered onto it. Each person paid about fifty cents to have his or her name used. After the quilt was finished it was sold to raise money for the church, or presented to a retiring minister. [C.C.F.C.S.]

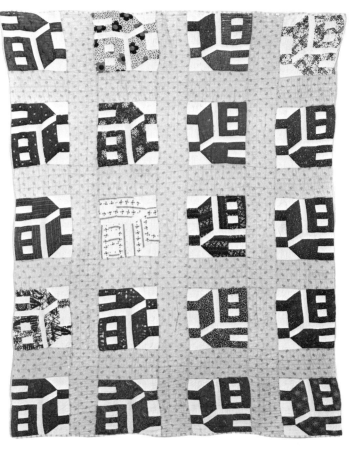

434 Little House: quilt, pieced; cotton; multicoloured; Frontenac County, 1st quarter 20th century. W. 132 cm, L. 172 cm (52, 68 in.). Two of the little houses have been replaced, probably because the originals wore out. The quilt appears to have been made from scraps of a little girl's dresses. [C.C.F.C.S.]

435 Garden Maze: quilt, pieced; wool and cotton; orange and black; Winchester area, Dundas County, 1st quarter 20th century. W. 165 cm, L. 180 cm (65, 71 in.). This is a rural quilt with an unusual colour combination. [C.C.F.C.S.]

436 Dresden Plate, or Aster: quilt, pieced and appliquéd; cotton; Gananoque, Leeds County, 20th century. W. 165 cm, L. 180 cm (65, 71 in.). This was a well-loved pattern. The deep peach coloured petals, with the same colour repeated in the centre of the flower, make this an attractive example of the pattern. The petals are lightly stuffed. [C.C.F.C.S.]

437

437 Crazy Wheels: quilt, pieced and appliquéd; cotton; Ontario County, ca. 1920. W. 152 cm, L. 200 cm (60, 79 in.). The wheels were pieced and then appliquéd with feather stitches. The little wheels running merrily along contribute to the quilt's overall gaiety. [S.S.M.]

438 Mosaic: quilt, pieced; cotton; Kingston, Frontenac County, 1st quarter 20th century. W. 157 cm, L. 190 cm (62, 75 in.). The design is formed by tiny hexagonal blocks arranged to resemble ancient floor tiles. [C.C.F.C.S.]

439

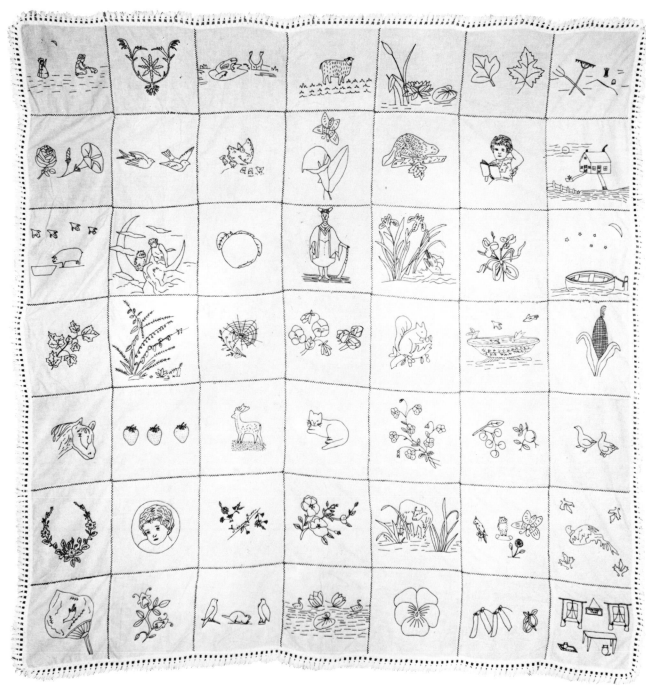

439 Bedspread: embroidered; cotton; Moscow area, Lennox and Addington County, ca. 1920. W. 170 cm, L. 185 cm, (67, 73 in.). Some of the designs are homedrawn, possibly by a child. She drew the scenes, animals and people dear to her. This type of bedspread was popular between 1890 and 1920, although embroidery transfers were more commonly used for the patterns. Exterior and interior views of the maker's house are shown. [L.A.S.]

440

440 Trip Around the World: quilt, pieced; cotton; Lennox and Addington County, 1st quarter 20th century. W. 175 cm, L. 212 cm (69, 83 in.). The colours are skillfully blended to carry the eye from the centre along the lines of the pattern to the outside border. [C.C.F.C.S.]

441

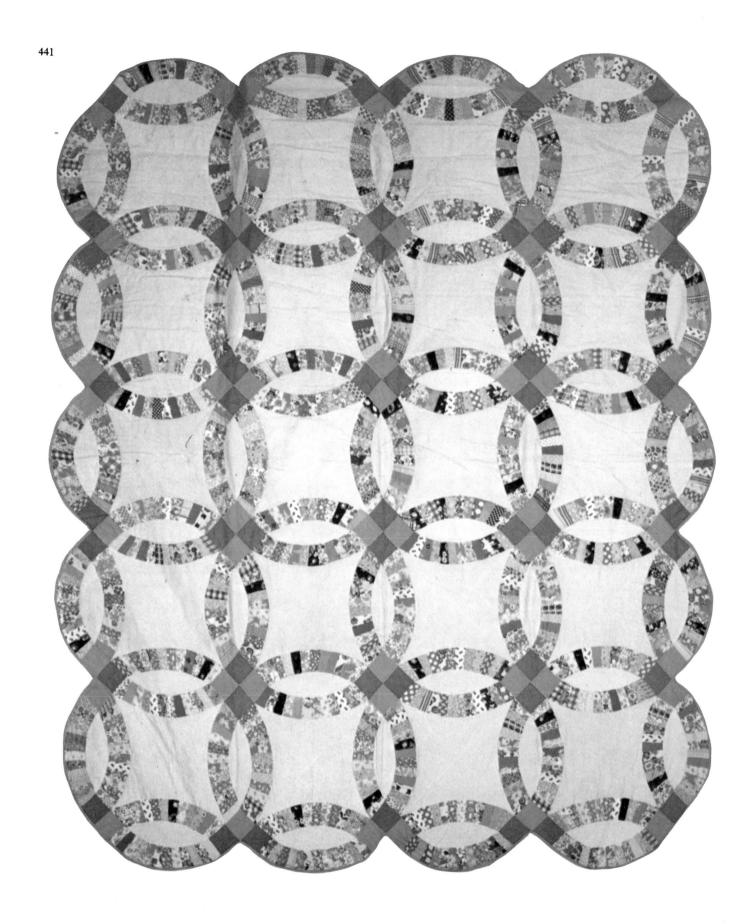

441 Double Wedding Ring: quilt, pieced and appliquéd; cotton: Picton, Prince Edward County, 1st quarter 20th century. W. 183 cm, L. 223 cm (72, 88 in.). The making of a Double Wedding Ring was considered quite a feather in one's cap in the early part of the century. [C.C.F.C.S.]

Notes

Notes to Chapter 1 (pages 13 to 18)

1 Quoted in Margaret Angus, "The McCauley Family of Kingston" in *Historic Kingston: Transactions of the Kingston Historical Society* (Belleville: Mika Publishing Company, 1974), V, p. 4.

2 R. C. M. Grant, *The Story of Martintown* (Published by the Author, 1974), p. 16.

3 Richard Preston, *Kingston Before the War of 1812* (Toronto: University of Toronto Press, 1959), pp. 67-68.

4 Ibid., p. 80.

5 John Ross Robertson, ed., *The Diary of Mrs. Simcoe* (Toronto: William Briggs, 1911), p. 184.

6 Ibid., p. 74.

7 William Canniff, *The Settlement of Upper Canada* (Toronto: Dudley & Burns, 1869), p. 212.

8 Walter S. Herrington, *History of the County of Lennox and Addington* (Toronto: Macmillan Company of Canada, 1913), p. 35.

9 Robertson, *Diary of Mrs. Simcoe*, p. 184.

10 Ibid., p. 256.

11 Canniff, *Settlement of Upper Canada*, p. 214.

12 Jean S. McGill, *A Pioneer History of the County of Lanark* (Toronto, 1969), p. 92.

13 H. H. Langton, ed., *The Journals of Anne Langton, A Gentlewoman in Upper Canada* (Toronto: Clarke, Irwin & Company, 1950), p. 88.

14 Ibid., p. 74.

15 Ibid., p. 98.

16 Ibid., p. 230.

17 [Catherine Parr Traill], *The Backwoods of Canada, Being Letters from the Wife of an Emigrant Officer* (London: Charles Knight, 1836), p. 151.

18 Ibid., p. 170.

19 John Howison, *Sketches of Upper Canada* (Edinburgh: Oliver & Boyd, 1821), p. 239.

20 McGill, *Pioneer History*, p. 67.

21 Ibid., p. 69.

Notes to Chapter 2 (pages 19 to 27)

1 Edwin Guillet, *The Pioneer Farmer and Backwoodsman* (Toronto: University of Toronto Press, 1963), pp. 198-199.

2 Herbert C. Burleigh, ed., *Samuel Sherwood's Account Book, 1785-1810* (Kingston: Dr. H.C. Burleigh, 1975), p. 60.

3 From an account book kept by A. Jones, Prescott, between 1829 and 1833, which is now in a private collection.

4 "Roderick Matheson's Letter Books, 1815-1851," in the author's collection.

5 William Dunlop, *Tiger Dunlop's Upper Canada* (Toronto: McClelland and Stewart, 1967), p. 129.

6 Ibid., pp. 16-17.

7 R. C. M. Grant, *The Story of Martintown* (Published by the Author, 1974), p. 39, p. 109.

8 In 1792, Samuel Sherwood sold David Palmer "a Spindle for wheel," see *Samuel Sherwood's Account Book*, p. 37.

9 Quoted from a letter in the author's collection.

10 John Howison, *Sketches of Upper Canada* (Edinburgh: Oliver & Boyd, 1821), p. 18.

11 [Catherine Parr Traill], *The Backwoods of Canada, Being Letters from the Wife of an Emigrant Officer* (London: Charles Knight, 1836), pp. 46-47.

12 E. C. Beer, "The Diary of J. B. Marks, 1825," in *Historic Kingston: Transactions of the Kingston Historical Society* (Belleville: Mika Publishing Company, 1974), VI, p. 30.

13 Walter S. Herrington, *History of the County of Lennox and Addington* (Toronto: Macmillan Company of Canada, 1913), p. 83.

14 *Ontario Historical Society*, Vol. 31 (1936), p. 52.

15 Quoted in Audrey Spencer, *Spinning and Weaving at Upper Canada Village* (St. Lawrence Parks Commission, 1964), p. 33.

16 Jean S. McGill, *A Pioneer History of the County of Lanark* (Toronto, 1969), p. 78.

17 Isabel Skelton, *William Bell* (Toronto: Ryerson Press, 1947), p. 152.

18 McGill, *A Pioneer History of the County of Lanark*, p. 127.

19 This information is based on an account book in the author's collection.

20 Susanna Moodie, *Life in the Clearings* (1853; rpt. Toronto: Macmillan Company of Canada, 1959), p. 235.

21 Samuel Strickland, *Twenty-Seven Years in Canada West* (1853; rpt. Edmonton: M. G. Hurtig, 1969), p. 292.

22 Ibid., p. 293.

23 Catherine Parr Traill, *The Canadian Settlers' Guide* (1855; rpt. Toronto: New Canadian Library Edition, 1969), p. 176.

Notes to Chapter 3 (pages 29 to 40)

1 J.F. Pringle, *Lunenburgh, or the Old Eastern District* (Cornwall: Standard Printing House, 1890), pp. 35-36.

2 Edward Allen Talbot, *Five Years Residence in the Canadas: Including a Tour Through Part of the United States of America, in the Year 1823* (London: Longman, Hurst, Rees, Orme, Brown and Green, 1824), II, 101.

3 Ibid., II, 92.

4 Catherine Parr Traill, *The Canadian Settlers' Guide* (1855; rpt. Toronto: New Canadian Library Edition, 1969), p. 21.

5 Philip Shackleton, *The Furniture of Old Ontario* (Toronto: Macmillan Company of Canada, 1973), p. 24.

6 Quoted from a letter in the author's collection.

7 Told to the author by Margaret Dewar (1857-1944), who had helped burn the beds in which her parents died.

8 John Howison, *Sketches of Upper Canada* (Edinburgh: Oliver & Boyd, 1821), p. 223.

9 Samuel Thompson, *Reminiscences of a Canadian Pioneer* (Toronto: Hunter, Rose & Company, 1844), pp. 43-44.

10 Sir James Alexander, *L'Acadie; or Seven Years Explorations in British America* (London: Henry Calhum, 1849), I, p. 187.

11 Susanna Moodie, *Roughing It in the Bush* (1852; rpt. Toronto: Bell and Cockburn, 1913), p. 98.

12 John Ross Robertson, ed., *The Diary of Mrs. Simcoe* (Toronto: William Briggs, 1911), pp. 101-105.

13 [Catherine Parr Traill], *The Backwoods of Canada, Being Letters from the Wife of an Emigrant Officer* (London: Charles Knight, 1836), p. 51.

14 John Bigsby, *Shoe and Canoe, Or Pictures of Travel in the Canadas* (London: Chapman and Hall, 1850), II, pp. 50-51.

15 Talbot, *Five Years Residence in the Canadas*, II, 263.

16 Moodie, *Roughing It in the Bush*, p. 114.

17 Ibid., p. 139.

18 [Michael Scherck], *Pen Pictures of Early Pioneer Life in Upper Canada* (Toronto: William Briggs, 1905), p. 133.

19 Herbert C. Burleigh, ed., *Samuel Sherwood's Account Book, 1785-1810* (Kingston: Dr. H. C. Burleigh, 1975), p. 77.

20 Joan MacKinnon, *Kingston Cabinetmakers, 1800-1867* (Ottawa: National Museum of Man, 1976), p. 15.

Notes to Chapter 4 (pages 41 to 44)

1 Thomas Fowler, *Journal of a Tour of North America* (Aberdeen: Lewis Smith, 1832), quoted in *Bulletin of the Association for the Preservation of Technology*, Vol. II, No. 2 (1975), p. 10.

2 *The Workwoman's Guide* (London: Simkin Marshall, and Co., 1840), p. 192.

3 From an account book kept in Prescott by a Mr. A. Jones for the years 1829-33. Now in a private collection.

4 *Kingston Gazette*, July 20, 1818.

5 Jeanne Minhinnick, *At Home in Upper Canada* (Toronto: Clarke, Irwin and Company, 1970), p. 19.

6 Jeanne Minhinnick (historical notes by Elizabeth Wylie), "Extracts from the McCauley Papers Relating to Furnishings, Architecture and Gardens," *Bulletin of the Association for the Preservation of Technology*, Vol. VI, No. 3 (1973), p. 68.

7 [M. Scherck], *Pen Pictures of Early Pioneer Life in Upper Canada* (Toronto: William Briggs, 1905), p. 133.

8 Susanna Moodie, *Life in the Clearings* (Toronto: Macmillan Company of Canada, 1959), p. 204.

9 H. H. Langton, ed., *The Journals of Anne Langton, A Gentlewoman in Upper Canada* (Toronto: Clarke, Irwin & Company, 1950), p. 44, p. 72.

10 Walter S. Herrington, *History of the County of Lennox and Addington* (Toronto: Macmillan Company of Canada, 1913), p. 83.

11 *York Gazette*, 1811.

12 E. A. Cruickshank, "Captain John Waldon Meyers, Loyalist Pioneer," *Ontario Historical Society*, Vol. XXXI (1936), pp. 52-53.

13 Herrington, *History of the County of Lennox and Addington*, p. 83.

Notes to Chapter 5 (pages 45 to 50)

1 H. H. Langton, ed., *The Journals of Anne Langton, A Gentlewoman in Upper Canada* (Toronto: Clarke, Irwin & Company, 1950), p. 9.

2 Catherine Parr Traill, *The Canadian Settlers' Guide* (1855; rpt. Toronto: New Canadian Library Edition, 1969), p. 33.

3 Susanna Moodie, *Roughing It in the Bush* (1852; rpt. Toronto: Bell and Cockburn, 1913), p. 30.

4 Ibid., p. 65.

5 Samuel Strickland, *Twenty-Seven Years in Canada West* (1853; rpt. Edmonton: M.G. Hurtig, 1969), II, 184.

6 Howard T. Pammett, "Assisted Emigration from Ireland to Upper Canada Under Peter Robinson in 1825," *Ontario Historical Society*, Vol. XXXI (1936), p. 196.

7 Traill, *Canadian Settlers' Guide*, p. 21.

8 William and Robert Chambers, "Emigration to Canada, and Other British American Possessions," *Information for the People*, No. 17 (1842), p. 265.

9 *York Gazette*, 1811. Sale at Hollyrood House owned by William Firth.

10 Edward Allen Talbot, *Five Years Residence in the Canadas; Including a Tour Through Part of the United States of America, in the Year 1823* (London: Longman, Hurst, Rees, Orme, Brown and Green, 1824), I, p. 118.

11 E. A. Cruickshank, "Captain John Waldon Meyers, Loyalist Pioneer," *Ontario Historical Society*, Vol. XXXI (1936), pp. 52-53.

12 From an inventory of furnishings in a general household list, Andrew Hurd, Augusta. A copy is in the author's collection.

13 From an inventory of furnishings in a general household list, Rachael Cronkhite, Prince Edward County, circa 1850. A copy is in the author's collection.

14 Edwin C. Guillet, *Pioneer Inns and Taverns* (Toronto, 1954), III, p. 34.

15 Thomas Flyn, comp., *Directory of the City of Kingston, 1857-1858*.

16 Joan MacKinnon, *Kingston Cabinetmakers, 1800-1867* (Ottawa: National Museum of Man, 1976), p. 69.

17 Langton, *The Journals of Anne Langton*, p. 231.

18 Ibid., p. 44.

19 Ibid., p. 182.

Notes to Chapter 6 (pages 51 to 56)

1 Herbert C. Burleigh, ed., *Samuel Sherwood's Account Book, 1785-1810* (Kingston: Dr. H. C. Burleigh, 1975), p. 41.

2 Ibid., p. 3.

3 "Roderick Mathewson's Letter Books, 1815-1851," author's collection.

4 William Canniff, *The Settlement of Upper Canada* (Toronto: Dudley & Burns, 1869), p. 213.

5 A. E. Cruickshank, "Captain John Waldon Meyers, Loyalist Pioneer,"

Ontario Historical Society, Vol. XXXI (1936), pp. 52-53.

6 *Glengarry News*, Alexandria, 1896.

7 Catherine Parr Traill, *The Canadian Settlers' Guide* (1855; rpt. Toronto: New Canadian Library Edition, 1969), p. 178.

8 Burleigh, *Samuel Sherwood's Account Book*, p. 11.

9 Cruickshank, "Captain John Waldon Meyers," pp. 52-53.

Notes to Chapter 7 (pages 59 to 78)
1 Information supplied by Blanche Connell, Grenville County.

2 A. E. Cruickshank, "Captain John Waldon Meyers, Loyalist Pioneer," *Ontario Historical Society*, Vol. XXXI (1936), p. 53.

3 Samuel Strickland, *Twenty-Seven Years in Canada West* (1853; rpt. Edmonton: M. G. Hurtig, 1969), pp. 295-96.

4 W. L. Stone, *Letters of Brunswick and Hessian Officers During the American Revolution* (Albany, N.Y., 1891), pp. 13, 16-20.

5 Susanna Moodie, *Roughing It in the Bush* (1852; rpt. Toronto: Bell and Cockburn, 1913), p. 128.

6 Ibid., p. 159.

7 Ibid., p. 525.

8 [Catherine Parr Traill], *The Backwoods of Canada, Being Letters from the Wife of an Emigrant Officer* (London: Charles Knight, 1836), pp. 72-73.

9 Samuel Thompson, *Reminiscences of a Canadian Pioneer* (Toronto: Hunter, Rose and Company, 1884), pp. 43-44.

10 Catherine Parr Traill, *The Canadian Settlers' Guide* (1855; rpt. Toronto: Canadian Library Edition, 1969), p. 8.

11 "Roderick Mathewson's Letter Books, 1815-1851," author's collection.

12 *Chronicle and Gazette and Kingston Commercial Advertiser*, Kingston, Ontario, March, 1842.

13 *Daily British Whig*, Kingston, Ontario, April 23, 1849.

14 *Metropolitan*, New York, January, 1873, p. 49.

15 H. B. Burnham, and D. K. Burnham, *Keep Me Warm One Night* (Toronto: University of Toronto Press, 1972), pp. 143-44.

16 Marion Wire, "The Old Coverlet in a New Place." Unfortunately, this article is contained in an unidentified magazine which has lost its covers and has no trace

of a date. It is certainly North American, and internal evidence suggests that it was written circa 1920.

17 Edith Fowke, comp., *The Penguin Book of Canadian Folk Songs* (Toronto: Penguin Books, 1973), p. 143.

Notes to Chapter 8 (pages 79 to 88)
1 "Roderick Mathewson's Letter Books, 1815-1851," in the author's collection.

2 Howard T. Pammett, "Assisted Emigration from Ireland to Upper Canada Under Peter Robinson in 1825," *Ontario Historical Society*, Vol. XXXI (1936), p. 206.

3 Author's collection.

4 Ibid.

5 Herbert C. Burleigh, ed., *Samuel Sherwood's Account Book, 1785-1810* (Kingston: Dr. H. C. Burleigh, 1975), passim.

6 These and similar unfamiliar terms are defined in the Glossary.

7 R. C. M. Grant, *The Story of Martintown* (Published by the Author, 1974), pp. 76-77.

8 Walter Herrington, *History of the County of Lennox and Addington* (Toronto: Macmillan Company of Canada, 1913), pp. 91-92.

9 Author's collection.

10 Ibid.

11 "Roderick Mathewson's Letter Books."

12 *History of Lennox and Addington*, pp. 76-77.

13 Author's collection.

14 Ibid.

15 See especially Susanna Moodie's disapproving description of a logging bee in *Roughing It in the Bush*, Chapter XV.

16 Susanna Moodie, *Life in the Clearings* (1853; rpt. Toronto: Macmillan Company of Canada, 1959), p. 17.

17 *Kingston Chronicle and Gazette*, March, 1842.

Notes to Chapter 10 (pages 99 to 107)
1 William Blake, "The Chimney Sweeper," 11. 1-4, in *Songs of Innocence and of Experience*, ed. Geoffrey Keynes (New York: Orion Press, 1971), pl. 12.

2 Song of Solomon 2: 1-3.

3 John Bunyan, *The Pilgrim's Progress* (Philadelphia: Henry Altimus, 1895), p. 121.

4 Quoted from letters by Alexander Cameron in the author's collection.

5 Susanna Moodie, *Roughing It in the Bush* (1852; rpt. Toronto: Bell and Cockburn, 1913), p. 34.

Notes to Chapter 11 (pages 109 to 116)
1 For those who are interested in pursuing this subject in an academic vein, the standard work is by Erwin Panofsky, *Studies in Iconology* (Oxford: Clarendon Press, 1962).

2 John 15:5.

3 Genesis 2:9.

4 This is an old version of "The Yellow Haired Laddie," originally published in Ramsey's *Tea Table Miscellany*, 1724, and reprinted in *Scot's Minstrelsie*, ed. John Greig (Edinburgh: Grange Publishing Works, 1892), I, 111.

5 Song of Solomon 2:9-13.

Notes to Chapter 12 (pages 117 to 132)
1 Averil Colby, *Patchwork* (London: B. T. Batsford, Limited, 1958), p. 28.

2 Job 38:7.

3 For a discussion of Wilno furniture, see Howard Pain, *The Heritage of Upper Canadian Furniture* (Toronto: Van Nostrand Reinhold, 1978), Ch. 5.

Notes to Epilogue (pages 133 to 134)
1 Christopher Marlowe (1564-93), "The Passionate Shepherd to His Love."

Glossary of Terms

Alum A mordant used to set dyes.

Amberina Glass An American art glass having transparent colours ranging from pale amber to ruby.

Appliqué The sewing of one textile over another.

Baize A coarse, open-made woollen material, or flannel, with a long nap, used for linings, bags, flourcloths and tablecloths.

Batt Cotton or wool fibre prepared in sheets for quilts, etc.

Bengal Stripes A kind of cloth or gingham woven with coloured stripes, also made in a mixture of linen and cotton. Originally imported from Bengal and name applied only to the pattern.

Binding A term used in sewing to denote the encasing of the edge of any material in a folded band of tape or other material which is cut on the bias and used to hide a raw edge.

Black Colburg Material composed of wool and cotton, or having a silk warp and woollen weft. Used for coat linings and dresses.

Bolster A long pillow placed across a bed or couch.

Bombazette One of the family of textiles called stuffs or worsted materials; a plain, thin, worsted, unglazed fabric.

Book Muslin A type of muslin used for embroidery.

Breaking Part of the process of freeing the rotted flax straw of the woody waste, usually accomplished by beating or crushing the straw.

Brown Holland A kind of linen originally imported from Holland; unbleached and either glazed or unglazed.

Calico Printed cotton, fine and closely woven.

Cambric A delicate linen textile of several kinds.

Carding Combing or disentangling the fibres of wool, hemp, etc. before spinning.

Chintz A fast-printed calico in which several different colours are applied to small designs. Printed on white or yellow ground, highly glazed.

Copperas A mordant used to set dyes.

Counterpane Bedspread.

Coverlet (Coverlid) A bedspread; commonly used for the type of handwoven, patterned bedspread which was made on a loom.

Crewel Worsted yarn, loosely twisted and used for embroidery, or an old embroidery stitch called after the yarn used.

Damask A twilled material decorated with ornamental devices, handwoven.

Delane A thin woollen fabric, but sometimes of a mixed material.

Denham (Denim) A twilled, hard-wearing cotton fabric.

Derry A coloured, woven, cotton cloth manufactured in blue and brown.

Diaper Fabric woven in a small diamond pattern.

Dimity A cotton fabric made either striped and cross-barred or plain and twilled; stout in texture with a raised design.

Distaff An implement employed in spinning flax, tow or wool. A staff around which the yarn was wound; in early times held under the arm of the spinner, later placed on a stand.

Doublecloth A coverlet having two layers of cloth, one cotton, one wool, that are woven simultaneously and tied together. Made between 1800 and 1850.

Drill A very strong linen twilled cloth, having a treble cord.

Durant A strong, worsted cloth made to imitate buff leather.

Echo Quilting Quilting done by following the outline of a pieced or appliquéd motif on the outer edge to make two or more outlines, each progressively larger.

Etoffe-du-Pays Country cloth; a coarse, woollen cloth worn by country people for work clothes.

Four-Harness Loom A loom is a machine or frame for weaving, and the harness is the apparatus operated to form a shed between the warp threads for the insertion of the weft threads. A four-harness loom was the size used in most families.

Fulling A manufacturing process to cleanse and thicken cloth, when done at home accomplished by thumping and wacking wet lengths of cloth on a long board.

Fustian A coarse, stout, twilled cotton fabric, including many varieties such as corduroy and jean; originally of linen and cotton, later of cotton alone.

Fustic A wood that yields a yellow dye; it was generally purchased in small chips.

Gingham A thin, chequered cloth made of linen whose threads have been dyed in the yarn, later made of cotton.

Hackle (Hetchel) A steel comb for separating the coarse flax fibres from the fine silky ones. Also a board with many long sharp teeth protuding from it; the flax fibres were drawn through them separating the coarse from the fine.

Hand-Brake (Hand-Break) A wooden instrument used to break the straw of the flax leaving the fibre uninjured. It consisted of several wooden bars mounted on a frame and a wooden knife with several blunt blades that were fitted between the bars.

Hank A certain measure of yarn, thread or cotton prepared for sale by winding off in lengths, twisting together and securing.

Jaconet A thin, closely woven, cotton textile of a quality between muslin and cambric.

Jacquard Loom A loom fitted with an apparatus that used perforated cards to facilitate the weaving of figured fabrics; invented by J. M. Jacquard.

Linsey-Woolsey A combination of linsey and woolsey woven into a coarse cloth. Linsey is a mixed material of wool and flax; woolsey is a mixture of cotton and wool.

Logewood A black dye made from a tree that grows in northern South America, Central America and Mexico.

Mackinaw A heavy, woollen cloth.

Madder A red dye obtained from the roots of the plant *Rubia Tinctorum*.

Merino A thin, woollen, twilled cloth made from the wool of the Spanish Merino sheep; also sometimes a mixture of silk and wool.

Moleskin A coarse, stout, twilled cotton fabric in which the pile has been cut short before the material is dyed.

Molten (Melton) A stout cloth suitable for menswear.

Mordant A substance used in dyeing to fix the colouring matter.

Moreen A coarse and strong cotton and worsted material, sometimes of very rich quality.

Muslin A thin and more or less transparent cotton textile made in many variations.

Orleans A mixture of wool and cotton designed for dress material; some varieties were made with a silk warp.

Overshot Weaving A technique employed in making coverlets using a plain ground (usually cotton) over which shoots an extra pattern of wool.

Picot Small loops that ornament laces. In quilting, a picot edging is made by folding small squares of cloth into triangles and sewing them along the edge of the quilt so that they overlap slightly.

Pieced Two pieces of material joined together.

Pilot Cloth An indigo blue woollen cloth, thick and twilled, with a nap on one side; used for greatcoats.

Point A symbol woven in the corner of a Hudson's Bay blanket to indicate the size and weight. A four point blanket would be larger than a three point blanket. Originally, the number of points indicated the number of skins required to buy the blanket.

Quilt A bedcover made of three layers: a top, a bottom and a filling in between.

Quilting Running stitches made in any material threefold in thickness.

Rateen A thick, woven material dressed like cloth, but the hair used in it is left showing in either a frizzed or unfrizzed state.

Ret The process of rotting the flax stalk so that the fibre can be separated from the bark and the inner part of the stem; done by immersing the plant in water for a length of time or leaving it out in the dew and rain.

Roving A soft strand of fibre that has been twisted, attenuated and freed of foreign matter preparatory to its conversion into yarn.

Russian Sheeting Very strong, coarse linen sheeting.

Sascony (Saxony) Cloth or flannel made from wool of the Merino sheep.

Scotch Sheeting Stout linen cloth used for bed linen.

Selvage The firmly finished edge of any manufactured textile, used to prevent the ravelling of the weft.

Serge A loosely woven, very durable, twilled material either in silk or wool.

Set As a verb, the act of putting a quilt together; as a noun, refers to the strips or squares joining the quilt blocks.

Shakedown Straw, blankets, etc. placed on the floor and used as a bed.

Shalon (Shalloon) A loosely woven, worsted material which is thin, short-napped and twilled; used for coat linings and dresses.

Silesia A fine Brown Holland, originally made in Silesia, Germany.

Skein A length of any kind of yarn wound off a hank, doubled and knotted.

Skeiner A wooden instrument such as a Niddy Noddy or hand reel for skeining yarn.

Slack Probably cotton thread of a weak, cheap variety used for basting.

Strouds Frequently Blue Strouds. A type of blanket made from 1759 for the Indian trade.

Swanskin Calico material, one side of which is fluffy.

Tartan A chequered pattern peculiar to the Scottish national costume.

Tester A canopy, especially over a four-poster bed.

Tick The cloth case of a mattress or pillow stuffed with hair, straw or feathers.

Tow The coarse and broken parts of flax or hemp prepared for spinning.

Turkey Twill Red cotton cambric woven with a pattern of small ribs.

Twill Diaper An all-over repeating design in large geometric motifs.

Valance A short curtain hung from the edge of a canopy, from the frame of a bed, etc.

Weft The transverse threads woven into the warp or lengthwise threads.

Witney Blankets made in Witney, Oxfordshire, England.

Wholecloth A quilt whose top was made all in one piece, or, if wide cloth was not available, in two lengths sewn together.

Acknowledgments

For permission to reproduce photographs of bed coverings in their possession, grateful acknowledgment is made to the following. (The abbreviations that follow the names have been used in the captions to the plates to identify the owners. The abbreviation P.C. indicates Private Collection.)

[A.S.]
Mrs. Alma Sargent
Latimer, Ontario

[C.B.]
Mr. and Mrs. Clay Benson
Port Hope, Ontario

[C.D.]
Dr. and Mrs. Charles Danby
Kingston, Ontario

[C.H.]
Mr. and Mrs. Charles Humber
Toronto, Ontario

[C.M.]
Mr. and Mrs. Charles McGuire
Cornwall, Ontario

[D.C.]
Diane Cumberland
Wilton, Ontario

[E.D.]
Miss Elsie Davidson
Kingston, Ontario

[F.S.H.]
Mr. and Mrs. F. S. Henemader
Vineland, Ontario

[G.D.]
Gwen Donaldson
Elginburg, Ontario

[H.H.]
Helen Holliday
Wolfe Island, Ontario

[I.D.]
Mrs. Isobel Day
Port Perry, Ontario

[I.W.]
Ila Wood
Kingston, Ontario

[J.B.]
Mrs. John Brock
Oshawa, Ontario

[J.D.]
Mr. and Mrs. Jack Davison
Harrowsmith, Ontario

[J.J.B.]
John and Jane Berry
Kingston, Ontario

[J.M.]
Jennifer McKendry
Kingston, Ontario

[J.R.P.H.]
J. R. Park Homestead
Essex, Ontario

[L.A.S.]
Mr. and Mrs. L. A. Skeoch
Glenburnie, Ontario

[M.B.T.K.]
Michael S. Bird and Terry Kobayashi
Kitchener, Ontario

[M.F.F.]
Mr. and Mrs. M. F. Feheley
Toronto, Ontario

[M.J.L.]
Marilyn and John Leverette
Moscow, Ontario

[M.J.S.]
Mel and Jean Shakespeare
Uxbridge, Ontario

[M.L.]
Mrs. Marjorie Larmon
Burgessville, Ontario

[M.S.W.]
Mildred S. Woolin
Kingston, Ontario

[N.L.P.]
Nancy-Lou Patterson
Waterloo, Ontario

[N.R.]
Mrs. Norman Ritchie
Inverary, Ontario

[P.B.]
Dr. and Mrs. Peter Bell
Sharbot Lake, Ontario

[P.S.]
Mr. and Mrs. Philip Shackleton
Ottawa, Ontario

[R.A.B.]
Rod and Aggie Brook
Toronto, Ontario

[R.B.]
Courtesy of Mr. and Mrs. Richard Bird
Corbyville, Ontario

[R.L.]
Mr. and Mrs. Robert Lambert
Orono, Ontario

[R.O.]
Mr. and Mrs. Robert O'Neill
Bowmanville, Ontario

[R.P.P.]
Ralph and Patricia Price
Port Perry, Ontario

[R.Y.]
Robert Young
Goodwood, Ontario

[S.R.H.]
Scinda Reynolds Hope
Goodwood, Ontario

[T.F.]
Courtesy of Mrs. Tillie Fripp
Perth, Ontario

[W.R.]
Mrs. Willa Ritchie
Inverary, Ontario

Acknowledgment is also made
to the following museums for
permission to reproduce material
in their collections.

[A.C.M.]
Archibald Campbell Museum
Perth, Ontario

[C.C.F.C.S.]
Canadian Centre for
Folk Culture Studies
National Museum of Man
Ottawa, Ontario

[N.G.C.]
National Gallery of Canada
Ottawa, Ontario

[N.M.M.]
National Museum of Man
Ottawa, Ontario

[P.E.C.M.]
Prince Edward County Museum
Picton, Ontario

[R.O.M.]
Royal Ontario Museum
Toronto, Ontario

*Plate 79, Gift of Mrs. George F.A. Reany;
Plate 87, Gift of the Ontario Spinners and
Weavers Cooperatives; Plate 88, Gift of
Mrs. C.R. Davis; Plate 259, Gift of Miss
Ellen Emsley*

[S.L.P.C.]
St. Lawrence Parks Commission

[S.S.M.]
Scugog Shores Museum
Port Perry, Ontario

[U.C.V.]
Upper Canada Village
Morrisburg, Ontario

Bibliography

Quilts and Textiles

BRETT, K. B. *Ontario Handwoven Textiles.* Toronto: Royal Ontario Museum, 1956.

BRETT, K. B. *Women's Costume in Ontario (1867-1907).* Toronto: University of Toronto Press, 1966.

BURNHAM, DOROTHY K. *Pieced Quilts of Ontario.* Toronto: Royal Ontario Museum, 1975.

BURNHAM, HAROLD B. *Handweaving in Pioneer Canada.* Toronto: Royal Ontario Museum, 1971.

BURNHAM, HAROLD B., and DOROTHY K. BURNHAM. *Keep Me Warm One Night.* Toronto: University of Toronto Press, 1972.

CARLISLE, LILIAN. *Pieced Works and Appliqué Quilts at Shelburne Museum, Vermont.* Shelburne: Shelburne Museum, 1957.

CAULFEILD, S.F.A., and BLANCHE C. SAWARD. *Encyclopedia of Victorian Needlework.* 2 Vols. 1882; rpt. New York: Dover Publications, 1972.

COLBY, AVERIL. *Patchwork.* London: B. T. Batsford, 1958.
_____. *Quilting.* New York: Charles Scribner's Sons, 1971.

CONROY, MARY. *Canada's Quilts.* Toronto: Griffin Press, 1976.

CUMMINGS, ABBOTT LOWELL. *Bed Hangings.* Boston: The Society for the Preservation of New England Antiquities, 1961.

DAVIS, MILDRED J. *Early American Embroidery Designs.* New York: Crown Publishers, 1969.

FENNELLY, CATHERINE. *Textiles in New England 1790-1840.* Sturbridge: Old Sturbridge Village Booklet Series, 1961.

FINLEY, RUTH E. *Old Patchwork Quilts and the Women Who Made Them.* Newton Centre, Mass.: Charles T. Brandford Company, 1970.

FLOUD, PETER. "Copperplate Bird Designs." *Antiques* (June 1957), 556-559.
_____. "Copperplate Floral Designs." *Antiques* (May 1957), 460-463.
_____. "Copperplate Pictorials." *Antiques* (March 1957), 238-241.
_____. "Pictorial Prints of the 1820s." *Antiques* (November 1957), 456-459.
_____. "The Pillar Print." *Antiques* (October 1957), 352-355.

GEHRET, ELLEN J., and ALAN G. KEYSER. *The Homespun Textile Tradition of the Pennsylvania Germans.* Landis Valley, Pa.: Pennsylvania Farm Museum, 1976.

HADERS, PHYLLIS. *Sunshine and Shadow: The Amish and Their Quilts.* New York: Universe Books, 1976.

HALL, CARRIE A., and ROSE KRETSINGER. *The Romance of the Patchwork Quilt in America.* Caldwell, Idaho: Caxton Printers, Ltd., 1935.

HOLSTEIN, JONATHAN. *The Pieced Quilt, A North American Tradition.* Toronto: McClelland and Stewart, 1973.

HOWE, MARGERY B. *Early American Embroideries in Deerfield.* Deerfield, Mass.: Heritage Foundation, 1963.

ICKIS, MARGUERITE. *The Standard Book of Quilt-Making and Collecting.* New York: Dover Publishers, 1949.

IVERSON, MARION DAY. "Bed Rugs in Colonial America." *Antiques* (January 1964), 107-109.

LANE, ROSE WILDER. *Woman's Day Book of American Needlework.* New York: Simon and Schuster, 1963.

MCKIM, RUBY. *101 Patchwork Patterns.* New York: Dover Publications, 1962.

MONTGOMERY, FLORENCE M. *Printed Textiles, English and American Cottons and Linens, 1700-1850.* New York: Viking Press, 1970.

ORLOFSKY, PATSY, and MYRON ORLOFSKY. *Quilts in America.* New York: McGraw-Hill, 1974.

PATTERSON, NANCY-LOU. "Log Cabin Quilts." *Canadian Collector* (Nov./Dec. 1977), 40-44.

PETTIT, FLORENCE H. *America's Indigo Blues: Resist-Printed and Dyed Textiles of the Eighteenth Century.* New York: Hastings House Publishers, 1974.

ROBERTSON, ELIZABETH WELLS. *American Quilts.* New York: Studio Publications, 1948.

SAFFORD, CARLETON L., and ROBERT BISHOP. *America's Quilts and Coverlets.* New York: E. P. Dutton & Company, 1972.

SPENCER, AUDREY. *Spinning and Weaving at Upper Canada Village.* Toronto: St. Lawrence Parks Commission, 1964.

SWAN, SUSAN BURROWS. *A Winterthur Guide to American Needlework.* New York: Crown Publishers, 1976.

WEBSTER, MARIE D. *Quilts: Their Story and How to Make Them.* New York: Doubleday, Page and Company, 1915.

History

ALEXANDER, SIR JAMES. *L'Acadie; Or Seven Years Explorations in British America.* 2 vols. London: Henry Calhum, 1849.

ANGUS, MARGARET. "The McCauley Family of Kingston," in *Historic Kingston:*

Transactions of the Kingston Historical Society, No. 5. Belleville: Mika Publishing Company, 1974, pp. 3-12.

BEER, E. C. "The Diary of J. B. Marks, 1825," in *Historic Kingston*, No. 6. Belleville: Mika Publishing Company, 1974, pp. 29-31.

BIGSBY, JOHN. *Shoe and Canoe, Or Pictures of Travel in the Canadas.* 2 vols. London: Chapman and Hall, 1850.

BURLEIGH, HERBERT C., ed. *Samuel Sherwood's Account Book, 1785-1810.* Kingston: Dr. H. C. Burleigh, 1975.

CANNIFF, WILLIAM. *The Settlement of Upper Canada.* Toronto: Dudley & Burns, 1869.

CARTER, J. S. *The Story of Dundas County.* Iroquois, Ontario, 1905.

CHAMBERS, WILLIAM, and ROBERT CHAMBERS. "Emigration to Canada, and Other British American Possessions." *Information for the People*, No. 17 (1842).

CROIL, JAMES. *Dundas, Or a Sketch of Canadian History.* Montreal: B. Dawson & Son, 1861.

CRUICKSHANK, E. A. "Captain John Waldon Meyers, Loyalist Pioneer." *Ontario Historical Society*, Vol. XXXI (1936), 11-55.

DUNLOP, WILLIAM. *Tiger Dunlop's Upper Canada.* Toronto: McClelland and Stewart, 1967.

FLYNN, THOMAS, comp. *Directory of the City of Kingston, 1857-1858.* Kingston, [1859?].

FOWLER, THOMAS. *Journal of a Tour of North America.* Aberdeen: Lewis Smith, 1832.

GRANT, R. C. M. *The Story of Martintown.* Published by the Author, 1974.

GRAY, HUGH. *Letters from Canada Written During a Residence There in the Years 1806, 1807 and 1808.* London: Longman, Hurst, Rees and Orme, 1809.

GUILLET, EDWIN C. *Early Life in Upper Canada.* Toronto: Ontario Publishing Company, 1933.
———. *The Pioneer Farmer and Backwoodsman.* Toronto: Ontario Publishing Company, 1963.
———. *Pioneer Inns and Taverns.* 3 vols. Toronto: Ontario Publishing Company, 1954.

HERRINGTON, WALTER S. *History of the County of Lennox and Addington.* Toronto: Macmillan Company of Canada, 1913.

HOWISON, JOHN. *Sketches of Upper Canada.* Edinburgh: Oliver & Boyd, 1821.

JAMESON, MRS. *Winter Studies and Summer Rambles in Canada.* London: Saunders and Otley, 1838.

LANGTON, H. H., ed. *The Journals of Anne Langton: A Gentlewoman in Upper Canada.* Toronto: Clarke, Irwin & Company, 1950.

LANGTON, W. A., ed. *Early Days in Upper Canada: Letters of John Langton from the Backwoods of Upper Canada and the Audit Office of the Province of Canada.* Toronto: Macmillan Company of Canada, 1926.

LIZARS, ROBINA and KATHLEEN MACFARLANE. *In the Days of the Canada Company: The Story of the Settlement of the Huron Tract and a View of the Social Life of the Period.* Toronto: William Briggs, 1896.

McGILL, JEAN S. *A Pioneer History of the County of Lanark.* Toronto: Published by the Author, 1969.

MOODIE, SUSANNA. *Life in the Clearings.* 1853; rpt. Toronto: Macmillan Company of Canada, 1959.
———. *Roughing It in the Bush.* 1852; rpt. Toronto: Bell and Cockburn, 1913.

MORTON, W. D. *Monk Letters and Journals 1863-1868.* Toronto: McClelland and Stewart, 1970.

PAMMETT, HOWARD T. "Assisted Emigration from Ireland to Upper Canada Under Peter Robinson in 1825." *Ontario Historical Society*, Vol. XXXI (1936), 178-214.

PRESTON, RICHARD. *Kingston Before the War of 1812.* Toronto: University of Toronto Press, 1959.

PRINGLE, J.F. *Lunenburgh, or the Old Eastern District.* Cornwall: Standard Printing House, 1890.

ROBERTSON, JOHN ROSS, ed. *The Diary of Mrs. John Graves Simcoe.* Toronto: William Briggs, 1911.

[SCHERCK, MICHAEL.] *Pen Pictures of Early Pioneer Life in Upper Canada, by a "Canuck".* Toronto: William Briggs, 1905.

SKELTON, ISABEL. *A Man Austere: William Bell, Parson and Pioneer.* Toronto: Ryerson Press, 1947.

STRICKLAND, SAMUEL. *Twenty-Seven Years in Canada West.* 2 vols. 1853; rpt. Edmonton: M. G. Hurtig, 1969.

TALBOT, EDWARD ALLEN. *Five Years Residence in the Canadas: Including a Tour Through Part of the United States of America, in the Year 1823.* 2 vols. London: Longman, Hurst, Rees, Orme, Brown and Green, 1824.

THOMPSON, SAMUEL. *Reminiscences of a Canadian Pioneer.* Toronto: Hunter, Rose & Company, 1844.

[TRAILL, CATHERINE PARR.] *The Backwoods of Canada, Being Letters from the Wife of an Emigrant Officer.* London: Charles Knight, 1836.

TRAILL, CATHERINE PARR. *The Canadian Settlers' Guide.* Toronto, 1855.
———. *The Workwoman's Guide.* London: Simkin Marshall, and Co., 1840.

General

BIRD, MICHAEL. *Ontario Fraktur: A Pennsylvania-German Folk Tradition in Early Canada.* Toronto: M. F. Feheley Publishers, 1977.

BULLFINCH, THOMAS. *The Age of Fable.* New York: The New American Library of World Literature, 1962.

FERGUSON, GEORGE. *Signs and Symbols in Christian Art.* New York: Oxford University Press, 1961.

FOWKE, EDITH, comp. *The Penguin Book of Canadian Folk Songs.* Toronto: Penguin Books, 1973.

GREENE, RICHARD LAWRENCE. "Fertility Symbols on the Hadley Chest." *Antiques* (August 1977), 250-257.

GREIG, JOHN, ed. *Scot's Minstrelsie.* 6 vols. Edinburgh: Grange Publishing Works, 1892.

LOUDON, J. C. *Furniture Designs.* Wakefield and London: S. R. Publishers and The Connoisseur, 1970.

MACKINNON, JOAN. *Kingston Cabinetmakers, 1800-1867.* Ottawa: National Museum of Man, 1976.

MINHINNICK, JEAN. *At Home in Upper Canada.* Toronto: Clarke, Irwin & Company, 1970.

MINHINNICK, JEAN and ELIZABETH WYLIE. "Extracts from the McCauley Papers Relating to Furnishings, Architecture and Gardens." *Bulletin of the Association for the Preservation of Technology*, Vol. VI, No. 3 (1973), 34-76.

PAIN, HOWARD *The Heritage of Upper Canadian Furniture.* Toronto: Van Nostrand Reinhold, 1978.

PALARDY, JEAN. *The Early Furniture of French Canada.* Toronto: Macmillan Company of Canada, 1963.

PANOFSKY, ERWIN. *Studies in Iconology.* Oxford: Clarendon Press, 1962.

PATTERSON, NANCY-LOU. *Organized Mennonite Traditional Arts of the Waterloo Region of Southern Ontario.* Kitchener: Waterloo Art Gallery, 1974.

SEZNEE, JEAN. *The Survival of the Pagan Gods: The Mythological Tradition and Its Place in Renaissance Humanism and Art.* New York: Harper & Row, 1953.

SHACKLETON, PHILIP. *The Furniture of Old Ontario.* Toronto: Macmillan Company of Canada, 1973.

Index

Numbers given in ordinary type refer to pages, those that are italicized indicate plates.